EDUCATION FOR WORLD PEACE

Edited by

Dr. Shireesh Pal Singh

Department of Education

Sri Guru Ram Rai P.G. College

Dehradun

DISCOVERY PUBLISHING HOUSE PVT. LTD.

NEW DELHI-110 002

Published by:
Tilak Wasan
DISCOVERY PUBLISHING HOUSE PVT. LTD.
4831/24, Ansari Road, Prahlad Street
Darya Ganj, New Delhi-110002 (India)
Phone: +91-11-23279245, 43764432
Fax: +91-11-23253475
E-mail: parul.wasan@gmail.com
discoverypublishinghouse@gmail.com
info@discoverypublishinggroup.com
web: www.discoverypublishinggroup.com

***First Edition:* 2011**
ISBN: 978-81-8356-732-9

Education for World Peace

Printed at:
Shree Balaji Art Press
Delhi

Foreword

In the 21st Century we have reached the pinnacle of technological advancement yet along with the positive achievements, we are also confronted with depressing influences such as inequality, materialism, stress, overwork and social pressure. As a result, many people are succumbing to negative emotions such as retaliation, intolerance, hatred, etc. The result of such negative emotions is aggression at an individual level and violence, disharmony and eventually terrorism at the collective level. The recent incidents in various parts of the world and the resultant media coverage has brought to fore the necessity of peace in society and the world at large. The intelligentsia as a whole has now started viewing peace education in more broadened and comprehensive manner.

Establishing peace at both the societal and global levels has become the foremost priority, as it is the only ways to achieve peace as a crucial factor for human survival. No excuse justifies the use of violence, in individual or collective life. We must maintain peace unilaterally, for nothing that we desire can be achieved without it, though at opposite poles, peace and violence result from human thinking. If we think of the end result, we would never indulge in violence. We should bear in mind that peace is in consonance with humanity, whereas violence means a descent to the animal level. Peaceful minds make for a peaceful world.

Once we become tolerant and obtain peace for our own sake, what that actually does is open up opportunities - it creates favourable conditions, which enable us to strive for our ideals, eventually attaining justice and other constructive ends. However, the important question in the minds of everyone is as how to solve this problem. People the world over are engaged in finding a workable solution to this menace. On the one hand, States are trying to crush the terror menace through legal action; and on the other hand, reformers are trying to curb it by engaging in condemnation. Both of these methods are, apparently, proving to be ineffective. Then what is the solution? The solution is to spread the ideology of peace throughout the world. The problem of terrorism is also based on a mindset which to be countered strategically. In fact, terrorism persists in one or other form until the mindset of violence is countered with the ideology of peace.

According to UNESCO, "violence begins from the mind". It must, therefore, be uprooted from the mind itself. In order to eliminate this root cause we need to initiate our efforts by re-engineering the minds of individuals, taking them away from the culture of violence and bringing closer to the culture of peace.

India has been historically contributing a great deal to world peace through the practice of *shanti* (peace) and *ahimsa* (non-violence) including the non-violence movement led by Mahatma Gandhi during independent struggle of India. After independence, India continued the crusade for the peace through the adoption of policy of *panchsheel* (five principles of peace) and non-alignment.

The book has been written in keeping with the desire of human beings to live in peace and coexistence. I hope that this book will provide necessary impetus to sensitize the youth of the country as a wakeup call. It may lead a movement for introducing peace education in curriculum at primary, secondary and tertiary levels. Today world has become a global village and therefore the violence is no more a local phenomenon. Hence the need for peace education as a counter strategy to the clandestine message of violence is more than ever before. Peace is a comprehensive process involving the upliftment of human consciousness and building of a truly human community at all the levels, not out of compulsion more out of self-convicted desire.

There are thirty four articles and research papers contributed by experts and scholars in the area. All the contributors deserved my appreciation for their scholarly contribution in rolling out this book with perfection, accuracy, relevance and significance.

Their contribution will go a long way in sensitizing readers about the need for peace and harmony in the society.

Prof. Sohanvir S. Chaudhary
Vice Chairperson
National Council for Teacher Education
New Delhi - 110 001

Preface

The research in the field of peace education is emerging of late in the educational institutions and some of the key concerns identified are absolutely relevant to be absorbed at school and personal levels.

While the whole world is developing in to an organized community, the concept of peace education should encompass the highly skewed definition of peace. The world community today is suffering more as a consequence of the indirect violence; people at large are suffering due to hunger, denial of human rights, gross military overspending and environmental degradation.

This broadening of concern amongst the intellectuals and thinkers of peace education has led to broader definition and workability of peace education.

The concept of peace in Indian Civilization is ancient and vedic hymns chanted during yajna discourses usually intone for all encompassing peace of universal nature. In his commentary on the Yoga Sutras, sage Vyasa defines ahimsa as "the absence of injuriousness (anabhidroha) toward all living beings (sarvabhuta) in all respects (sarvatha) and for all times (sarvada)."

Beliefs, attitudes and actions interact to produce peace or violence. The Brihadaranyaka Upanishad (IV, 4, ii, 6) says: "Here they say that a person consists of desires. And as is his desire, so is his will. And as is his will, so are his deed; and whatever deed he does, that he will reap." Every belief creates certain attitudes. Those attitudes govern all of our actions. Man's actions can thus be traced to his inmost beliefs about himself and about the world around him. If those beliefs are erroneous, his actions will not be in tune with the universal dharma.

For instance, the belief in the existence of an all-pervasive Divinity throughout the universe creates an attitude of reverence, benevolence and compassion for all animate and inanimate beings. This equals ahimsa, non-hurtfulness. The belief in the duality of heaven and hell, the white forces and the dark forces, creates the attitude that we must be on our guard, and that we are justified in giving injury, physically and emotionally to others whom we judge to be bad, pagan or unworthy for other reasons. Such thinking leads to rationalizing so-called righteous wars and conflicts. We can sum this up from the Hindu, Buddhist and Jain traditions: ahimsa is higher consciousness, and himsa, hurtfulness, is lower consciousness.

During the modern times, our Father of nation- Mahatma Gandhi himself became embodiment of peace and instrumental in advocating for peace through long and short term political strategies. His autobiography "My experiments with Truth" is a testimony towards his inherent desire to be at peace with his self and the social and political environment in which he willingly moved around.

In the current context too, finding stability and peace is certainly the greatest collective challenge that mankind has ever faced. Conflict is unavoidable, but violence is not. In many cases, the energy stemming from conflict can be directed towards achieving peace led positive change. People need to be taught peace and presenting them with the alternatives for resolving conflict, that violence is not a necessary means to achieve their goals and peace education is a means of achieving this end.

Peace education raises awareness of the roots and causes of conflict, and it provides people with the necessary skills and knowledge how to respond to conflict. Through channeling this energy into programs that rebuild the community and strengthen bonds between communities, peace education can inspire people to look to the future for a better tomorrow. It can stimulate and revitalize morale and work towards developing the infrastructure of developing economies. The United Nations and its partners can encourage this directed effort for peace by raising standards and initiating programs that catalyze the growth of a truly universal culture of peace.

Despite these challenges, it is a clinical fact that fine arts and among them music and dance also make a significant contribution to the peace-building capacities of the people at large.

The possibilities for deploying music and dance as alternative modes of engaging in dialogue and thus resolving conflict are enormous and the world should discuss how participation in artistic forums can aid in the construction of new identities for themselves and others; and the space emerged thus serves as an important factor intricately related to identity and dialogue and which could be expanded further throughout different communities to create other places that enable these sorts of changes.

The creation of peace is a long, ongoing process that will take years to accomplish, but at least the generations to come will have the chance to experience its benefits. It must become our united goal as human beings to live with one another in peace and harmony. Through the generations to come that will benefit from the fruits of our efforts towards creating a world of peace, it can still be a rewarding effort to present before you this compilation on the necessity of imparting peace education across the diverse spectrum of human populace.

Dr. Shireesh Pal Singh

Contents

CHAPTER 1

Reasons for a Philosophy of Peace Education

*Dr. Shireesh Pal Singh
**Dr. Kamla Kant Yadav

Introduction

Perhaps peace education thinkers think peace can be taught like war is taught, but the reality is that neither war nor peace can be taught since they are learning concepts. Violence and war are products of the mis-education of a privileged minority and the non-education of a poor majority in many parts of the world.

Currently, peace education is rarely practiced in the educational institutions of undemocratic nation-states, and even where there are democracies, its implementation is limited. It is a positive sign that peace education thinkers may correct, amend or set right the true nature of peace education as a concept and adopt the right methodology of learning for peace education rather than focussing excessively on pedagogy.

* Dr. Shireesh Pal Singh, born in 1982 and did his Master Degree in Botany and Education from Chaudhary Charan Singh University, Meerut. Followed by NET in Education.He has got gold medal in M.Ed. He was awarded Ph.D degree in Education from HNB Garhwal University. He is working as a teacher educator for the last 4 years. Presently he is working as a lecturer in education in S.G.R.R.(P.G.) College Dehradun.

** Dr. Kamala Kant Yadav had M.A. and B.Ed from Deen Dayal Uppadhyay, M.Ed from Maharshi Dayanand Sarswati University, Ajmer, M.Com and Ph.D (Education) from Bikaner University, Bikaneer and worked in Indian Air Force in the rank of Junior Warrant Officer and performed the various duty like Ops adjt, In charge training. He worked two years as lecturer in education in Jawahar Vidyapeeth Teacher's Training College Knore, Udaipur (Raj). Presently he is working in Kendriya Vidyalaya, Dibrugarh as primary teacher.

A great variety of theories, definitions and practices are referred to in peace education. Since both 'peace' and 'education' are abstractions without any concrete and absolute meaning, it is not surprising that it is rather difficult to find widespread agreement about what peace education actually is.

History of Peace Education

Throughout history humans have taught each other conflict resolution techniques to avoid violence. Peace education is the process of teaching people about the threats of violence and strategies for peace. Peace educators try to build consensus about what peace strategies can bring maximum benefit to a group.

Peace education activities that attempt to end violence and hostilities can be carried out informally within communities or formally within institutional places of learning, like schools or colleges. Peace education has been practiced informally by generations of humans who want to resolve conflicts in ways that do not use deadly force. Indigenous peoples have conflict resolution traditions that have been passed down through millennia that help promote peace within their communities.

Rather than killing each other over their disputes, they employ non-violent dispute mechanisms that they hand down from generation to generation through informal peace education activities. Although there are no written records, human beings throughout history have employed community-based peace education strategies to preserve their knowledge of conflict resolution tactics that promote their security.

Definition of Peace Education

Peace education is the process of acquiring the *values*, the *knowledge* and developing the *attitudes, skills, and behaviours* to live in harmony with oneself, with others, and with the natural environment.

The philosophy of peace education can be defined, most simply, as the elaboration of reasons why we ought to be committed to peace education. To some extent, all writers on peace and peace education may be said to be articulating reasons why we ought to be committed to peace education. However, if we think of an organised philosophy of peace education, this implies that such reasons for the commitment to peace education as organised within the context of established philosophical traditions. A philosophy of peace education is thus more than a personal statement of the importance of peace education, as valuable as this might be.

Ian Harris and John Synott have described peace education as a series of 'teaching encounters' that draw from people:

- Their desire for peace;
- Non-violent alternatives for managing conflict; and
- Skills for critical analysis of structural arrangements that produce and legitimate injustice and inequality.

Importance of Peace Education

There are numerous *United Nations* declarations or instruments which confirm the importance of peace education. *Koichiro Matsuura,* the current Director-General of *UNESCO,* wrote of peace education as being of "fundamental importance to the mission of UNESCO and the United Nations". Peace education as a right is something which is now increasingly emphasised by peace researchers such as *Betty Reardon* and *Douglas Roche.* There has also been a recent meshing peace education and human rights education.

James Page suggests peace education be thought of as "encouraging a commitment to peace as a settled disposition and enhancing the confidence of the individual as an individual agent of peace; as informing the student on the consequences of war and social injustice; as informing the student on the value of peaceful and just social structures and working to uphold or develop such social structures; as encouraging the student to leave the world and to imagine a peaceful future; and as caring for the student and encouraging the student to care for others".

Contents Peace Education

What content is to be learned in peace education? No *absolute* answer is to be found in the literature about peace education or anywhere else on this topic. In the initial phase of developing its peace education programme, UNESCO (1974) proposed using a macro approach and selecting "the most important problems of mankind":

(*a*) The equality of rights of peoples, and the right of peoples to self-determination;

(*b*) The maintenance of peace; different types of war and their causes and effects; disarmament; the inadmissibility of using science and technology for warlike purposes and their use for the purposes of peace and progress; the nature and effect of economic, cultural and political relations between countries and the importance of international law for these relations, particularly for the maintenance of peace;

(*c*) Action to ensure the exercise and observance of human rights, including those of refugees; racialism and its eradication; the fight against discrimination in its various forms;

(*d*) Economic growth and social development and their relation to social justice; colonialism and decolonisation; ways and means of assisting developing countries; the struggle against illiteracy; the campaign against disease and famine; the fight for a better quality of life and the highest attainable standard of health; population growth and related questions;

(*e*) The use, management and conservation of natural resources, pollution of the environment;

(*f*) Preservation of the cultural heritage of mankind; and

(*g*) The role and methods of action of the United Nations system in effort to solve such problems and possibilities for strengthening and furthering its action.

This proposal for peace education content is globally oriented, and the major problems of humankind are explicitly macro. How specific circumstances appear at various levels on the micro-macro spectrum is a most difficult and interesting problem involving questions of cause and effect between the levels. What, for instance, are the effects of enemy images propagated by governments for legitimating a war in shaping our consciousness? Or, in another example, what was the impact of the micro-level mobilisation of peace demonstrators against the war in Iraq on February 15, 2003? This protest evolved into a macro force in terms of sheer numbers of people mobilised around the world, in spite of being hidden in the micro realities of, for example, the 2 million inhabitants of London and neighbouring towns that gathered in Hyde Park. The hidden force of the morning had manifested itself by the evening, turning micro-level phenomena into a global movement. It was not strong enough to stop the war at that time, but these events add to others in a continuous flow of resistance against certain kinds of international behaviours.

It is evident that proposals for peace education content vary in relation to the macro-micro dimension. For instance, some peace educators define the content in terms of international and global problems whereas others define the content in relation to the everyday life and the context of the individual. In both cases, the initial disintegration of micro and macro may be temporary or permanent. If it is permanent, the segregation has an epistemological status, and if it is temporary, it may be grounded in a methodological belief that a complex problem needs to be simplified at the beginning of the educational experience. Thus, the goal may or may not be to understand the micro context in light of the macro context and vice versa, depending upon the duration of the strong segregation of micro-macro phenomena. In all cases, the strength and degree of permanence of any classification of this sort would carry with it a message of power on behalf of those who have made the decision to keep the categories apart.

Such integration or non-integration of "here and now" with "there and then" is a major choice to make concerning the content. Further, it is important if one chooses to depart from the "here and now" context or the "there and then" context because this choice may influence the understanding of the totality, especially in regard to the question of causal relationships between micro and macro phenomena. Starting with "here and now," situations may give the impression that these are important in the explanation of the global totality, whereas starting with "there are then" may imply more emphasis upon seeing the global reality as a cause of micro phenomena.

Reasons for a Philosophy of Peace Education

The reasons for developing a philosophy of peace education are, at one level, similar to the reasons for developing a philosophy for any educational activity. Put simply, if the state and civil society are expected to commit resources to peace education, then it is reasonable that the state and civil society be told why this is important. Peace education is often mentioned within United Nations instruments as being of central importance, although it most instances this is an assumed importance The importance of peace and education for peace may well be obvious to some, although it does nevertheless need to be argued.

In addition to this, there is a special reason for articulating an educational philosophy with regard to peace education: peace education is often prone to accusations of political correctness (something which we might define as fashionable morality) or constituting a form of indoctrination. If indeed peace education is to be regarded as more than political correctness or indoctrination, then a well developed philosophy of peace education is one way of countering this accusation. In developing a philosophy of peace education, we are arguably engaging in an apologetics of peace education and subtly also an apologetics of peace.

The Expansive Nature of a Philosophy of Peace Education

One of the central problems for articulating a philosophy of peace education is the definition problem of peace education, in much same way that the definition of peace is a problem for peace research. Working from Galtungian theory, peace is now generally taken to include direct peace, structural peace and cultural peace. So too, peace education may be taken to include development education, futures education, educational for international understanding, human rights education, inclusive education and environmental education. One problem which flows from this is whether a philosophy of peace education ought to constitute a philosophy of the expansive understanding of peace education and, if so, how ought the definitional boundaries be drawn.

A related problem for a philosophy of peace education is the closeness of peace education to peace advocacy, especially if we think of education operating within formal and informal contexts. For education within formal contexts, it is relatively easy to distinguish peace education from peace advocacy, although the distinction is not so straightforward for education within an informal context. In some respects peace education is a form of peace advocacy. This expanded notion of the philosophy of peace education is not something we ought necessarily to feel uneasy about: the leading figure of modern educational philosophy, John Dewey, famously equated philosophy with the philosophy-of-education (MW9:331-342), suggesting that philosophy may be described as a general theory of education (338) and that philosophy substantially originated in response to educational questions (339).

Form of Peace Education

In some peace education projects, more emphasis is placed on teaching methods and learning than on the content as such. This is often grounded upon the principle that the educational interaction should be in harmony with the idea of peace. This could mean that teacher and students should be equal partners in the educational process. The teacher would be in dialogue with the students about a problem that interests both parties. The teacher does not necessarily have to be an expert who knows all about the problem. It should be apparent that any human, including a teacher, cannot be expected to possess all knowledge about the solution of societal problems. Only historic and diagnostic knowledge can be reproduced. Knowledge in the other categories has to be produced by all the participants in the educational situation. This reproduction and production of knowledge cannot be done only by the teacher if propaganda for and/or indoctrination of specific views are to be avoided.

This means that some knowledge about solving a social, political, economic or cultural problem can only be given through the active participation of those who are suffering the consequences of the problem and whose interest in solving the problem is not purely academic, but also emotional and practical. Thus, problem solving in this sense involves knowledge already produced in science about objective realities as well as knowledge to be produced in the educational setting. It is to be expected that the latter most often would apply to knowledge about the future (what will be, what ought to be) as well as to tactical and strategic knowledge. These three, as well as the realisation of the action, may be seen as more dependent upon subjective viewpoints than upon 'academic' knowledge about historical and present circumstances. Peace education forms are in contradiction to anti-dialogical methods, resulting in the reproduction of prescribed 'old' knowledge and the lack of production of 'new' knowledge. This might, in the long run, be an example of cultural violence if learner participation in developing the content (including action itself) is denied. It would mean that autonomy and creativity are not rewarded (or are directly or indirectly punished). This again might result in inactive learners without the possibility of engaging themselves in problem solving.

Peace education projects introduced in such situations might place special emphasis upon changing the educational form. Important goals might be to encourage the participation of the students in decision-making about both form and content. In this sense, education for peace is more a question of method or forms of communication than of content, *i.e.* it would center on the solution of problems in which participants are engaged. Which problems are selected is highly dependent upon the subjective viewpoints of the participants themselves, and this would mean that the content of peace education would vary greatly depending on the group's social, political, economic and cultural situation.

James Page (2004, 2008) has suggested five possible ethical or philosophical foundations for peace education: virtue ethics, whereby peace may be interpreted as a virtue, and/or virtue is interpreted as peacefulness, and peace education as education in that virtue; consequentialist ethics, whereby peace education may be interpreted as education regarding the consequences of our action and inaction, both as individuals and collectivities; conservative political ethics, whereby peace education may be interpreted as emphasising the importance of the evolution of social institutions and the importance of ordered and lawful social change; aesthetic ethics, whereby peace may be interpreted as something beautiful and valuable in itself, and peace education as emphasising the importance of that beauty and value; and the ethics of care, whereby care may be interpreted as a core element in peace, and peace education as encouraging trust and engagement with the other.

Organisational Structure

The formal educational system in most countries is characterised by the following: the division of knowledge into specific subjects; teachers with specific competencies in these subjects; the grouping of students into classes; and the division of time into periods and breaks. These basic characteristics (others could be added) are important structural components, which allow for only certain types of initiatives for introducing peace education into the curriculum. Thus, it is possible to change the content of a specific subject in such a way that it would deal more with the subject of peace. Such change in the content might not have any significance for the other components such as the methods employed, the division of knowledge into subjects and the division of time into periods and breaks.

If, however, the form of education is regarded as a problem, as well as the way knowledge has been divided into subjects, the peace educator runs into other problems of a structural nature, *i.e.* the peace education project might contradict the basic characteristics of the structure in which it is introduced. If, for instance, a peace education project is based on the principles of problem orientation and participatory decision-making, it could not, without problems, be introduced into a school system which rigidly practices the division into subjects, classes, and periods.

It would be extremely difficult to realise problem-oriented and participatory education through a prescribed plan for a subject, carried out by a teacher in a rigidly-structured classroom situation with thirty students, in periods of 45 minutes each. Apart from the rigidity imposed by these three components (subject, class, time), the greatest barrier for peace education projects might be the rules laid down in educational systems concerning evaluation of the students, through which students are sorted into categories according to their achievement in terms of grades (this is not the place to discuss the sorting function of the school and its role in the reproduction of inequalities in society).

Through this discussion about organisational structure, it should be clear that a peace education project might be in harmony or disharmony with it. Therefore, it is possible that so many disharmonies exist that the structure itself must be changed before peace education can be introduced. The question then arises whether the organisational structure can be changed through changes in form and content, or whether this is impossible until changes are brought about in the society which has produced an educational structure antagonistic to problem orientation and dialogue.

Conclusion

Peace education is the process of acquiring the *values*, the *knowledge* and developing the *attitudes, skills, and behaviours* to live in harmony with oneself, with others, and with the natural environment.

Peace education has been practiced informally by generations of humans who want to resolve conflicts in ways that do not use deadly force. It is often mentioned within United Nations instruments as being of central importance, although in most instances this is an assumed importance. True peace education makes humans whole and is a life-long endeavour. It is the core aspect of all types of education. Peace education includes all the elements that constitute human life. Thus peace cannot be taught, but is learnt by both teachers and students through dialogue, discussion and practice.

Any human, including a teacher, cannot be expected to possess all knowledge about the solution of societal problems. Only historic and diagnostic knowledge can be reproduced. So knowledge about solving a social, political, economic or cultural problem can only be given through the active participation of those who are suffering the consequences of the problem and whose interest in solving the problem is not purely academic, but also emotional and practical.

REFERENCES

1. Aspeslagh, R. (1999). Peace Education. In Young Seek Choue, (Ed.)
2. Bhave, V. (1996). Thoughts on Education. Varanasi : Sarva Seva Sangh Prakashan.

3. Buckman, P. (Ed.). (1975). *Education Without Schools.* New Delhi : Rupa and Company.
4. Dewey, J. (1959). Quoted in Saryu Prasad Chaube, *Pashchatya Shiksha Ka Itihas* (History of Western Education).
5. Galtung, J. (1974). On Peace Education. In C. Wulf (Ed.), *Handbook on Peace Education.*
6. Gandhi, M.K. (1942). *Non-violence in Peace and War,* Vol. I. Ahmedabad : Navajivan Publishing House.
7. Hurst, J. (1999). Pedagogy for Peace.
8. Johnson, M.L. (1998). *Trends in Peace Education.* Bloomington : Indiana University.
9. Prasad, S.N. (1976). Peace Education : An Alternative to War Education. *Peace Progress.*
10. *World Encyclopaedia of Peace* Oceana Publications, Inc New York.
11. Wulf, C. (Ed.) (1974). *Handbook on Peace Education.* Frankfurt/ Main : International Peace Research Association.

CHAPTER 2

Need, Curriculum and Content of Peace Education in Schools

*Dr. Saroj Yadav

Peace is the most vital thing in human life. It is a calm and relaxed state of mind. Peace consists of positive thoughts, pure feelings and good wishes. It is the need of the hour to sow the seeds of peace among students. It has been said that if we are to reach real place in the world, we shall have to begin with the children.

Most disputes between the people are solved without violence but not all. If we are to move away from violence as a way of solving disputes at home and abroad, it is essential to work together to help young people learn how deal with conflict creatively and non-violently. Violence comes in different forms and the fear of violence can be as damaging as violence itself. Violence is embedded in our society not only as a method to solve conflict, but in sports, entertainment and literature. Conflict is inevitable in human affairs but violence is not. Conflict can be positive and creative force for change. Conflict can be approached as a challenge, offering people the change to be inventive and creative and to develop in ways they might not have thought of. Dealing with conflict creatively, is a vital part of peace education. To prevent the continued cycle of violence, education must promote peace, tolerance and understanding to help create a better society for all.

The overall aim of peace education is to help build a peaceful world. Awareness of values and attitudes underpin

* Lecturer, Deptt. of Education, C.S.J.M. University, Kanpur.

peace education and need to be addressed through the curriculum and the whole school. Education for peace is founded on some values and attitudes. Wars, shooting in schools, natural disasters, death at sporting events etc. are the tragic outcomes and will never happen anywhere and definitely will not impact the children and the youth we care about. We would like to protect those young minds from pain and horror of difficult situations. We would like to ensure that they have happy, innocent and carefree lives.

The school community is not always a neutral setting for children. School can facilitate a pupil's journey of discovering about their own identity, other people and the world around them. This helps children to formulte their own view of world and to manage and articulates their own emotions. The school community can also reinforce the development of aggressive response to conflict.

Values and Attitudes Required for Peace Education

Values and attitudes underpin peace education and need to be addressed through curriculum and the whole school.

1. Respect for others regardless of race, gender, age, nationality, class, sexuality, appearance, political and religious belief, physical and mental ability.
2. Empathy—Willingness to understand the views of others from their standpoint.
3. Self-esteem—Accepting the intrinsic value of oneself.
4. Commitment to social justice, equity and non-violence.
5. Concern for the environment and understanding of our place in the eco-system.
6. Commitment to equality.

Assumptions of Peace Education

1. Children can be self-disciplined and motivated. Peace is implicitly part of much education but this peace element must be made for explicit.

2. To prevent violent relationship at any level—personally, locally, nationally and internationally.
3. Children's moral development can be enhanced by the appropriate curriculum, teaching methods, relationships in the classroom and school as a whole.

Key Skills Required for Peace Education

1. Identifying biases, problem solving, sharing and co-operation, shared decision-making, analysis and critical thinking, enhancing the self-esteem of one-self and others.
2. Creative self-expression.
3. Ability to imagine life beyond the present and work towards a vision.
4. Understandings the links between the personal, local and international communicating through observations.
5. Honest talk and sensitive learning.
6. Self-reflection.
7. Independent research.
8. Empathy.
9. Self-reflection.
10. Conflict resolution strategies.
11. Ability to act on ideas.
12. Positive emotional expression.
13. Non-violent action in relation to problem solving.

Aims of Peace Education

In the classroom, peace education aims to develop skills, attitudes and knowledge with co-operative and participatory learning methods and an environment to tolerance, care and respect. Through dialogue and explorations, teachers and students engage in a journey of shared learning. Students are neutral and empowered to take responsibilities for their own growth and achievement, while teachers care for the well-being of all students. The practice of peace education is an effort to promote the total welfare of students, equitable treatment of youth and promote individual and social responsibilities for both educator and learner. Through pedagogy and social action, peace educators demonstrate that there are alternatives of violence.

Needs of Peace Education in Schools

1. To create frameworks for achieving peaceful and creative societies.
2. To understand the nature and origin of violence and its effects on both victims and perpetrator.
3. To sharpen awareness about the existence of un-peaceful relationship between people and within and between schools.
4. To investigate the causes of conflicts and non-violence embedded vision within perceptions, values and attitudes of individuals as well as within social and political structure of society.
5. To encourage the search for alternative or possible non-violent skills.
6. To equip children and adults with personal conflict relation skill.
7. To develop the abilities to act on ideas.
8. To show positive self-expression.
9. To understand the links between the personal, local and global, communicating through careful observations.
10. To make able for the imagination of life beyond the present and work towards a vision.
11. To encourage the search for truth.
12. To equip children and adults with personal misunder-standings.

Challenges and Opportunities of Peace Education

Peace Education does not teach students what to think, but rather what to think critically. In the process, it's holistically and participatory approach may conflict with more traditional curriculum design or strict standard-based schooling. Peace Education aims not to reproduce but to transform. It consists of people consciously striving to educate their successors not for existing state of affairs, so as to make possible a future better humanity. So with this task come significant challenges and opportunities for all involved.

One way to meet challenges of peace education is to build bridges to support among key participants. Just as learning takes place in a broader social context and not exclusively in schools and classrooms, so peace education relies on families, communities and social network to affect positive and lasting change. The notion, "Think globally, act locally" is central to educating for a culture of peace, in that it links theory with practice, international issues to individual efforts. As a peace educator one need not to work alone. The international peace education community is active and growing through networks, publications, global campaigns, national initiatives and international programmes. Concerned citizens, educators, activists of all ages around the world are promoting and building peace through education.

Peace education does not provide a complete answer, as it appears to offer a long-term solution to threats here and now. It depends on millions of students being educated, ideally in every country, to work to change from violent to peaceful behaviour. This takes time and effort. The good news is that more and more countries are waking up to the need of peace education. Many international organisations such as United Nation's educational, scientific and cultural organisations continue to promote peace education.

Teachers are the role models for students and hence they can help their students handle the day to day situations in a non-violent way. Arrogance and aggression, which propel violence, are the two vices that can be controlled by peace education. Students come across trying situations at their home, educational institutions and other places and tend to commit crime. Teachers must understand the multicultural, multiethnic and multi religious problems in society are not to dealt with in isolation in bits and pieces of only peace education programme, but being interconnected with all other problems of peace and violence, are addressed in the programme. The teacher must be cognizant and wholly supportive of the basic nature and aims of peace education.

In the land of Mahatma Gandhi, the apostle of non-violence, teachers are now getting trained to teach peace as a subject to students. Peace education is now a part of teacher training programme of the National council of educational training and research (NCERT), which formulates school curricula and teacher training programme in India. The program has already trained over 70 teachers from across the country. Experts from various fields teach the participating teachers how to handle violent students, react to their queries, help them counter social evils and respect others, thereby promoting social cohesion. The programmes primary goal is to shape up the child's life cohesively. That will be possible only if some extra efforts are made. Peace education program is an effort in that direction.

Peace is living in harmony and not fighting with others. It consists of pure feelings, positive thoughts and good wishes. Peace education is more effective when it is adapted according to the social and cultural context and the needs of the society. It is enriched by those social, cultural and spiritual values along with universal human values.

Themes of Peace Education

Themes of Peace Education include interethnic harmony, human rights and democratic decision-making processes. The programme should give particular attention to issues of worldview, human nature, individual and collective development. It should also include the psychological, moral, ethical and spiritual causes of violence and war. The combined approach lays the critical foundation for the creation of both a culture of peace and a culture of healing.

Through this process, participating teachers from each country become partner with peace education specialists, researchers, curriculum designers and e-learning experts in an ongoing programme of curriculum designing approach and evaluation.

Content of Theory Based Peace Education

Content of theory based Peace education can include the following areas—

1. Role of value system in religious and secular world views, the history and present day struggle for justice and equality in race and gender.
2. The ethics of science and technology.
3. Understanding of the causes of violence and war.
4. Local, national and international disputes.
5. The theory of conflict resolution.
6. Political and social change.
7. The economics of war and oppressions.
8. Human rights and citizenship.
9. Non-violence, Peacemaking in media, literature and arts.

Content of Practical Expressions of Peace-making for Use in Peace Education

1. Models of peace-making-local, national and international.
2. Models of peace history.
3. The role of United Nations and non-government organisations for peace.

4. Models showing how community groups affect peaceful change.
5. Vocations for peaceful change.
6. The role of personal and community health and nutrition in a healthy society.
7. Understanding other cultures through language, custom and stories and also by parenting and child care.
8. Peer mediation and conflict resolution skills for children in class room.

Process, Content and Methodology of Peace Education

1. Active learning/Participatory method.
2. Experimental learning
3. Partnership in learning with pupil participation.
4. Dialogue, Story telling and response to stories.
5. Self-expression.
6. Project work focussed on identifying questions and researching answers.
7. Encouragement of the use of source material.
8. Exchange with children from other cultures using their own medium.
9. Creative teaching and learning.
10. Whole school approach including all staff and links with the wider community.

Peace education brings together multiple traditions of pedagogy, theories of education and international initiations for the advancement of human development through learning. It is fundamentally dynamic, interdisciplinary and multicultural. It grows out of the work of educators such as John Dewey, Maria Montessori, Johan Galton and many others.

Building on principles and practices that have evolved over time, responding to different historical circumstances, peace education aims to cultivate the knowledge, skills and attitudes needed to achieve and sustain a global culture of peace. The following diagram helps to visualise the core relationship between violence and peace—

Voilence Direct	Peace Negative
Personal—Terrorism, murder, ethnic cleansing Institutional—War, State sponsored terror, industrial destruction of plants and animal life.	Absence of personal and institutional violence.

Indirect	Positive
Structural—Sexism, discrimination, poverty, racism, lack of education and health services, hunger.	Presence of well being, justice, gender equality and human rights.

Curriculum of Peace Education

English

Reading and writing: Past and present experiences of peace as seen from a variety of viewpoints; communication with other people—particularly those given authority, to express opinions about present and future decisions for peace in societies at all levels.

Speaking and listening: Working collaboratively with others to reach consensus, particularly over controversial and cross-cultural issues.

Science

Processes of obtaining, analysing and evaluating evidence and making predictions develop social skills for peace and collaborative citizenship; learning about science in everyday life and how to treat living things and the environment with care and sensitivity require awareness of the ethics of science and social responsibility.

History and Geography

Historical knowledge and understanding can be used for explicit learning about experiences of war-making and peace-building in the past; historical skills of interpretation, enquiry and communication can all develop skills for relating learning from the past to planning the future.

Geographical skills of using and interpreting sources can help develop awareness of messages and meaning from different perspectives; learning about places can show how environment and economic factors affect social welfare in different ways in different parts of the world and so help understanding of how local, national and international conflicts may arise and may be resolved peacefully.

Languages and Expressive Arts

Communicating skills and knowledge of a modern foreign language can help young learners express feelings and areas of agreement or disagreement, particularly with first-language speakers, building international exchange and understanding; developing cultural awareness can increase appreciation of values in different societies.

In Art—as in Design Technology—investigating and making can be practiced collaboratively in the classroom. Knowledge and understanding of the arts and crafts of a diversity of societies can heighten sensitivity to different ways of seeing the world and so contribute to future perceptions of peace.

In Music, performing and composing can be collaborative skills, while listening and appraising can encourage appreciation of other cultural values.

Design and Information Technology

Design and making skills can be developed collaboratively through group projects which practice discussion and consensus building.

In Information Technology, communicating and handling information can give great scope for exchanging ideas and experiences with others, particularly other young people across the world.

Maths

Processes of collecting, presenting, interpreting data and calculating probabilities can develop skills in communicating meaning with integrity which contribute to peaceful relationships between different groups of people.

Physical Education

Healthy lifestyles, positive attitudes and safe practice can all help develop in young learners a sense of fairness and consideration of others.

Whole Curriculum

Peace education should also be fundamental to the whole life of a school, in Religious and Moral Education, in learning about Citizenship and Community Service, Equal Opportunities and Global Awareness.

Peace is understood not only as the absence of traditional form of direct violence, but also a positive presence of educating and about all aspects of peace constitute peace education. The following diagram illustrate among the central knowledge, skill, attitudes of peace education, which are drawn from the basic of the learning objectives in the learning units.

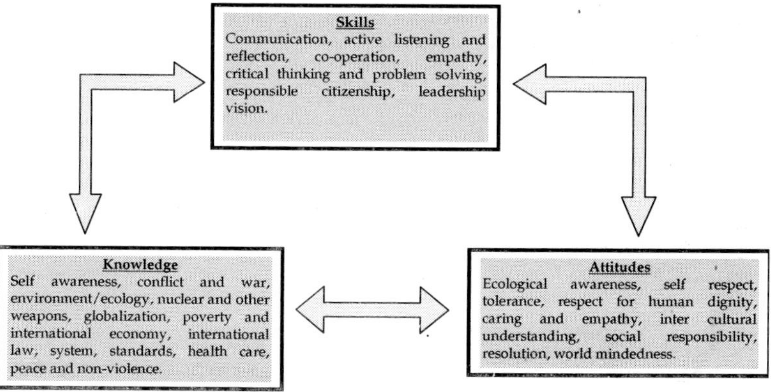

REFERENCES

1. Education for Peace, International Education for Peace Institutions. http//www.ef. pinternational.org/about/curriculum.html.
2. How You Can Teach Peace: The Seville Statement 1989.
3. http//wwwexpressindia.com/news/fullstory.
4. msn.Education; http//www.education. in.msn.com/schoolcolleges/article.aspx.
5. Peace education; http//www.un.org/cyberschoolbus/peace/index.asp.
6. Teacher as learner;http//www.un.org/cyberschoolbus/peace/frame.htm.
7. Tips for Developing Peace Education Curricula; Some Lessons from Vietnam, Melisso.c.Tyler, University of Melbourne, A.Halafoff, Monash. Australian Curruiculum Studies Vol. 3, 2005, University of Melbourne Legal Studies Research Paper, No. 164.
8. A Student Guide to Peace Education, United Nations Cyber Schoolbus.
9. Bernard Crick; Education for Citizenship and Teaching of Democracy in Schools, Sep. 1998.
10. Education for Peace, International Education for Peace Institutions. http//www.ef. pinternational.org/about/curriculum.html.
11. Learn peace:Looking at Peace Education, http//www.ppu.org.uk/learn/peaceed/pe.
12. Peace Education to be Introduced in Schools, Press Trust of India, 25 April, 2005.
13. Values and Visions: Spiritual Development and Global Awareness in the Primary School, 1993.

CHAPTER 3

Peace Education : A New Approach in Education

*Syed Hayath Basha

Introduction

Peace education encompasses the key concepts of education and peace. While it is possible to define education as a process of systematic institutionalised transmission of knowledge and skills, as well as of basic values and norms that are accepted in a certain society, the concept of peace is less clearly defined. Many writers make an important distinction between positive and negative peace. Negative peace is defined as the absence of large-scale physical violence—the absence of the condition of war. Positive peace involves the development of a society in which, except for the absence of direct violence, there is no structural violence or social injustice. Accordingly, peace education could be defined as an interdisciplinary area of education whose goal is institutionalised and no non institutionalised teaching about peace and for peace. Peace education aims to help students acquire skills for non-violent conflict resolution and to reinforce these skills for active and responsible action in the society for the promotion of the values of peace. Therefore, unlike the concept of conflict resolution, which can be considered to be retroactive—trying to solve a conflict after it has already occurred—peace education, has a more proactive approach. Its aim is to prevent a conflict in advance or rather to educate individuals and a society for a

* RTA, School of Education, Indira Gandhi National Open University, New Delhi.

peaceful existence on the basis of non-violence, tolerance, equality, respect for differences, and social justice. (www.encyclopedia.com)

It is a truism that one cannot give what he/she does not have. Conversely, one cannot be at peace with others and the world if he/she is not at peace with himself/herself. Many people find themselves in trouble with others because of their inability to control themselves: an inability to stay calm amidst external pressures. Some people become easily confused, fretful and violent when suddenly under pressure, then wonder afterwards why in the world they have harmed others and why they cannot seem to account for their actions. Reactions of this kind may be indicative of a person's need to look inwards—harmonising thoughts, motives, words and actions—to get in touch with the inner self where peace, strength and truth reside. Peace from within consists of pure thoughts, pure feelings, and pure motives and wishes. (*UNESCO, 1998 p. 24*)

A culture of peace is necessary for a meaningful life together. In a world where there is great diversity in personal, social and cultural ways of being and living, possession of significant human values can overcome these differences and ensure peace and solidarity.

The process of peace building starts from within the heart of each individual, when this is shared with other groups and cultures.

Meaning and Nature of Peace Education

Peace education, then, is best thought of not as a distinct 'subject' in the curriculum, nor as an initiative separate from basic education, but as process to be mainstreamed into all quality educational experiences (although the actual approach used to introduce peace education will be determined by local circumstances).

The term *'education'* in this context refers to any process–whether in schools, or in informal or non-formal educational contexts—that develops in children or adults the knowledge, skills, attitudes and values leading to behaviour change.

The term *'peace'* does not merely imply the absence of overt violence (sometimes referred to as 'negative peace'). It also encompasses the presence of social, economic and political justice which are essential to the notion of 'positive peace'.

Peace Education means to *learn about* and to learn *for* peace.

(*a*) ***Learning about*** peace means obtaining knowledge and understanding of what contributes to peace, what damages it, what leads to war, what does 'peace' mean on each level anyway, what is my role in it, and how are the different levels connected?

(*b*) ***Learning for peace*** means learning the skills, attitudes and values that one needs in order to contribute to peace and help maintain it. For instance, this means learning to deal with conflicts without the recourse to violence, learning to think creatively, learning to apply the methods of active non-violence or learning to deal with cultural differences in a constructive way.

Peace: Avoiding the Way of Negation

'Peace' is a word that is uttered almost as frequently as 'truth', 'beauty', and 'love'. It may be just as elusive to define as these other virtues. Common synonyms for peace include 'amity,' 'Friendship', 'concord', 'tranquility,' 'repose', 'quiescence,' 'truce', 'pacification', and 'neutrality'. Likewise peacemaker is the pacifier, mediator, intermediary, and intercessor. While some of these descriptions are appropriate, they are still quite limited in describing both the nature of peace and the role of the peacemaker. Any attempt to articulate the nature of peace and peacemaking, therefore, must address those conditions that are favourable to their emergence. Freedom, human rights, and justice are among such prerequisites. Also included are proactive strategies such as conflict resolution, non-violent action, community building and democratisation of authority.

Definitions

Peace education is defined in a different way by the eminent educationists and philosophers. There are some well-known definitions which have been mentioned below:

- Peace must begin with each one of us. Though quiet and serious reflection on its meaning, new and creative ways can be found to foster understanding, friendship and co-operation among all people.

  —(*Javier Perez de Cuellar*)

- Peace Education includes development of knowledge, insight and skills as well as the building up of opinions and attitudes, deriving from norms and values embedded in peace and directed to the realization of a humane and peaceful world.

  —*Lennart Vriens and Robert Aspeslagh*

- The Vanities of the world are transient, but they alone live who live for others, the rest are more dead than alive. —*Swami Vivekananda*

- Let us learn to make the whole world as our own. No one is a stranger. —*Mahatma Gandhi*

- Where the mind is without fear and the head is held high, into that kingdom of freedom my father let my country awake. —*Rabindranath Tagore*

- Peace and human progress do not come about by themselves. It entails a will for peace. At the dawn of disarmament as the basis for the establishment of peace in the world must be accompanied by a new vision of peace. —*Rodrigo Carazo*

- Peace education in UNICEF refers to the process of promoting the knowledge, skills, attitudes and values needed to bring about behaviour changes that will enable children, youth and adults to prevent conflict and violence, both overt and structural; to resolve conflict peacefully; and to create the conditions conducive to peace, whether at an intrapersonal, intergroup, national or international level. —*UNICEF (1999)*

- Our scientific power has outrun our spiritual power. We have guide missiles and misguided men.

  —*Martin Luther King, Jr.*

- Peace is not merely the absence of war but the presence of justice, of law, of order-in short, of government.

  —*Albert Einstein*

- The abolition of war requires the development of effective nonviolent alternatives to military struggle.

  —*Gene Sharp*

- Unless every member of our global family is peaceful, our peace is incomplete. —*Sri Sri (2008)*

The Nature of Peace Education

The nature of peace education is creation of a new dimension across the curriculum, a concern that may be explored in different ways with any age group and in any subject through which students may be discussed the nature of peace. Particularly, in small groups they are identifying and sharing personal experiences of peace: moments of joy, shared endeavour, giving and receiving, creating and celebrating. They then brainstorm some of the main obstacles to peace, such as fear, prejudice, aggression and indoctrination. The teacher is leading them through a guided fantasy in which they imagine the world as they would like it to be in thirty years' time. 'There is no way to peace, peace is the way'. The stress in education for peace is thus as much on method as on content. The curriculum has some important objectives. They are clearly mentioned in the below diagram (*See on next page*).

Being clear about one's needs and able to relate assertively rather than aggressively is also at the heart of good education for peace. Such matters need to be pursued across the

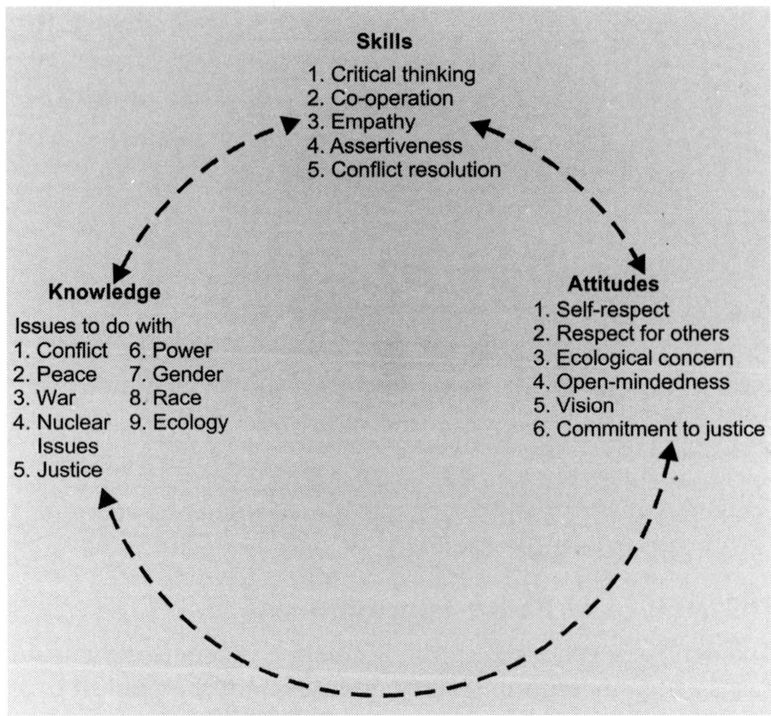

Source: http://www.ppu.org.uk

curriculum by both subject specialists and generalist teachers. They are equally important at both primary and secondary level. They are also, of course, extremely pertinent to issues involving the school as a community and in the community, whether in relation to staff-student relationships, staff-staff relationships, or vandalism, crime, and football violence.

Curriculum objectives play vital role and have paramount place in the field of peace education. They are clearly described here.

SKILLS

There are various skills which can be developed among students to impart peace education. Some of them are as mentioned below:

1. Critical thinking : It has much importance to impart peace among students. Students should be able to approach issues with an open and critical mind and be willing to change their opinions in the face of new evidence and rational argument. They should be able to recognize and challenge bias, indoctrination, and propaganda.

2. Co-operations : Students should be able to appreciate the value of co-operating on shared tasks and be able to work co-operatively with other individuals and groups in order to achieve a common goal.

3. Empathy : Students should be able to imagine sensitively the viewpoints and feelings of other people, particularly those belonging to groups, cultures, and nations other than their own.

4. Assertiveness : Students should be able to communicate clearly and assertively with others, that is not in an aggressive way, which denies the rights of others, or in a non-assertive manner which denies their own rights.

5. Conflict resolutions : Students should be able to analyse different conflicts in an objective and systematic way and be able to suggest a range of solutions to them. Where appropriate they should be able to implement solutions themselves.

6. Political literacy : Students should be developing the ability to influence decision-making thoughtfully, both within their own lives and in their local community, and also at national and international levels.

ATTITUDES

1. Self-respect : Students should have a sense of their own worth and pride in their own particular social, cultural, and family background.

2. Respect for others : Students should have a sense of the worth of others, particularly of those with social, cultural, and family backgrounds different from their own.

3. Ecological concern : Students should have a sense of respect for the natural environment and our overall place in the web of life. They should also have a sense of responsibility for both the local and global environment.

4. Open-mindedness : Students should be willing to approach different sources of information, people, and events with a critical but open mind.

5. Vision : Students should be open to and value various dreams and visions of what a better world might look like, not only in their own community but also in other communities, and in the world as a whole.

6. Commitment to justice : Students should value genuinely democratic principles and processes and be ready to work for a more just and peaceful world at local, national, and international levels.

KNOWLEDGE

1. Conflict : Students should study a variety of contemporary conflict situations from the personal to the global and attempts being made to resolve them. They should also know about ways of resolving conflicts non-violently in everyday life.

2. Peace : Students should study different concepts of peace, both as a state of being and as an active process, on scales from the personal to the global. They should look at examples of the work of individuals and groups who are actively working for peace.

3. War : Students should explore some of the key issues and ethical dilemmas to do with conventional war. They should look at the effects of militarism on both individuals and groups and on scales ranging from the local to the global.

4. Nuclear issues : Students should learn about a wide range of nuclear issues and be aware of the key viewpoints on defence and disarmament. They should understand the effects of nuclear war and appreciate the efforts of individuals, groups, and governments to work towards a nuclear-free world.

5. Justice : Students should study a range of situations illustrating injustice, on scales from the personal to the global. They should look at the work of individuals and groups involved in the struggle for justice today.

6. Power : Students should study issues to do with power in the world today and ways in which its unequal distribution affects people's life chances. They should explore ways in which people and groups have regained power over their own lives.

7. Gender : Students should study issues to do with discrimination based on gender. They should understand the historical background to this and the ways in which sexism operates to the advantage of men and the disadvantage of women.

8. Race : Students should study issues to do with discrimination based on race. They should understand the historical background to this and the ways in which racism operates to the advantage of white people and to the disadvantage of black.

9. Environment : Students should have a concern for the environmental welfare of the entire world's people and the natural systems on which they depend. They should be able to make rational judgments concerning environmental issues and participate effectively in environmental politics.

10. Futures : Students should study a range of alternative futures, both probable and preferable. They should understand which scenarios are most likely to lead to a more just and less violent world and what changes are necessary to bring this about.

Approaches of Peace Education

There are numerous approaches to peace education. Some of them are as mentioned below:

• **A Holistic Approach :** Often attempts to bring peace in society are confined to the realms of politics and economics. The focus has been on establishing an outer atmosphere for peace rather than creating peace from within, thus making the means bigger than the end itself. This vision of Sri Sri envisages the process of peace in its totality by reaching out to individuals, families, communities, nations and humanity as a whole. Sri Sri has rightly said that *"Unless every member of our global family is peaceful, our peace is incomplete,"*.

All the initiatives taken up by Sri Sri have an underlying goal of achieving holistic peace. His approach places sustainable development and social upliftment alongside value education. This has created happy, healthy individuals who have attained a decent standard of living and received essential education and life skills so that their proclivity to fight is eliminated.

• **Teacher College (TC) approach to Peace Education :** The three formative dimensions of the TC approach to peace education arise from this rationale of social need and educational responsibility. The three dimensions are the substantive problematic from which content is derived, a philosophy of education grounded in the role of education in social change, and a pedagogy that is consistent with the philosophy and most relevant to the problematic.

1. The Central Problematic : It is violence as it has been conceptualised and studied by peace research, outlining its systemic nature and it multiple manifestations. The substantive purposes of peace education are to provide a knowledge base drawn largely from peace research and based in a grounding of the relevant issues of peace, development, education and other academic disciplines. So, the knowledge is comprehensive and interdisciplinary in scope.

2. The Philosophy of peace education : It is in the Dewey tradition, seeking to prepare learners for active and responsible citizenship in the process of addressing the problematic. It is based on an inquiry into the normative principles (non-violence, human rights, social, economic, political and ecological justice, etc.) that inform peace education and asserts the need for an intentional interrelationship between pedagogy and content. One of its primary purposes is the development of agency, in the sense of the concept as articulated by Maxine Green, to capacitate learners to take action in the larger society.

3. The Pedagogy : It is the most unique and special quality of the TC approach, is an adaptation of critical pedagogy with roots in Freire and elements of forms of inquiry practiced in various academic disciplines and some sub fields of peace research, such as the problem inquiry developed by world order studies. This pedagogy is primarily directed toward developing student capacities for critical thinking, inquiry, and reflective skills that enable students not only to understand the relevant issues and obstacles to peace, but more importantly to develop skills and abilities to confront these issues, envision realistic alternatives and devise and implement strategies for the realisation of the alternatives.

Holistic and Comprehensive Dimensions

The Peace Education Programmes at Teachers College emphasise the integral relationship between pedagogy and content that is essential to its transformative nature. Drawing from the rich field of peace studies, Peace Education goes beyond learning about peace to teaching for a culture of peace. Peace education openly acknowledges its purpose as education to facilitate the achievement of peace and a related set of social values, largely through learning to recognise, confront and practice alternatives to multiple forms of violence.

Peace Education in Practice

Schooling and other educational experiences that reflect UNICEF's approach to peace education should:

- Function as 'zones of peace', where children are safe from conflict in the community;

- Uphold children's basic rights as enumerated in the CRC;
- Develop a climate, within the school or other learning environment, that models peaceful and rights—respectful behaviour in the relationships between all members of the school community: teachers, administrators, other staff, parents, and children;
- Demonstrate the principles of equality and non-discrimination in administrative policies and practices;
- Draw on the knowledge of peace building that already exists in the community, including means of dealing with conflict that are effective, non-violent, and rooted in the local culture;
- Handle conflicts—whether between children, or between children and adults— in a non-violent manner that respects the rights and dignity of all involved;
- Integrate an understanding of peace, human rights, social justice and global issues throughout the curriculum whenever possible;
- Provide a forum for the explicit discussion of values of peace and social justice;
- Use teaching and learning methods that promote participation, cooperation, problem-solving and respect for differences;
- Allow opportunities for children to put peace-making into practice, both in the educational setting and in the wider community;
- Provide opportunities for continuous reflection and professional development of all educators in relation to issues of peace, justice and rights.

Conclusion

Thus, Peace Education has been defined by the eminent educationists in different ways. Of course, it is not a particular subject in schools like Science, Maths, Physics, History, Geography and etc. Peace may be negative and positive. So, we should have to create peace among students in a positive way while teaching the subjects, because the world has lot of critical and complicated problems for each and every individual. Hence, the class teacher should take onus of creating peace and can change their attitude towards positive peace not only within the four walls of a class, but also outside of the class, and make them as humane. There are numerous approaches to peace education such as Holistic approach, TC approach, inter-disciplinary approach, YMCA approach, negative approach, positive approach and many more.

REFERENCES

1. Gangrade, K.D. (2008) *Gandhian Perspectives on Global Interdependence, Peace and Role of Professional Social Work*: Delhi, Authors Press.
2. http://en.wikipedia.org/wiki/peace_education retrieved on 28-10-2009
3. http://www.spaceforpeace.net/download.php?f=146147ed21c9d16f9557f31fa5878886 retrieved on 28-10-2009.
4. http://www.spaceforpeace.net/pe.phtml retrieved on 28-10-2009.
5. http://www.ppu.org.uk/learn/peaceed/pe_which1.html retrieved on 28-10-2009
6. http://www.ppu.org.uk/learn/peaceed/pe_which1.html retrieved on 28-10-2009.
7. http://www.encyclopedia.com /doc/1G2-3403200482.html retrieved on 28-10-2009.
8. http://www.firstschool.ws/activities/firststeps/peaceeducation.htm retrieved on 30-10-2009.
9. http;//www.unicef.org/girlseducation/files/peaceEducation.pdf retrieved on 28-10-2009.
10. http://www.artofliving.org/intl/Intiatives/ServiceProjects/ConflictResolution/PeacebyPeace/tabid?93/Default.aspex retrieved on 02-11-2009)
11. http://www.tc.columbia.edu/Peaceed/Philosophy.htm retrieved on 02-11-2009

12. Rajput, J.S. (edt. 2004) *Encyclopaedia of Indian Education:* NCERT Vol. II, (L-Z).

13. UNESCO (1998) *"Learning to Live Together in Peace and Harmony"*, A UNESCO-APNIEVE Sourcebook:Bankong,UNESCO Principal Regional Office for ASIA and the Pacific

FURTHER READINGS

1. Woolen, D.C. (1985, spring) "Education and Peace in the Thought of Johan Gatung", *Currents: Issues in Education and Human Development Education and Peace,* Vol. 3, No. 2, pp. 7-20.

2. Burns, Robin J., and Aspeslagh, Robert, eds. 1996. *Three Decades of Peace Education Around the World: An Anthology.* New York: Garland.

3. Dugan, MÁire A., and Carey, Dennis. 1996. *"Toward a Definition of Peace Studies."* In Three Decades of Peace Education Around the World: An Anthology, ed. Robin J. Burns and Robert Aspeslagh. New York: Garland.

4. Rajan, V. (1972). War and Peace: Adult Education in Peace Education. *Millennium Journal of International Studies,* 1(3), 50-66.

5. http://mendind.nic.in/haa/t05/i2/haat05i2p38.pdf retrieved on 30-10-2009.

6. Cremin, P., 1993. *'Promoting Education for Peace.'* In Cremin, P., ed., 1993, Education for Peace. Educational Studies Association of Ireland and the Irish Peace Institute.

7. Cremin, P., ed., 1993, Education for Peace. Educational Studies Association of Ireland and the Irish Peace Institute.

8. Fateem, Elham, 1993. 'Concepts of Peace and Violence: Focus Group Discussions on a Sample of Children, Parents, Teachers and Front-line Workers with Children'. Cairo: The National Center for Children's Culture (Ministry of Culture) and UNICEF.

9. Lederach, J. P., 1995. Preparing for Peace: Conflict Transformation Across Cultures. Syracuse, New York: Syracuse University Press.

10. Regan, C., 1993. 'Peace education: A Global Imperative'. In Cremin, P., ed., 1993.

CHAPTER 4

Peace Education for All

*Dr. P.P. Satyanarayana Rao

Peace education is an era of 21st century to bring down the stress level and flaring-up situations and enable the people to enjoy their life peacefully in a meaningful way. Peace education will give much importance to the human values and make the individuals to think about values, rather than violence and hatredness. Peace education play an important role in promoting the culture of peace, non-violence and tolerance by which human beings learns to live together with peace and harmony at individual level, which will intern effect at global level. Peacefulness is a calm, cool and relaxed state of situation and willingness to live together in harmony by treating all are one and accepting companionship. It will grow with positive understanding, acceptance, non-violence, tolerance and forgiveness.

In general, Peace Education may be defined as 'the process of acquiring the values, the knowledge and developing the attitudes, skills and behaviours to live in harmony with oneself, with others and with the natural environment' (*Source:* Wikipaedia, the Encyclopaedia).

James Page suggests Peace Education be thought as, 'encouraging a commitment to peace as a settled disposition and enhancing the confidence of the individual as an individual agent of peace; as informing the student on the consequences

---

* Dr. P.P. Satyanarayana Rao is Associate Professor, Department of Education, Andhra University, Visakhapatnam-530003.

of war and social injustice; as informing the student on the value of peaceful and just social structures and working to uphold or develop such social structures; as encouraging the student to leave the world and to imagine a peaceful future; and as caring for the student and encouraging the student to care for others' (*Source:* Wikipaedia, the Encyclopaedia).

Ian Harris and John Synott have described peace education as a series of 'teaching encounters' that draw from people towards 'their desire for peace, non-violent alternatives for managing conflict, and skills for critical analysis of structural arrangements that produce and legitimate injustice and inequality' (*Source:* Wikipaedia, the Encyclopaedia).

Dale Hudson defined peace education as 'education that actualises children's potentialities in helping them learn how to make peace with themselves and with others, to live in harmony and unity with self, humankind and with nature. This definition rests on the following principles: 1. The cardinal prerequisite for world peace is the unity of humankind. 2. World order can be founded only on the consciousness of the oneness of humankind. The oneness of humankind has at least three major aspects: [first] All human beings belong to the same species and all humans are related, at least as close as 50th cousins, [second] A common spiritual capacity, [third] A common home—planet earth' (Quoted by Dr. H. T. D. Rost, Baha'i Academy, New Era Development Institute, Panchgani, in his lecture on Peace Education in Norway, 2006). The above stated sentences are best suitable for children, adolescents and adults in promoting peace at all levels.

National and International organisations are making serious effort to promote peace education may be in terms of different names *viz.*, Peace Education, Human Rights Education, Environmental Education, International Education, Development Education, Conflict Resolve Education, Global Education for Liberation and Empowerment, Social Justice Education etc., to attain peace at all stages and to all equally.

All these labels are working for a common cause of spreading peace to one and all from grass-roots level to global level.

The Preamble of United Nations declares 'to save succeeding generations from the scourge of war, which twice in our lifetime has brought untold sorrow to mankind, and to reaffirm faith in fundamental human rights, in the dignity and worth of the human person, in the equal rights of men and women and of nations large and small, and to establish conditions under which justice and respect for the obligations arising from treaties and other sources of international law can be maintained, and to promote social progress and better standards of life in larger freedom" and to attain the ends 'to practice tolerance and live together in peace with one another as good neighbours, and to unite our strength to maintain international peace and security, and to ensure by the acceptance of principles and the institution of methods, that armed force shall not be used, save in the common interest, and to employ international machinery for the promotion of the economic and social advancement of all peoples' (United Nations Chapter). "Education shall be directed to the full development of the human personality and to the strengthening of respect for human rights and fundamental freedoms. It shall promote understanding, tolerance and friendship among all nations, racial or religious groups, and shall further the activities of the United Nations for the maintenance of peace" (Article 26, Universal Declaration of Human Rights).

The Preamble to the Constitution of UNESCO declares that 'Since wars begin in the minds of men, it is in the minds of men that the defences of peace must be constructed'. In the International Congress on 'Peace in the Minds of Men' held at Yamoussoukro, Cote d'Ivoire (1989), UNESCO has elaborated the notion of 'Culture of Peace' The Congress invites States, intergovernmental and non-governmental organisations, the scientific, educational and cultural communities of the world, and all individuals to 'help construct a new vision of peace by developing a peace culture based on the universal values of respect for life, liberty, justice, solidarity, tolerance, human rights and equality between women and men' and 'to promote education and research for this vision'.

The Congress recommends that UNESCO make the fullest possible contribution to all peace programmes. It recommends in particular that the following proposals be examined:

1. The endorsement of the Seville Statement on Violence (1986) first stage in an important process of reflection tending to refute the myth that organised human violence is biologically determined. This Statement should be disseminated in as many languages as possible together with appropriate explanatory material. The process of reflection should be pursued through the convening of an interdisciplinary seminar to study the cultural and social origins of violence.
2. The promotion of education and research in the field of peace. This activity should be conducted using an interdisciplinary approach and should be aimed at studying the inter-relationship between peace, human rights, disarmament, development and the environment.
3. The further development of the UNESCO-UNEP International Environmental Education Programme, in co-operation with Member States, in particular to implement the International Strategy for Action in the Field of Environmental Education and Training for the 1990s. This should incorporate fully the new vision of peace.
4. Study of the establishment with the United Nations University of an international institute of peace and human rights education, particularly aimed at training future cadres through a system of exchanges, teaching and internships.

5. The compilation of texts from all cultures, highlighting the common lessons they yield on the themes of peace, tolerance and fraternity.
6. The development of measures for the enhanced application of existing and potential United Nations—and, in particular, UNESCO—international instruments relating to human rights, peace, the environment and development and those encouraging recourse to legal remedies, dialogue, mediation and the peaceful settlement of disputes.

The Hague Agenda for Peace and Justice for 21st Century (UN Document: Ref A/54/98) is a significant contribution in this field. The Hague Appeal for Peace conference has called and campaign 'to support the United Nations Decade for a Culture of Peace and Non-violence for the Children of the World and to introduce peace and human rights education into all educational institutions, including medical and law schools'. "A culture of peace will be achieved when citizens of the world understand global problems, have the skills to resolve conflicts and struggle for justice non-violently, live by international standards of human rights and equity, appreciate cultural diversity, and respect the Earth and each other. Such learning can only be achieved with systematic education for peace"—Statement of Hague Appeal for Global Campaign for Peace Education.

UNICEF refer Peace education is ' the process of promoting the knowledge, skills, attitudes and values needed to bring about behaviour changes that will enable children, youth and adults to prevent conflict and violence, both overt and structural; to resolve conflict peacefully; and to create the conditions conducive to peace, whether at an intrapersonal, interpersonal, intergroup, national or international level'.

UNICEF and UNESCO are taking special care in promoting education for peace. UNICEF concentrating on schooling and other educational institutions to initiate to:

- Function as 'Zones of Peace', where children are safe from violent conflict.
- Uphold children's basic rights as outlined in the CRC.
- Develop a climate, within the school or other learning environment, that models peaceful and rights—respectful behaviour in the relationships between all members of the school community: teachers, administrators, other staff, parents, and children.
- Demonstrate the principles of equality and non-discrimination in administrative policies and practices.
- Draw on the knowledge of peace-building that exists in the community, including means of dealing with conflict that are effective, non-violent and rooted in the local culture.
- Handle conflicts in ways that respect the rights and dignity of all involved.
- Integrate an understanding of peace, human rights, social justice and global issues throughout the curriculum whenever possible.
- Provide a forum for the explicit discussion of values of peace and social justice.
- Use teaching and learning methods that stress participation, Cupertino, problem-solving and respect for differences.
- Allow opportunities for children to put peace-making into practice, both in the educational setting and in the wider community.
- Provide opportunities for continuous reflection and professional development of all educators in relation to issues of peace, justice and rights. (*Source:* 'Peace Education in UNICEF' working paper, 1999).

As per UN Document (UN Doc/A/RES/52/15), the year 2000 is the International Year for the 'Culture of Peace' and United Nations General Assemble has declared that the period

2001-2010 is the International Decade of the Culture of Peace and Non-Violence for the Children of the World (UN Doc A/RES/53/25). The United Nations called on every country to 'ensure that children from an early age benefit from education to enable them to resolve any dispute peacefully and in a spirit of respect for human dignity and tolerance'.

The initiative effort of UN has inspired various Institutions, Non-Governmental Organisations, Educational institutions and many more to take-up the task of peace education in teaching, practice and research in building-up the 'Culture of Peace' in the life's of humankind. Different national and international organisations are making serious efforts to promote peace education to attain peace at all stages and to all.

The long historical Independence Movement in India is an example to prove that Indians are practicing Peace (Shanti) and Non-Violence (Ahimsa) and continuing the same principles as followers of Gandhiji, since Indians treat (feel) Mahatma Gandhi as 'Father of the Nation'. But till 1958, no institution or university or research center has established either Peace Research Units or any course related to Peace Education. As per UNESCO World Directory of Peace Research and Training Institute (1994), on 1959 first institute 'Gandhi Shanti Pratishthan' was established at New Delhi to promote studies and research on peace. And from then onwards, various institutions, Universities and research centers are taking-up the task of 'Peace Education' in a constructed way to enable the people to enjoy the fruits of peace in a meaningful way.

Government of India and especially National Council of Educational Training and Research (NCERT) and other organisations are making serious efforts for widespread of peace education to develop the culture of peace from childhood. NCERT has realised the need of the hour at school level and organising orientation programmes for the teachers and mainly training the teachers in conflict resolution techniques, techniques of conflict management, ways and means to undermine violence, controlling arrogance and aggression etc., and inturn the teachers are expected to teach, guide and practice both at school and at community level.

National Council of Educational Training and Research (NCERT) have made Peace Education as part of Teacher Training Programme. Programme Co-coordinator Daya Pant has stated, "Peace is the most vital thing in human life. It is the need of the hour to sow the seeds of peace among students. Teachers under the peace education programme are taught the nitty-gritty of inculcating peace among students in a holistic manner".

NCERT spokesman Bishnucharan Patro said, "The programme's primary goal is to shape up the child's life cohesively. That will be possible only if some extra efforts are made. Our peace education programme is an effort in that direction. It is open to teachers of all streams".

Prof. Sushama Gulati, Head of Department of Educational Psychology and Foundations of Education at NCERT has stated "There will be an orientation programme for teachers that will include techniques of conflict management and controlling arrogance and aggression. They will pass on the experience to their students." She said that 'the teachers are the role models for students and hence they can help their pupils handle the day-to-day situations in a non-violent way. Arrogance and aggression, which propel violence, are two vices that can be controlled by value-based education. Further, she stated, "Crimes by students is a global concern. The students come across trying situations at their home, educational institutions and other places and tend to commit crime. If they are trained in matters pertaining to social justice, human rights, self-respect, inter-cultural harmony, balancing between rights and responsibilities, the students will restrain themselves from any conflict with law. And this course deals with these issues". Prof. Sushama Gulati has rightly pointed out the importance of peace education at school level. If the child or youth are not trained/educated properly about conflict management and conflict resolution techniques at younger age, they may become violent adults with dysfunctional and deviant in social behaviour. Generally, children will learn prejudices from schoolmates, parents, their peers and prejudice-prone personalities. Peace educators should understand the causes of prejudices and should be able to take-up remedial measures to prevent/reduce the level prejudice to make them as good citizens of the state.

On April, 2007, Community Based Institution for Peace Education (CIPE) at its meeting (held at Shillong) has recommended that, "Peace Education is a field of the theory and practice of education related to the idea of promoting knowledge, values, attitudes and skills conducive to peace and non-violence and to an active commitment to the building of a cooperative and caring democratic society. It is targeted towards the empowerment of an individual and the promotion of social well-being through the protection of human dignity for all, the promotion of social justice, equality, civil responsibility and solidarity and the accepting of a dynamic global perspective, by utilizing the concepts and practices of peaceful conflict-resolution and non-violence". The above stated recommendation reveals the importance of Peace Education in this complex society. In this modern complex society domestic violence, environmental destruction, crimes, riots, wars, conflict, hatredness are bombarding the individual's day-to-day life and creating caius and confusion and frightening situation. The purpose of peace education will not be served unless/until people develop belief and will-power in it and everybody should make multifaceted effort starting from children. Peace educators should take all pre-cautionary measures in framing the peace education curriculum and proper programming for effective spread of message among the members of the society, since the prime aim of peace education is to achieve unity in diversity and culture of peace both at individual level and at societal level.

Peace education not only concentrate on the causes and consequences of war and violence, but also it concentrate on the nature and reasons of unrest, violence, prejudice, ethnic hatred, discrimination, dehumanization poverty, humiliation, gender inequality, rape, social disparities, genocide, conflict, threat to life, ethnic conflict, terrorism, inequality and injustice, international conflicts, national conflicts, regional conflicts, riots, war, brutal killing, calamities, arms usage, bombing etc. and egocentric is another cause for conflict or aggression, since they don't care, don't recognise and don't consider the interests and views of others, by keeping 'self-interest' in their minds.

The peace education is the only way and 'Culture of Peace' can be achieved by peaceful talks, kindness, soft feelings, soft expressions, self-discipline, positive thinking about others, encouraging good and positive relation with others, co-operation and co-ordination among themselves, effective communication, convincing or motivating or avoiding unreasonable personalities, sharing feelings, understanding other's feelings, respect each other, encouraging group feelings and group culture, humanism, ethnic relation by developing the feeling of all are one and one for all.

Peace education not only develops peace in life style, but also develops knowledge about the society, surroundings, present state of affairs, principles, policies, rights, duties, responsibilities, socialisation, unity, harmony, love towards humankind, justice, reciprocity, empathy, fairness, non-violence, universal human values, moral values, forgiveness, rights of child, liberation, solidarity, tolerance, ethics, peaceful conflict resolution, unilateral disarmaments, respect towards law and order, peaceful co-existence, problem-solving both at individual level and at societal level.

In other words, peace education not only concentrate on the causes and consequences of unpeaceful incidents, but also it study the nature of it and its forms in depth to understand and to create awareness on the root cause of it. Inner peace (peace of mind) and outer peace (peace in society) should go together to enjoy the real fruits of humankind at full length.

Peace education plays a vital role in promoting love and affection, trustworthiness, justice to all by overcoming or replacing hatredness, injustice, falsehood, and unreliability. To achieve the peaceful situation either between the individuals or in the nation or between the nations, one should have positive attitudes towards victim and perpetrator, accepting the intrinsic values of others and should be able to respect each other as 'We should treat others as we ourselves would wish to be treated'.

As part of Peace Education, Peace Educators will act as Peace-keeping, Peace-making and Peace-building personalities to promote peace at all levels irrespective of caste, creed, color, religion and region. At wider perspective, peace can achieved either at individual or at Nation or even at Global level by developing peace-making and peace-keeping skills and practicing as part of our day-to-day life. A. J. Muste has rightly stated that 'There is no way to Peace. Peace is the way' (*Source:* wikipaedia, the Encyclopaedia).

REFERENCES

1. 'Education for Peace', National Council of Educational Research and Training, New Delhi, 2002.
2. 'Education for Peace', National Council of Educational Research and Training, New Delhi, 2005.
3. Harris, Ian and Synott, John (2002), 'Peace Education for a New Century: Social Alternatives 21 (1): 3-6 (as quoted in Wikipaedia, the Enclopaedia).
4. Harris, I an and Mary Lee Morrison, 'Peace Education', Second Edition, McFarland and Company Inc., Publishers, North Carolina, 2003.
5. International Congress Report on, 'Peace in the Minds of Men', held at Yamoussoukro, Cote d'Ivoire (1989).
6. 'National Curriculum Framework', National Council of Educational Research and Training, New Delhi, 2005.
7. Page, James S. (2008) *Peace Education: Exploring Ethical and Philosophical Foundations,* Information Age Publishing. p. 189 (as quoted in wikipaedia, the Encyclopaedia).

8. 'Peace Education in UNICEF', Working Paper, Education Section Programme Division, UNICEF, New York, June 1999.
9. 'Peace Education Activities for Children: A Teacher's Guide', New Era Development Institute, Panchgani, India, 2002.
10. 'Perspectives on Human Rights', edited by Vijay K. Gupta published by Vikas Publishing House Pvt. Ltd., New Delhi, 1996.
11. Prasad, Surya Nath, 'Development of Peace Education in India (Since Independence)', Peace Education Miniprint No. 95, 1998.
12. Sudhakar, Sumathi, Usha Jesudasan and Fathima Muzaffer, 'Living in Harmony: A Course on Peace and Value Education', Book 4, Oxford University Press, New Delhi, 2006.
13. United Nations Cyber School Bus.
14. United Nations Educational, Scientific and Cultural Organisation, 2001.

CHAPTER 5

Suggestive Activities in Promoting Peace Education

*Dr. J.D. Singh

Peace education leads to peaceful living. As teacher educators, we are constantly looking for engaging and meaningful topics to use in our classrooms. Peace Education offers us topics and issues that touch the lives of our students every day such as resolving conflicts, clarifying values, and understanding diversity. The classroom also offers us the opportunity to help students address these issues through activities and tasks that are related to the content and that require the practice of language skills, social interaction skills, and critical thinking skills. Peace education is based on a philosophy that teaches non-violence, love, compassion, trust, fairness, cooperation and reverence for the human family and all life on our planet.

But a few questions to be answered: Are we giving adequate attention today to teach peace? Are our schools really interested in producing a peaceful young generation? Is it enough having mere peace concepts in the curriculum? This is a matter of debate? Is Government of India as a member of United Nation striving towards peace in schools, colleges and universities and how the UN bodies are making efforts to incorporate the Peace education as an integral part of the curriculum?

The General Assembly of the United Nations proclaimed the years 2001-2010 "the International Decade for a Culture of Peace and Non-violence for the Children of the World".

* Lecturer, G.V. College of Education (CTE), Sangaria-335063 (Rajasthan).

The United Nations has called on every country to "ensure that children, from an early age, benefit from education to enable them to resolve any dispute peacefully and in a spirit of respect for human dignity and of tolerance". It defines a culture of peace as "all the values, attitudes and forms of behaviour that reflect respect for life, for human dignity and for all human rights, the rejection of violence in all its forms and commitment to the principles of freedom, justice, solidarity, tolerance and understanding between people".

Global peace has become a major concern these days. There is a general restlessness in the entire world which is leading to widespread violence. Empathy for others, democratic living, secular values have been relegated to the background. Educatinoal process seems to have lost track of the original purpose of bringing out the best in each individual. Instead, even schooling is seen as a part of the rat race for which we are preparing the posterity. Under these circumstances, there is a great need to reconsider our own objectives of education and ensure that the principles of right living and non-violence are incorporated into the process of education.

Meaning of Peace Education

Peace is the inner state of calm that remains despite external circumstances. It is cultivated through the development of inner qualities that result in a peaceful state of mind. Peace education may be defined as the process of acquiring the values, the knowledge and developing the attitudes, skills, and behaviours to live in harmony with oneself, with others, and with the natural environment.

When mankind matures, it leaves behind itself adolescent views of the world, and a more mature and peaceful civilisation is born. Peace is possible only in mature societies where a universal world view and the mentality are in place. A civilisation of peace is possible where universal love exists, a love which does not exclude anyone and which is addressed to everyone. The more we create love and unity in diversity, the less there will be hate and wars.

Peace education encompasses the key concepts of education and peace. While it is possible to define education as a process of systematic institutionalised transmission of knowledge and skills, as well as of basic values and norms that are accepted in a certain society, the concept of peace is less clearly defined.

Peace is not simply the absence of war but a condition in which people are free from the fear of potential and actual violence—a condition where justice flourishes.

Peace Education is concerned with helping learners to develop an awareness of the processes and skills that are necessary for achieving understanding, tolerance, and good-will in the world today. Educating for peace means :

- Examining and discussing our values and attitudes towards diversity, cultural differences, tolerance, and human dignity;
- Developing language and social interaction skills to promote peaceful relations among people, among nations, and between human beings and the natural environment;
- Learning to solve problems and to think critically regarding issues of conflict and violence.

Peace education in UNICEF refers to "the process of promoting the knowledge, skills, attitudes and values needed to bring about behaviour changes that will enable children, youth and adults to prevent conflict and violence, both overt and structural; to resolve conflict peacefully; and to create the conditions conducive to peace, whether at an intrapersonal, interpersonal, intergroup, national or international level". This definition represents a convergence of ideas that have been developed through the practical experiences of UNICEF peace education programmes.

Quotes on Peace Education

Educationists, leaders and preachers have opined about peace education are ahead—

"To laugh often and love much; to win the respect of intelligent persons and the affection of children, to earn the approbation of honest critics; to appreciate beauty; to give of one's self, to leave the world a bit better, whether by a healthy child, a garden patch or a redeemed social condition; to have played and laughed with enthusiasm and sung with exultation; to know even one life has breathed easier because you have lived—that is to have succeeded." *—Ralph Waldo Emerson*

"Be the change you want to see in the world. It is possible to live in peace." *—Mahatma Gandhi (1869-1948)*

"Peace education plants positive seeds (*i.e.* thoughts, techniques) that shift behaviour towards non-violent responses." *—Anonymous*

"Our most basic common link is that we all inherit this small planet, we all breathe the same air, we all cherish our children's future." *—President John F. Kennedy*

His Holiness the Dalai Lama explains that as "we feel love and kindness towards others, it not only makes others feel loved and cared for, but it helps us also to develop inner happiness and peace."

"Peace is the marriage of the people and the planet, with all attendant vows." *— Anonymous*

"There is no trust more sacred than the one the world holds with children. There is no duty more important than ensuring that their rights are respected, that their welfare is protected, that their lives are free from fear and want and that they grow up in peace." *— Kofi Annan*

"Democracy is an objective. Democratisation is a process. Democratisation serves the cause of peace because it offers the possibility of justice and of progressive change without force." *— Boutros Boutros-Ghali*

"Human Beings, indeed all sentient beings, have the right to pursue happiness and live in peace and freedom."

—*The XIV Dalai Lama*

"Peace cannot be kept by force. It can only be achieved by understanding." —*Albert Einstein (1879-1955)*

"One day we must come to see that peace is not merely a distant goal that we seek, but that it is a means by which we arrive at that goal. We must pursue peaceful ends through peaceful means."

—*Martin Luther King, Jr. (1929-1968)*

"Establishing lasting peace is the work of education; all politics can do is keep us out of war."

—*Maria Montessori (1870-1952)*

"If we have no peace, it is because we have forgotten that we belong to each other."

—*Mother Theresa (1910-1997)*

According to UNESCO, a peace oriented education... ".....should attempt to reduce the willingness to use violence in individuals and to reveal and remove the infrastructures which cause violence in human relations at all levels of society and amongst nations."

The term 'peace education' can cover many areas, from advocacy to law reform, from basic education to social justice. It is generally agreed that there is a difference between peace education and peace building. Peace education is an attempt to change people's behaviours; peace building incorporates social and economic justice (and legal reform where necessary).

Purposes of Peace Education

Peace education programme can enable people to think constructively about issues, both physical and social, that need solutions and to develop constructive attitudes of living in community. With this understanding young people will be better equipped to stand up to the culture of war in society and, we hope, be determined 'not to support any kind of war' and be encouraged 'to work for the removal of all causes of war'. It also includes teaching young people positive communication skills that they can use throughout their lives. Teaching students about how to achieve peace empowers them to seek alternatives to violence, so they can build a more peaceful future. It lays the foundation for a culture of peace. Peace education aims to help students acquire skills for non-violent conflict resolution and to reinforce these skills for active and responsible action in the society for the promotion of the values of peace. Our global existence depends on learning to live together without the threat of violence and conflict. Educators have the unique opportunity to promote peaceful co-existence by bringing the processes of peacemaking and peacekeeping to the attention of their students in the classroom. The overall aim of Education for Peace is to help build a peaceful world. The major purposes of Peace Education are as follows:

- to build, maintain, and restore relationships at all levels of human interaction;
- to create a better learning environment where conflict and relationships may be explored;
- education as a catalyst for activating a democratic and secular culture;
- to create a more peaceful world where all of us may become agents for change. Education for Peace gives us the skills that will assist in achieving peaceful societies;
- to develop positive approaches towards dealing with conflicts—from the personal to the international;
- creating frameworks for achieving peace and peaceful, creative societies;
- to make learners aware of the basis of conflict and how to resolve conflict in their daily lives;
- empowering people with the skills, attitudes, and knowledge;

- to investigate the causes of conflicts and violence embedded within perceptions, values and attitudes of individuals as well as within social and political structures of society;
- nurturing in students the social skills and outlook needed to live together in harmony;
- reinforcing social justice, as envisaged in the Constitution;
- to build a sustainable environment and protect it from exploitation and war;
- to create safe environments, both physically and emotionally, that nurture each individual;
- promoting national integration through education; and education for peace as a lifestyle movement;
- to prepare students to become good citizens of their communities, nations, and the world with skills to promote peace and human dignity on all levels of interaction;
- to use the classroom as a microcosm of a just world order, in which the global values of positive interdependence, social justice, and participation in decision-making processes are learned and practiced.

Examples of Peace Education Activities

The purpose of the initiative is to help significantly reduce the human costs of violence in our country and abroad through education (*i.e.* what we are trying to achieve). The suggested objects are: The advancement of education in the methods of achieving the peaceful resolution of conflict, within families, communities and throughout the world, by means of educational programmes, research programmes, educational media programmes, schools, conferences and resource libraries, and other learning materials. Schools, universities and existing educational institutions may undertake activities for developing and disseminating peace. Details of main activities in peace education include:

- development of instructional videos, audios, books, newsletters and other publications.
- using of new technologies to promote peace-minded quality education.
- training in empowerment, leadership, governance, public accountability, social accountability, peace informatics, peace psychology, ethics, change management.
- raising funds for the above activities, from individuals, corporations and businesses, other registered charities, sales of goods and services, government grants or contracts.
- service-learning in peace education responding to real community needs as identified by the community, by utilising reflection to combine service and training, through a collaborative process involving faculty, students, administrators, and staff and community partners.
- establishing peace societies and similar institutions to build peace.
- undertaking research in the field of peace, for educational purposes and available to the public.
- supporting development of country-based educational materials, curricula, and teaching manuals for Peace Education.
- establishing and maintaining peace resource libraries.
- providing scholarships and prizes for scholastic achievements in peace and future studies.
- advancing peace science and related institutions, including maintaining related learned societies.
- providing models of peace and promoting the preservation of peaceful environments.

- creating a historical account of students' human rights and peace education initiatives.
- development and dissemination of peace education curricula.
- establishing workshops, conferences and other venues for communicating, networking, information dissemination, development and instruction.
- capacity building to promote democratic youth leadership, training of child broadcasters, and parents' education for conflict mediation and non-violence.
- formal training and instruction through establishing, operating and supporting classes, schools, colleges, universities, and other similar institutions.
- organising and providing formal and informal peace and future studies instruction.
- exploring human rights workers and peace activists strategies through storytelling.
- to develop children's skills for conflict resolution, offer alternative behaviours to youth, and build pressure for changes in public policy through youth involvement in peace-building at community and national levels.
- Using puppets puts the problem at a safe enough distance from children's' lives and them to become more creative in generating solutions.

Role of UNICEF and UNESCO in Peace Education

The international role in peace education is also expanding. There is a recognition that education has been used politically and, unless challenged, the persistence of divergent views of history can be a source of latent conflict. In other words, peace education is an integral part of the work of the United Nations. Through a humanising process of teaching and learning, peace educators facilitate human development. They strive to counteract the dehumanisation of poverty, prejudice, discrimination, rape, violence, and war. Originally aimed at eliminating the possibility of global extinction through nuclear war, peace education currently addresses the broader objective of building a culture of peace.

UNICEF and UNESCO are particularly active advocates of education for peace. UNICEF describes peace education as schooling and other educational initiatives that:

- Function as 'zones of peace', where children are safe from violent conflict;
- Develop a climate that models peaceful and respectful behaviour among all members of the learning community;
- Demonstrate the principles of equality and non-discrimination in administrative policies and practices;
- Draw on the knowledge of peace building that exists in the community, including means of dealing with conflict that are effective, non-violent, and rooted in the local culture;
- Handle conflicts in ways that respect the rights and dignity of all involved Integrate an understanding of peace, human rights, social justice and global issues throughout the curriculum whenever possible;
- Provide a forum for the explicit discussion of values of peace and social justice;
- Use teaching and learning methods that stress participation, problem-solving and respect for differences;
- Enable children to put peace-making into practice in the educational setting as well as in the wider community;
- Generate opportunities for continuous reflection and professional development of all educators in relation to issues of peace, justice and rights. (*Peace Education in UNICEF Working Paper Series, July 1999*)

Peace education is an integral part of the UNICEF vision of quality basic education. The 1990 World Declaration on

Education for All, clearly states that basic learning needs comprise not only essential tools such as literacy and numeracy, but also the knowledge, skills, attitudes and values required to live and work in dignity and to participate in development. It further states that the satisfaction of those needs implies a responsibility to promote social justice, acceptance of differences, and peace.

A RATIONALE FOR PEACE EDUCATION IN UNICEF

Article 29 of the Convention on the Rights of the Child (1989) states:

"...the education of the child shall be directed to...the preparation of the child for responsible life in a free society, in the spirit of understanding, peace, tolerance, equality of sexes, and friendship among all peoples..."

The 1990 World Declaration on Education for All says that:

"Every person—child, youth and adult—shall be able to benefit from educational opportunities designed to meet their basic learning needs. These needs comprise both essential learning tools (such as literacy, oral expression, numeracy, and problem solving) and the basic learning content (such as knowledge, skills, values, and attitudes) required by human beings to be able to survive, to develop their full capacities, to live and work in dignity, to participate fully in development, to improve the quality of their lives, to make informed decisions, and to continue learning ...The satisfaction of these needs empowers individuals in any society and confers upon them a responsibility to ... further the cause of social justice, ... to be tolerant towards social political and religious systems which differ from their own, ensuring that commonly accepted humanistic values and human rights are upheld, and to work for international peace and solidarity in an interdependent world."

The 1996 study by Graça Machel on *The Impact of Armed Conflict on Children* reaffirmed the importance of education in shaping a peaceful future:

"...Both the content and the process of education should promote peace, social justice, respect for human rights and the acceptance of responsibility. Children need to learn skills of negotiation, problem solving, critical thinking and communication that will enable them to resolve conflicts without resorting to violence."

The UNICEF 'Anti-war Agenda', set out in *The State of the World's Children 1996,* declares:

"...Disputes may be inevitable, but violence is not. To prevent continued cycles of conflict, education must seek to promote peace and tolerance, not fuel hatred and suspicion."

Since 1990, a number of UNICEF documents have confirmed this vision of basic education as a process that encompasses the knowledge, skills attitudes and values needed to live peacefully in an interdependent world. 'The Future Global Agenda for Children—Imperatives for the Twenty-first Century' (UNICEF 1999, E/ICEF/1999/10) makes a commitment to "... ensure that education and learning processes help to form both human capital for economic growth and social capital for tolerance, respect for others and the right of each individual to participate with equality within family, community and economic life; ... and to challenge the culture of violence that threatens to destroy family and community life in so many countries." Peace education must address the prevention and resolution of all forms of conflict and violence, whether overt or structural, from the interpersonal level to the societal and global level.

Much of the work of UNESCO is centred on the promotion of education for peace, human rights, and democracy. The notion of a 'culture of peace' was first elaborated for UNESCO at the International Congress on Peace in the Minds of Men, held at Yamoussoukro, Cote d'Ivoire, in 1989. The Yamoussoukro Declaration called on UNESCO to 'construct a new vision of peace by developing a peace culture based on the universal values of respect for life, liberty, justice, solidarity, tolerance, human rights and equality between women and men' and to promote education and research for this vision. (UNESCO and a Culture of Peace, UNESCO Publishing, 1995).

Therefore, The UNESCO has instituted peace education prize. The purpose of the UNESCO Prize for Peace Education is to promote all forms of action designed to construct the defences of peace in the minds of men by rewarding a particularly outstanding example of activity designed to alert public opinion and mobilise the conscience of humankind in the cause of peace, in accordance with the spirit of the Constitution of the United Nations Educational, Scientific and Cultural Organisation and the United Nations Charter. The UNESCO is committed to the education of the peace. It is publishing a lot of resource material and circulating worldwide for mass awareness. The library and documentation centre in India is a catalyst for the publication for material for the teachers and resource persons. UNESCO as a technical support agency is imparting skill based training to the resource persons and preparing them for the good of the society.

Underlying all of this work in the field of peace education are the efforts of committed educators, researchers, activists, and members of global civil society. Acting in partnership with the United Nations and its Specialised Agencies, Non-governmental Organisations (NGOs), educational institutions, and citizen networks have advanced education for peace by linking ideals with extensive research and practice. The International Peace Research Association, founded with support from UNESCO, has a Peace Education Commission that brings together educators working to promote a culture of peace. The Peace Education Network, based in London, also works alongside the UN in promoting peace through education. Overall, the participation of global civil society in building a culture of peace is essential.

Role of Teacher in Improving the School Peace Environment

Peace education is most effective when the skills of peace and conflict resolution are learned actively and are modelled by the school environment in which they are taught. In a number of countries, emphasis is placed on improving the school environment so that it becomes a microcosm of the more peaceful and just society that is the objective of peace education. This creates a consistency between the messages of the curriculum and the school setting, between the overt and the 'hidden' curriculum. Interventions on the level of the school environment tend to address how children's rights are either upheld or denied in school, discipline methods, how the classroom and school day is organised, and how decisions are made. Training of teachers and administrators is critical to enabling teachers to examine these issues from the perspective of peace education. Aiming to arm teachers with skills to promote a sense of harmony with oneself and social environment among students for avoiding conflict with law, there will be an orientation programme on 'peace education' for teachers that will include techniques of conflict management and controlling arrogance and aggression. Teachers are the role models for students and hence they can help their pupils handle the day-to-day situations in a non-violent way.

First, the teacher must understand that multicultural, multiethnic, and multi-religious problems in society are not to be dealt with in isolation in bits and pieces of a good peace education programme but, being interconnected with all other problems of peace and violence, are addressed in the whole programme. For example, developing such qualities as compassion and service to others can help reduce racial, religious, or other prejudices, but students of all backgrounds must take part in the programme. Activities in school can improve students' performance through peace education.

Second, the teacher must be cognizant and wholly supportive of the basic nature and aims of peace education. It follows that, in this view, the teacher of peace education in an apparently diverse society must keep certain basic aims in mind: the achievement of a unified, peaceful society both globally and within the nation, where world citizenship is fostered and 'unity in diversity' is recognised and practiced.

Third, the teacher should constantly keep in mind that the attainment of any aim is conditioned upon knowledge, volition, and action. The power needed to accomplish a peaceful world is the unification of humankind. To this end, the teacher must use his or volition and will-power. In the words of Sarvepalli Radhakrishnan, we should "... will peace with our whole body and soul, our feelings and instincts, our flesh and its affections." Then we should act intelligently to reduce intercultural, interethnic, and inter-religious violence, bringing a greater degree of unity and harmony in society. To accomplish this, the teacher should develop qualities such as tolerance, respect of and appreciation of others, being fair and open-minded, and being able and willing to consider other points of view looking beyond his or her own self-interest. In other words, the teacher must be sincerely attempting to be free of prejudice. Implementing peace education in the classroom can be achieved several ways:

- Using topics that raise the issues related to peace and cultural understanding in our classrooms, a teachers can give students basic information to help them develop positive attitudes and values related to 'peaceful' living.
- Engaging in activities that encourage cooperation, consensus building, and reflective listening gives students the skills they need to meet and resolve conflicts.
- Confronting issues and problems related to the topics will provide opportunities for students to develop problem-solving skills and critical thinking skills to express themselves clearly and convincingly.

In our experience, when a teacher becomes deeply and regularly involved in teaching peace education, this can cause that teacher to take a long, deep look at his or her values and beliefs. Clearly, it can center a person on one's own thoughts, words, and deeds. In order to be a model for the students, the teacher has the opportunity of transformation and change of the inner self. Then the students can be helped to understand and feel what is a peaceful person who is a peacemaker, and the teacher will have a powerful, positive influence on hundreds and thousands of children and youth.

Peace education is now a part of the teacher-training programme of the National Council of Educational Training and Research (NCERT), which formulates school curricula and teacher training programmes in India. In the land of Mahatma Gandhi, the apostle of non-violence, teachers are now getting trained to teach peace as a subject to students. The six-week long programme was first started at the NCERT headquarters in New Delhi during the summer vacation in 2006 and was repeated the next years. It is the need of the hour to sow the seeds of peace among students. Teachers under the peace education programme are taught the nitty-gritty of inculcating peace among students in a holistic manner. The best way to shape them up effectively for positive goals is through their teachers. There is a need to train teachers accordingly.

Suggestions

Reviews of research on effective school-based, skill-oriented conflict resolution programmes suggest that important points may include:

1. According to UN, peace education must be the core objective of every member country so as to imbibe the social, cultural and traditional and intellectual values among the students.
2. Peace education should not mean the education of the peace of mind only but for preparing the young minds for the mutual dialogue and understanding in

intellectual arena. Peace education is more effective and meaningful when it is adopted according to the social and cultural context and the needs of a country. It should be enriched by its cultural and spiritual values together with the universal human values. It should also be globally relevant.

3. National Curriculum Framework (NCF) (2005) by NCERT asserts that education must be able to promote values that foster peace, humanness and tolerance in a multicultural society. So that training programmes should organise regularly for the teachers on peace education in the country in which the objective is to build the peace for self and empowerment.
4. Peace education should be used to focus efforts in programme development, as well as to give a sense of the wide range of activities that can promote peace through many different learning contexts.
5. The interpersonal relationships, and the style and approaches to teaching are as important as the content of the curriculum. This means: Policy documents with references to Education for Peace should be displayed throughout the school and referred to regularly in lessons and in activities such as themed assemblies, school plays and concerts.
6. The components of Education for Peace must be implicit in all school structures including the school ethos and anti-bullying strategy. All adults in the school should model what is being taught about respecting others and resolving conflict non-violently.

Conclusion

Peace education brings together multiple traditions of pedagogy, theories of education and international initiatives to help teachers and students understand the complex dynamics of international affairs and the various forms of violence and its alternatives. Its activities seek to move students away from modes of thinking and acting that promote warring to ways of behaving that create a peaceful global order. In the classroom, it takes a variety of forms including courses on violence prevention emphasising peacekeeping strategies and courses on non-violence that build in students' minds a consciousness that desires peace. Peace education involves the use of teaching tools designed to bring about a more peaceful society. In spite of its tremendous growth in the twentieth century, peace education has not really taken hold in school systems around the world. We should use United Nations mandates to stimulate formal school-based peace education activities.

Peace education is a diverse field that includes the theoretical, research, and practical activities of experts from many disciplines. Peace educators no longer solely concern themselves with interstate rivalry but also study ways to resolve intra-state violence and the chaos that comes from identity and religious based conflicts. Peace can be developed through active, meaningful engagement with other people and working towards a common goal. A culture of peace will be achieved when citizens of the world understand global problems, have the skills to resolve conflicts and struggle for justice non-violently, live by international standards of human rights and equity, appreciate cultural diversity, and respect the Earth and each other. Such learning can only be achieved with systematic education for peace.

REFERENCES

1. Bartal, D. (2002), *The Elusive Nature of Peace Education:* In G. Salomon and B. Nevo (Eds.), *Peace Education: The Concepts, Principles, and Practices Around the World* (pp. 27-36). Mahwah, NJ: Lawrence Erlbaum Associates.
2. Brocke-Utne, B. (1985), *Educating for Peace: A Feminist Perspective* New York: Pergamon Press.
3. Harris, I., and M. Morrison (2003), *Peace Education* (2nd edition). Jefferson, NC: McFarland & Co.
4. Montessori, M. (1974), *Education for a New World*. (Thiruvanmiyur, India: Kalakshetra Press).

5. Reardon, B. (1988), *Comprehensive Peace Education: Educating for Global Responsibility*. New York: Teachers College Press.

6. Salomon, G. (2002), *The Nature of Peace Education:* Not All Programmes are Created Equal. In G. Salomon & B. Nevo (Eds.), *Peace Education: The concepts, principles, and practices around the world.* (pp. 3-14) Mahwah, NJ: Lawrence Erlbaum Associates.

7. Balasooriya, A. S. (2001), *Learning the Way of Peace:* A Teachers' Guide to Peace Education. New Delhi: United Nations Educational, Scientific and Cultural Organisation.

8. www.humanrightsandpeacestore.org.

9. www.ineesite.org/edcon/peace.asp

CHAPTER 6

Peace Educatior in Present Era for World Peace

*Mr. Adnan Khan Lodi

The object of this paper is *first,* to try the define world peace and to clarity its various rarefactions both in its negative sense, which implies the absence of war in a positive ways the factors that's seek to prevent war and promote world peace; *secondly* to discuss the various theories connected with world peace and *thirdly,* to discuss the importance of peace education and *Fourthly,* to discuss the task of peace education. In promoting world peace.

What is the Meant by War and Peace?

Tagore Rightly Said "Where the mind is with out fear and the head is held high, into that kingdom of freedom my father let me country awake".

War is a state of hostility between nation (or within nation or within individual characterized by fighting, destruction or bloodshed. war are often caused by real/perceived injustice hatred, poverty and the desire for power. On the other hand, peace is an ideal of freedom and happiness among and within all nations and people. world peace is an utopian idea of planetary non-violence by which nations willingly cooperate, either voluntarily or by virtue of a system of government which prevents warfare. World peace may simply mean the resolution of global and regional conflict through non-violent means or it may mean the end of violence among all individuals.

---

*Sr. Lecturer, Deptt. of Teacher Education, Vivek College, Bijnor (U.P.).

World Peace Theory

Many theories for achieving world peace have been proposed. world peace is claimed to be the inevitable results of certain political ideologies. some of these are given below :

1. **The Democratic Peace Theory :** The proponents of this theory claim that's democracies never or rarely wags against each other. Former U.S. President George W. Bush said "the march of democracy will lead to world peace." there have been no wars between well-established liberal democracies. An increasing number of nation have become democratic since the industrial revolution. there are, however, several expectations to the above theory.
2. **Capitalism Peace Theory :** A.Y.N. Rand in her 'Capitalism peace theory' holds that's the major wars of history were started by the more controlled economic of the time against the free ones and that's capitalism gave mankind the longest period of peace in history—a period during which there were no wars, involving the entire civilised world from the end of the Napoleonic wars in 1815 to the outbreak of World War I in 1914. This theory ignores the fact that's there was no pure capitalism in the 19th century and that's there were colonial wars.
3. **Cobdenism :** This theory claims that's by removing tariffs and creating international free trade, wars would become impossible, because free trend prevents a nation from becoming self-sufficient, which is a requirement for long wars. For example, one country produce fire arms and another produce ammunition, the two could not fight each other, because the former would be unable to obtain weapons.
4. **Mutual Assured Destruction (MAD) :** This is a doctrine of military strategy in which a full scale use of nuclear weapons by two opposing side would effectively result in the destruction of both the attacker and the defender.

5. **Isolationism and Non-inter Ventronism :** Proponents of this theory claim that many nations can peacefully exist, if they focus on domestic affairs and do not try to impose their will on other nations non-interventionism advocates combining free tread with political and military non-interference.
6. **Self-organised Peace :** World peace can be ensured by having a self-organised network of mutually supportive mechanism, resulting in a viable politico-social fabric and enabling anyone to participate irrespective of his cultural background, religious, doctrine, political affiliation or age.
7. **Globalisation :** Many country such as China, Italy and United States and Germany and Britain have unified into single nation state. Nations of the European Union have also blurred their boundaries and have now a common currency. the Euro. it is hoped that's further globalisation will bring about a unified world order.

Religious Views of World Peace

Different religious leaders have expressed a desire to end violence and ensure world peace.

The *Bhai* faith prescribed a world embracing collective security arrangement for the establishment of lasting peace.

The *Buddhist* believe that world peace within our mined. Buddha said, "peace comes from within". Do not seek it without. Anger and other negative states of the mind are the cause of wars and fighting. we can live-in peace and harmony only if we abandon the anger in our minds and learn to love each other.

The Christian ideal promotes peace through goodwill and by sharing the faith with other, as well as forgiving those who try to break peace.

Hinduism hold that's the world is one family (*Vasudhev kutumbakam*). Only base minds see dichotomies and divisions.

The more we seek wisdom, the more we become inclusive and free our internal spirits from worldly illusion s or Maya. world peace can only be achieved through internal means by liberating oneself from artificial boundaries that's separate us.

Sikhism all beings and creatures are his; he belongs to all. God is contained within all. (Guru Granth Sahib 425 and 706) the special feature of Sikhism is that's it goes beyond the framework of caste classification and moves in humility.

Islam there is only one God. having common parents Adam and eve is the greatest reason for humans to live together with peace and brotherhood. The Quran recognises the whole of humanity as one family.

Judaism holds that's when the messiah comes all nations will be united in peace.

Importance of Peace

Peace is important because it precisely means human life. Among the basic rights of mankind the first one is protecting life. This right is infringed around the world today. Some developed countries claiming they are protecting and serving this right, interfere with these underdeveloped third-world countries but in fact they infringes this right because during these interferences hundreds even thousands of innocent people dies this is only because of economical ambitions. What if peace is kept in total agreement by all nations? In these conditions, by all means development continues totally, all around the world. For this reason, 'someone' rejects and tries to prevent this development and therefore peace is prevented. The most important factor that reflects the importance of peace is psychological comfort. If you don't have psychological comfort at first you are stressed then depressed and then may go crazy and have a suicide. Because if a person doesn't have this psychological comfort and living with the fear of death, he cannot do anything correctly; he cannot go anywhere and in the end and begin to lose the control of himself, his logic and his brain. Even he cannot eat because of that fear so the importance of our psychological balance is the most important so no-one can say "I am trying to give these people their freedom"—you know to whom these words belong to—and then fall hundreds of bombs to my head. Today, in Turkey nearly half of the national budget and 95% of national lottery incomes—the amount of money is 450 million dollars—is spent to defending industry and armament expands. But if just 10 per cent of this money is left to education, education budget will multiply twice. As in this example the percentage of money that is spent for weapon and war toys, is always high than any other expands. Anyway, but if peace is permanent like all other goods, the services of healthcare and education work continually. By this way people gather around a specific aim. Human learns to have respect for other's ideas, religions, point of views and most importantly learns to have respect for other's freedom. Finally, importance of peace is seen clearly and opposite of peace 'war' is understood to be end of existence of every kind of creature. One can easily see that peace is necessity but why it cannot be provided? Answer of this question is up to you. Does anyone have one? The answer consists of everything we count from the beginning the ambitions and greed of mankind.

Ways to Prevent War and Promote Peace Education in the World

"The destiny of India is now being shaped in her classroom "this is the opening sentence of the Kothari Education commission Report (1964-66). What kind of disting has been actually shaped during that last forty years—

1. **Improved communication :** Improved communication may make all difference between our extinction or survival
2. **Acquiring knowledge :** Peace will evolve through knowledge. knowledge combined with enlightenment lags to wisdom. Wisdom is peace.

3. **Granting freedom to others :** Abraham Lincoln said, "those who deny freedom to others, deserve it not for item selves; and under a just gods cannot long retain it."
4. **Means and ends :** Martin Luther king said, The means we use to reach our ends are extremely importance.
5. **Conflict prevention and conflict resolution :** It required that's we eliminate the nature of the hostilities and attempt to create harmony and equality between the various parties. Injective should be resoled either through negotiation, meditation, arbitration, community conference, negotiated rule making, international law or as a last resort, military action.
6. **Youth development strategies :** This can help our future adults form repeating the mistakes we have made that's led to wars.
7. By suggesting alternative to governments and politician who advocate wars as the main solution to civil and international conflict.
8. By creating a true world economy, we could ends starvation, reduce poverty, creative jobs and work towards common goals such as world-wide justice, peace education, pollution control and planet management.

Globalised Education and World Peace

A phenomenon that's we have witnessed in recent times is that's of Globalization in higher education is defined as the process of political, cultural, technological and economic development that's directly affects higher education in the globalise world like other fields of society. It has affected education greatly. It transformed world trade in the latter past of the 20th century and had a profound impact on education at the start of the 21st century. innovative forms of education, computer and communication technologies, Internet have all accelerated the process of education. Some of the implications of globalisation of education and world peace have been examined below:

1. Information and innovation are highly knowledge intensive. This calls for manpower educated centers are emerging in the developing countries. Students and scholars go abroad to learn technology. Foreign experts are imported to teach locals and locals personnel are trained in multinational companies.
2. Developing countries specially the newly industrialising are increasing their size of higher education specially in science and technology.
3. The developed country universities are drawing heavily on undergraduates of developing countries. Sixty per cent graduate students of the U.S.A. are foreign nationals.
4. Scientists and engineers trained in Universities of the developing countries are being employed in multinational firms.
5. The newly industrialised countries are adopting their own innovation strategies.

Consequences of Globalisation

While globalisation is intended to break the barriers between nation, it has also some undesirable feature.

- As a result of globalisation, polities and ideology have a subordinate role to profits and market driven economy. The globalise world of higher education is highly unequal because nationally and internationally the powerful institutions of higher education, the so-called innovative centers dominate the production and distribution of knowledge and the weaker ones follow them.
- Globalisation has created a global market place for students and scholars. Most students pay tuition enriching the coffer of the host countries and draining their own some 80 per cent of students from China and India *donor* return home. The U.S.A identifies the best talent of the world and facilitates their immigration to the U.S.A.

- The limited financial capacity of the governments in developing countries could not meet the demand for massive expansive. As a result many profit making self financed institution of questionable quality have sprung up.
- Another consequence of globalisation is the inter nationalisation of curriculum and requires the content method and structure to meet international norms. Instructional material and approaches to research in both soft and hard disciplines are influenced by developed countries.
- Sometimes we witness racial discrimination in the developed countries against students coming from developed countries as recently happened in Australia.

The Role of Science and Humanities in World Peace

The world of today is in peril due to global warming disease, poverty, *stared* of terrorism and shortage of food and water. science can reduce the magnitude of these problems. Micro chip has reduce the need for *paper this saving* forest. alternative energy sources will reduce the use of fossil fuel and there by carbon emission and development in bio-technology will reduce shortage of food.

We also need social and human science, fine art, culture and philosophy. In this consumerist market- friendly society greed and corruption,brutal exploitation of natural resources, discrimination and unequal distribution will lead the world to destruction. if corrective means are not adopted through education in morals and ethics.

Conclusion

Lets us remember the message contained in the preamble of the charts of the U.N.O. that's says,

> *"wars are born in the minds of men, and it is there that the citadels of peace must be made."*

Can world peace be achieved ? this question is more important in this time now we can say, In the modern day world, peace is a phenomenon that eludes us. In spite of our best efforts strife and dissension dominate the world. History is dotted with great wars since the dawn of civilisation. The *Ramayana, The Mahabharata and the Iliad* describe the Epic wars.

It is, however obvious that success in peace education depend upon the enthusiasm and commitment of teachers and government and parents. Peace education/inculcation is not an additional subject. it should permanent all works and activities in education institution link a guardian angel.

During the last century, we have witnessed two world wars. Alexander and Nepoleon wanted to conquer the whole world. Even today we witness hostilities and rivalries among great nations that contribute a threat to world peace. What is the remedy? Probably globalisation is a step in the right direction, while avoiding its pitfalls.

REFERENCES

1. Nair, Gopinath (2009) *"Peace Education and Conflict Resolution in School"* Health Administration—Vol. XVII, No. 1, pp. 1-38-42.
2. Mishra, Loknath(2009) *"Peace Education—Framework for Teacher"* APH Publication Corporation, New Delhi.
3. S.R, Rohidekar (1995) *"Inculcation of Values–How"* Sri Rukma Prakashana, Bangalore.
4. Bowett, D. W. (1972) *"The Search for Peace"* London and Boston, Routledge and Kegan
5. Bell, Ralirh.G(1970) *"Alternative to War"* New York, McGraw Hill.
6. A, Mortimer, J(1944) *"How to Think About War and Peace "* New York, Simon and Schuster.
7. Mishra, Loknath (2009) *"Encyclopaedia of Peace Education"* APH Publication Corporation,New Delhi.

CHAPTER 7

Peace Education in this Era of Globalisation

*Km. Ambika Bhatt

The Concept of Peace Education

Peace Education means to *learn about* and to *learn for peace. Learning about peace* means obtaining knowledge and understanding of what contributes to peace, what damages it, what leads to war, what does 'peace' mean on each level anyway, what is my role in it, and how are the different levels connected? *Learning for peace* means learning the skills, attitudes and values that one needs in order to contribute to peace and help maintain it. For example, this means learning to deal with conflicts without the recourse to violence, learning to think creatively, learning to apply the methods of active non-violence or learning to deal with cultural differences in a constructive way. Peace is a way of living together, in which people give their fellow creatures the space and, if necessary, the mutual support to live their lives to the full. Peace education may be defined as the *process of acquiring the values, the knowledge and developing the attitudes, skills, and behaviours to live in harmony with oneself, with others, and with the natural environment.* Ian Harris and John Synott have described peace education as a series of "teaching encounters" that draw from people:

- their desire for peace;
- non-violent alternatives for managing conflict; and

* Research Scholar, Department of Education, Birla Constitute, Srinagar Garhwal, H.N.B.G.U. Srinagar Garhwal.

- skills for critical analysis of structural arrangements that produce and legitimate injustice and inequality.

James Page suggests peace education be thought of as "encouraging a commitment to peace as a settled disposition and enhancing the confidence of the individual as an individual agent of peace; as informing the student on the consequences of war and social injustice; as informing the student on the value of peaceful and just social structures and working to uphold or develop such social structures; as encouraging the student to leave the world and to imagine a peaceful future; and as caring for the student and encouraging the student to care for others". Peace education is based on a philosophy that teaches non-violence, love, compassion, trust, fairness, cooperation and reverence for the human family and all life on our planet. Peace education leads to peaceful living. There is a question that what is the difference between *peace studies* and *peace education?* How do these two concepts overlap? Earlier within the International Peace Research Association peace education was seen as a means for propagating the findings of peace researchers. *Peace education* is quickly becoming a field of its own as teachers all over the world are looking to insights from peace theory to help them make their schools more peaceful and resolve bloody disputes in civil societies. Students in *peace studies* classes learn about the causes of war and alternatives to violence. Peace educators figure out how to teach those concepts to different age levels in different contexts. Insights into the international sphere provided by peace studies may not seem relevant to educators whose schools and communities are experiencing violence and whose students are being shot. How do the micro issues of violence relate to the broader macro cultures that glorify violence throughout the world?

Peace education in UNICEF refers to the process of promoting the knowledge, skills, attitudes and values needed to bring about behaviour changes that will enable children, youth and adults to prevent conflict and violence, both overt and structural; to resolve conflict peacefully; and to create the conditions conducive to peace, whether at an intrapersonal, interpersonal, intergroup, national or international level.

A RATIONALE FOR PEACE EDUCATION IN UNICEF

- **Article 29 of the Convention on the Rights of the Child (1989) states :**"...the education of the child shall be directed to...the preparation of the child for responsible life in a free society, in the spirit of understanding, peace, tolerance, equality of sexes, and friendship among all peoples..."
- **The 1990 World Declaration on Education for All says that :** "Every person—child, youth and adult—shall be able to benefit from educational opportunities designed to meet their basic learning needs. These needs comprise both essential learning tools (such as literacy, oral expression, numeracy, and problem solving) and the basic learning content (such as knowledge, skills, values, and attitudes) required by human beings to be able to survive, to develop their full capacities, to live and work in dignity, to participate fully in development, to improve the quality of their lives, to make informed decisions, and to continue learning ... The satisfaction of these needs empowers individuals in any society and confers upon them a responsibility to ... further the cause of social justice, ... to be tolerant towards social, political and religious systems which differ from their own, ensuring that commonly accepted humanistic values and human rights are upheld, and to work for international peace and solidarity in an interdependent world."
- **The 1996 study by Graça Machel on *The Impact of Armed Conflict on Children* reaffirmed the importance of education in shaping a peaceful future :** "... Both the content and the process of education should promote peace, social justice,

respect for human rights and the acceptance of responsibility. Children need to learn skills of negotiation, problem solving, critical thinking and communication that will enable them to resolve conflicts without resorting to violence."

- **The UNICEF 'Anti-war Agenda', set out in *The State of the World's Children, 1996,* declares :**"...Disputes may be inevitable, but violence is not. To prevent continued cycles of conflict, education must seek to promote peace and tolerance, not fuel hatred and suspicion."

Origins

In 1945, the United Nations was established to "save succeeding generations from the scourge of war", "to reaffirm faith in the ... dignity and worth of the human person [and] in the equal rights of men and women", "to establish conditions under which justice and respect for the obligations arising from treaties and other sources of international law can be maintained", and "to promote social progress and better standards of life in larger freedom..."*(Preamble to the UN Charter).* Peace education has developed as a means to achieve these goals. It is education that is "directed to the full development of the human personality and to the strengthening of respect for human rights and fundamental freedoms". It promotes "understanding, tolerance and friendship among all nations, racial or religious groups" and furthers "the activities of the United Nations for the maintenance of peace." *(Article 26, Universal Declaration of Human Rights)*

In other words, peace education is an integral part of the work of the United Nations. Through a humanising process of teaching and learning, peace educators facilitate human development. They strive to counteract the dehumanisation of poverty, prejudice, discrimination, rape, violence, and war. Originally aimed at eliminating the possibility of global extinction through nuclear war, peace education currently addresses the broader objective of building a culture of peace. In this global effort, progressive educators world-wide are teaching the values, standards and principles articulated in fundamental UN instruments such as the *UN Charter*, Human Rights documents, the *Convention on the Elimination of All forms of Discrimination Against Women (CEDAW), the Convention on the Rights of the Child* (CRC), the World Declaration on Education for All, and many others.

In various parts of the world, peace education has been referred to as Education for Conflict Resolution, International Understanding, and Human Rights; Global Education; Critical Pedagogy; Education for Liberation and Empowerment; Social Justice Education; Environmental Education; Life Skills Education; Disarmament and Development Education; and more. These various labels illuminate the depth and diversity of the field. Using the term *peace education* helps co-ordinate such global initiatives and unite educators in the common practice of educating for a culture of peace.

UNICEF and *UNESCO* are particularly active advocates of education for peace. *UNICEF describes* peace education as schooling and other educational initiatives that:

- Function as 'zones of peace', where children are safe from violent conflict.
- Uphold children's basic rights as outlined in the CRC.
- Develop a climate that models peaceful and respectful behaviour among all members of the learning community.
- Demonstrate the principles of equality and non-discrimination in administrative policies and practices.
- Draw on the knowledge of peace-building that exists in the community, including means of dealing. With conflict that are effective, non-violent, and rooted in the local culture.
- Handle conflicts in ways that respect the rights and dignity of all involved.

- Integrate an understanding of peace, human rights, social justice and global issues throughout the curriculum whenever possible.
- Provide a forum for the explicit discussion of values of peace and social justice.
- Use teaching and learning methods that stress participation, Cupertino, problem-solving and respect for differences.
- Enable children to put peace-making into practice in the educational setting as well as in the wider community.
- Generate opportunities for continuous reflection and professional development of all educators in relation to issues of peace, justice and rights. (*Peace Education in UNICEF Working Paper Series, July 1999*)

"A culture of peace will be achieved when citizens of the world understand global problems, have the skills to resolve conflicts and struggle for justice non-violently, live by international standards of human rights and equity, appreciate cultural diversity, and respect the Earth and each other. Such learning can only be achieved with systematic education for peace."
—Hague Appeal for Peace Global Campaign for Peace Education

Aim of Peace Education

Peace Education is about empowering people with the skills, attitudes, and knowledge. Building on principles and practices that have evolved over time, responding to different historical circumstances, peace education aims to cultivate the knowledge, skills, and attitudes needed to achieve and sustain a global culture of peace. Understanding and transforming violence is central, so these are the aims of peace education:

- to build, maintain, and restore relationships at all levels of human interaction.
- to develop positive approaches towards dealing with conflicts—from the personal to the international.
- to create safe environments, both physically and

emotionally, that nurture each individual.

- to create a safe world based on justice and human rights.
- to build a sustainable environment and protect it from exploitation and war.

Content of Peace Education

Peace education content generally include instruction in conflict resolution; cooperation and interdependence; global awareness; and social and ecological responsibility. Peace education in the United States has evolved since its early nineteenth century beginnings. In the early years, peace education was promoted by a small group of New England educators, writers, and thinkers who shared a vision of the world without war or violence.

> *"If peace is both the destination and the journey then what we teach and how we teach it must not be separated in our preparations for working with pupils."*
>
> **—Patrick Whitaker, British Educational Advisor and former teacher**

Peace education brings together multiple traditions of pedagogy, theories of education, and international initiatives for the advancement of human development through learning.

Violence	Peace
(Direct) **Personal:** assault, rape, brutality, terrorism, murder, ethnic clansing, **Institutional:** war, state-sponsored terror, industrial destruction of plant and animal life.	*(Negative)* Absence of personal and institutional violence
(Indirect) **Structural:** sexism racism, discrimination, poverty, hunger, lack of education and health services.	*(Positive)* Presence of wellbeing, social justice, gender equity, human rights

It is fundamentally dynamic, interdisciplinary, and multicultural and grows out of the work of educators such as John Dewey, Maria Montessori, Paulo Freire, Johan Galtung, Elise and Kenneth Boulding, and many others. The present diagram helps to visualise the core relationship between violence and peace which shows that what should be the ingredient of peace-education content. Peace is understood not only as the absence of traditional forms of direct violence, but also as a positive presence. Educating for and about all aspects of peace constitutes peace education.

> *"It is understandable that in Hiroshima and Nagasaki peace education is almost exclusively equated with anti-nuclear bomb education. For many teachers, who were victims and survivors of the A-bomb attack, the core of peace education is nothing more than telling others about their own personal experience in August 1945."* **—Mitsuo Okamoto, Japanese peace educator**

In the classroom, peace education aims to develop skills, attitudes, and knowledge with co-operative and participatory learning methods and an environment of tolerance, care, and respect. Through dialogue and exploration, teachers and students engage in a journey of shared learning. Students are nurtured and empowered to take responsibility for their own growth and achievement while teachers care for the wellbeing of all students. The practice of peace education is an opportunity to promote the total welfare of students, advocate for their just and equitable treatment of youth, and promote individual and social responsibility for both educators and learners. Through pedagogy and social action, peace educators demonstrate that there are alternatives to violence. The following diagram illustrates the relationships among the central knowledge, skills, and attitudes of peace education which constitutes the content of peace education. They are drawn from educational initiatives all over the world and form the basis of the learning objectives in the Teaching Units of the *Learner as Teacher* section. Various aspects of peace education may even serve to enhance learning across subjects. Ultimately, educating for peace is as varied as the teachers who practice it.

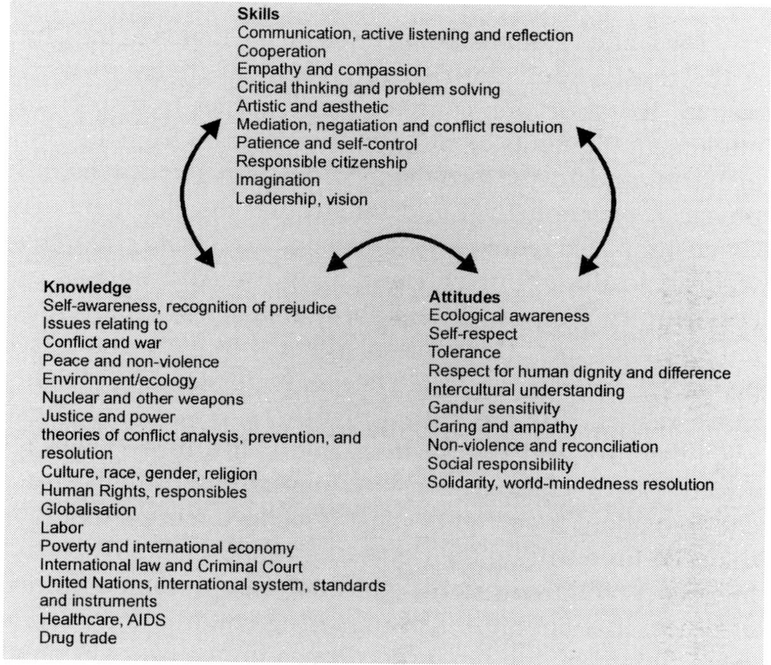

Need of Peace Education

Over the past couple of decades our schools, like our governments have focussed on global economic restructuring and concerned themselves with promoting an economically and technologically competitive citizenry. But global developments, intensified by the events of 9-11, have highlighted the need for global citizens who are educated for peace, not just economic competitiveness. The ideal global citizen is one who understands the importance of respecting human rights, and who is prepared to work cooperatively to end poverty, to improve the health and well-being of the world's children, to reclaim and protect the environment, and to effect peaceful co-existence among individuals, peoples and states. We have the opportunity to work toward developing such global citizens through the systematic inclusion of children's rights education—in form of peace education—in our schools.

The United Nations Convention on the Rights of the Child is the most widely ratified international treaty in world history. Its ratification commits states parties to respect and implement the rights of children to protection from all forms of harm, and to the provision of basic needs for healthy physical, psychological and intellectual development. The Convention also requires states parties to educate children as well as adults about children's rights. And here is our opportunity. Empirical data show that when children are taught about their Convention rights within a rights-based pedagogy, they demonstrate a deeper understanding of rights, more respect for the rights of others, a sense of social responsibility and the participation skills appropriate for effective democratic citizenship. Similarly, those who teach children about their rights come to believe more strongly in the need for ensuring the rights of all children are respected. In essence, children's rights education can promote a culture of peace. It is one means of preparing children for a world characterised by mutual respect based on the belief in rights for all, and thus characterised by peace. If globalisation is to equitably benefit all cultural and ethnic groups within a society, and around the world, intercultural respect and solidarity clearly need to be developed. Reardon discusses —the value of human relationships which starts "with interconnections between the human order and the natural order and emphasising a human order of positive relationships...that make it possible for all to pursue the realisation of individual and communal human potential". *(Reardon, 1988, p. 59).*

There is an urgent need for peace education so that globalisation problems such as the violation of human rights, poverty, environmental destruction, and structural violence can be alleviated and eventually eliminated. Peace education is necessary in order to resolve global issues, to preserve the environment, to safeguard human rights, and to ensure peace within and between countries. In a time of economic interdependency, world citizens have to learn to work co-operatively in culturally diversified settings. Peace education can assist in the development of social harmony, equity, and social justice as alternatives to tensions and wars.

> *"As far as this configurational way of thinking is concerned, successful government, in the sense of achieving or approaching a situation in which the fundamental values of society are met, and the peaceful coexistence of people become one. The objectives of government (...) are one and the same with the conditions for peace. The different state objectives and aims encompassed by government are linked up to the Senghaas' peace theory using a "civilising hexagon", which demonstrates a good and working internal state order and the ability for peace-orientated foreign affairs. (...)*

In modern era of globalisation and privatisation the need of peace education can be shown in following form:

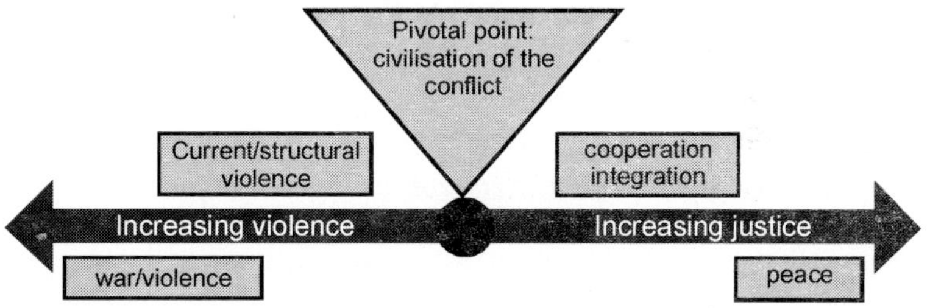

There is thus no shortage of official statements on the need and importance of peace education. There are numerous *United Nations* declarations or instruments which confirm the need as well as the importance of peace education.[1][2] *Koichiro Matsuura,* the current Director-General of *UNESCO,* wrote of peace education as being of "fundamental importance to the mission of UNESCO and the United Nations".[3] Peace education as a right is something which is now increasingly emphasised by peace researchers such as Betty Reardon [4]

and *Douglas Roche* [5] There has also been a recent meshing peace education and human rights education [6].

"If we are to reach real peace in this world, if we are to declare war on war, we must begin with the children." **—(Gandhi)**

"Think about what kind of world you want to live and work in. What do you need to know to build that world? Demand that your teachers teach you that." **—(Peter Kropotkin)**

"Establishing a lasting peace is the work of education; all politics can do is keep us out of war." **—(Maria Montessori)**

"Just as we teach literacy and numeracy today, we must teach students to learn to think critically; respect diversity; understand global, cultural and economic interdependence; analyse media, examine the nature of violence and learn ways for us all to live more peacefully."

—(Global Campaign for Peace Education)

"Since wars begin in the minds of men and women, it is in the minds of men and women that the defences of peace must be constructed." **—(UNESCO)**

"They shall beat their swords into ploughshares, and spears into pruning hooks; nation shall not rise up against nation, neither shall they learn war any more."

—(Prophet Isaiah)

"Violence begets violence, toughness begets toughness....It is either non-violence or non-existence."

—(Martin Luther King Jr)

"Peace education has evolved into studying violence in all its manifestations and educating to counteract the war system for the creation of a peace system." **—(Leonisa Ardizzone)**

"Peace is in our hands. It just takes education."

—(Educating for Peace)

"A culture of peace will be achieved when the citizens of the world understand global problems, have the skills to resolve conflict constructively, know and live by international standards of human rights, gender and racial equality; appreciate cultural

> *diversity and respect the integrity of the Earth.... Such learning cannot be achieved without the intentional, sustained and systematic education for peace."*
>
> —**(Global Campaign for Peace Education)**

Why Teach Peace ?

- In 2003 there were 36 wars in 28 countries (www.ploughshares.ca).
- 11/2 million children have died in such wars in the past decade.
- Small arms kill one person per minute.
- 30,000 nuclear warheads – 5,000 on hair-trigger alert— still threaten the planet.

The hundreds of billions of dollars spent on war and efforts to protect ourselves from it do not work. Here's what has to change, to move to a world where real peace has a chance, which also show us the need of peace education:

Culture of war & violence	Culture of peace & non-violence
1. belief in power based on force.......	1. belief that peace is possible and can be learned
2. acceptance of an "enemy".......	2. reconciliation, tolerance, cultural understanding
3. authoritarian government.......	3. democratic participation, cooperation
4. secrecy and propaganda.......	4. free flow of information, critical awareness
5. reliance on arms.......	5. negotiation, disarmament, non-violence
6. exploitation of people.......	6. the same human rights for all
7. exploitation of nature.......	7. respect for the Earth, sustainable development
8. male domination.......	8. equality of men and women
(derived from UNESCO Programme of Action on a Culture of Peace www.unesco.org/cp and the Culture of Peace News Network)	

What's Happening NOW Regarding the Peace Education?

In August 2004 *Peace Camp Canada* was in full swing in Ottawa. A Palestinian-Israeli experiment initiated by Ottawa teenagers, it brought young people from both communities to live, eat, argue and sightsee together. In Toronto Muslim,

Christian and Jewish 11-years olds from Israel met other youngsters and learned about each other's lives and faiths. *Kids4peace* first set up letter writing between children in Canada and Israel, then organised the visit. The *Faculty of Education at the University of Ottawa* is beginning its second year of teaching peace and global education to student teachers with an Institute, *Educating for Peace and Global Awareness, Sept. 23-24.* Courses in peace and global education are reinforced by on-campus workshops and lectures and an annual country weekend retreat. (www.education.uottawa.ca) *Resources for Peace Education* is the theme of the third annual national *Conference on Peace Education,* to be held Nov. 18-22 at McMaster University in Hamilton ON. There will also be a training session for leaders and a national symposium on the culture of peace. *Creating a Culture of Peace: a Peace Curriculum for Manitoba Teachers – Middle Years (grades 5-8)* has been produced by *Project Peacemakers,* an affiliate of Project Ploughshares in Winnipeg. The group has produced other resources for schools and communities, relating especially to children and war(www.projectpeacemakers.org). A *University of Victoria* conference *"Learning and the World We Want" (2003)* called on teachers, school administrators and other educators to include the study of modern war and the requirements for a culture of peace in their curricula, publications, conferences and seminars. *Children's Creative Response to Conflict (www.ccrccrc.ca)* works with the Ottawa District School Board and community groups to provide conflict resolution programmes for children, parents and teachers. CCRC helped organise leadership training in conflict resolution for 22 Northern Irish and Canadian young people from various faiths and backgrounds who had experienced conflict.

Peace Education in Era of Globalisation

The impact of globalisation will be understood more clearly by first defining the term, though it is interpreted differently by different authors. Some claim that globalisation means the competition of companies—nationally and internationally,—

to maximise profit. It is also identified as a process of the international integration of economies by means of the social restructuring of the modes of production, distribution, and consumption of goods and services on a global scale; this restructuring is accomplished in part through the removal of trade restrictions and the opening of national borders to allow capital to flow freely between countries (Burbules, and Torres 2000; Carnoy, 1999; Hirst, and Thompson, 1996; Scholte, 2000; Sanders, 1996; Tujan, 1998). Some authors suggest that globalisation is not merely a process of economic integration, but the actual universalisation and commodification of knowledge, technology and communication, culture, health care, heritage, genetic codes, and natural resources such as land, forests, air, and water (Barlow, and Clarke 2002; Reiser, and Davies 1944; Smith, 2000). A third definition equates globalisation to westernisation and modernisation, where existing local social structures and cultures are destroyed and replaced by the social structures of capitalism, rationalism, industrialism, and the imperialism of such social institutions as McDonald's, Hollywood, CNN, and the like(Schiller, 1991; Scholte, 2000; Spybey, 1996; Taylor, 2000). Globalisation is the process by which all peoples and communities come to experience an increasingly common economic, social and cultural environment. By definition, the process affects everybody throughout the world. A more integrated world community brings both benefits and problems for all; it affects the balance of economic, political and cultural power between nations, communities and individuals and it can both enhance and limit freedoms and human rights.

The international monetary organisations such as the IMF and the World Bank and the regional organisations like the Asian Development Bank (ADB) play a dominant role in influencing the debt-receiving countries (developing countries) when it comes to their educational practice. The intensity of the influence of these organisations can vary depending on the existing educational policy of the aid receiving countries. The processes of globalisation have both positive and negative effects on young people and their right to education. Improvements in communication technology and educational delivery have the potential to improve the quality of education and make it increasingly accessible. Global human rights movements, the UN's Education for All goals and the Global Campaign for Education (GCE)2 have placed pressure on key players to ensure young people have access to quality educational resources and are able to attend schooling without harassment and discrimination (Dos Santos 2001).

The impacts of globalisation on youth and education "[have] a lot to do with your 'starting point' in the world-whether you are on the advantaged or disadvantaged side of things" *(Niel, C. 2002: IYP submission, Australia).* For the advantaged, "young people live in a knowledge society and benefit from this. They have lots of choices and have a proper education" *(Gennaio, Guiliano 2002: IYP submission, Italy).* However, the positive effects of globalisation are countered by the negative impacts of factors such as higher costs of provision, national budget misallocation, poor resource mobilisation, privatisation, international debt and economic instability. Although the roots of globalisation can be traced back to the Enlightenment era of eighteenth-century Europe (Gray in Smith, 2000), the impact of globalisation has never garnered as much attention as it has in the last sixty years or so.

Since globalisation is here to stay, efforts should be continually made to mitigate its destructive effects. This challenge has been taken up through global education or peace education efforts initiated by people at the grassroots level, in the upper echelon of governments and societies, and by peoples' movements, religious groups, non-governmental organisations (NGOs), and others. Many schools have added global education to their social studies curriculum, while others have integrated it into other subject areas. However, greater awareness of and participation in the movement is required, particularly on the part of First World countries.

Simultaneously, more education and conscientisation is necessary in Third World countries. It has taken centuries to realise the encroachment of globalisation into world systems; it may take longer to mollify its negative effects.

The increased awareness aimed to motivate citizens to take action in solidarity with Third World citizens to transform the structures of injustices and foster a fairer world system. It was in this social context that the movement called development education (sometimes referred to as popular education) emerged(Arnold, 1991; Cronkhite, 1991; Osler, 1994; Zachariah, 1983). Development education

> *refers to the teaching and learning processes relating to issues in development [and seeks] to make [people] more aware of the problems of development and to assist in the formation of attitudes and behaviours that will facilitate the constructive transformation of the many relationships between rich and poor countries or [individuals] (Ariyaratne, 1991, p. 5).*

In recent decades, a growing number of critical educators, including those in development education, have argued for a more holistic framework of consciousness-raising through peace education. Peace education—delivered formally in classrooms, informally in communities, as well as in boardrooms—tries to address the globalisation issues. Some of its gains, big and small, give us reason to be hopeful. Peace educators today cannot avoid dealing with the effects of war and other consequences of militarisation. Massive global spending on weapons and other military technologies clearly diverts valuable resources away from many nations' basic needs. As Floresca-Cawagas and Toh (1993) note *"peace education motivates citizens to become more aware of the anti-development effects of militarisation, and hence lobby for the conversion of arms expenditures into programmes which satisfy the basic needs of the poor, (e.g., food, housing, health care, jobs, education)" (p. 7).*

There is now widespread consensus among peace, global, and development educators that future development projects must promote sustainability (Fine, 2001; Shiva, 1991). Peace education also tries to address the issue of environmental destruction, among others, through formal education. Development education is conducted within a peace education framework and centres on issues of intercultural/'ethno-racial' conflicts. Ethnic diversity is found, in some degree in most, if not all, of the world's countries. However, there are increasing numbers of examples of conflicts between cultural groups that have lead to ethnic cleansing and genocide (e.g., Rwanda, Bosnia, India, Iraq, Kosovo). The empowerment component that lies at the heart of peace education coaches citizens to exercise their social, political, and economic rights (Floresca-Cawagas, and Toh, 1989). It helps people to develop knowledge, skills, and attitudes that will ideally free them from hunger, from abuses and exploitation, and from structural violence as they take greater control over the direction in which their lives are headed (Selby, 1993). Global education, or peace education, puts "great emphasis on participatory and experiential modes of learning, which foster both pupil autonomy and the development of critical thinking skills. Effective learning is seen as arising out of affirmation of each pupil's individual worth, the development of a wide range of cooperative skills, the ability to discuss and debate issues, to reflect critically on everyday life and events in the wider world, and to act as responsible citizens," observes Hicks (1993, p. 20). Citizens are empowered when they are given the chance to participate in the decision-making processes, especially on those that directly affect them.

Finally, a holistic model of peace, or global, education is ideal, especially one that DePass et al (1991) describe:

> *to develop a "partnership between professional development educators, ... schools, and the broad range of social movements.... What is required of partnerships is mutual respect and common recognition of common important goals. When the right to life and viable community is threatened anywhere, by nature, social, or political cause, we have a common goal and a common responsibility to protect and support those who are threatened (pp. 1-2).*

Peace education must not only involve school personnel, but also the community, private citizens, governments, business and everyone else since for it to be effective, it must be taught holistically.

Conclusion

To establish the peace overall the world in era of globalisation or internationalisation is a difficult task, but yet we can think about it by using the education as an agent for it, so we can make following efforts:

...In Our Schools

FOR TEACHERS

Resources teachers have found useful:

- Teaching Young Children to Care, K-6.
- Elementary Perspectives, teaching concepts of peace and conflict, K-6.
- Open Minds to Equality, K-6.
- The Friendly Classroom for a Small Planet, K-6.
- Conflict Resolution in the Middle School, Gr 6-8.
- Conflict in Context: local to global security and peacemaking, Gr 9-12.
- Learning to Abolish War : teaching toward a culture of peace, Gr 1-12.
- Tolerance–The Threshold of Peace,Gr 1-12.

It's where most young people spend most of their time. School helps shape a person's character. Classrooms and schoolyards are places where every child can be heard, where conflict can be resolved positively, where critical skills can be learned among friends. Teachers can *teach peace* by integrating the values, facts and methods of peace and global education into the curriculum.

Many teachers are already doing so, for instance:

In *elementary grades* children learn to cooperate and share through games and role-playing. They recognise their responsibilities for making their classroom a peaceful place, and begin to handle positively their own conflicts. In *middle school* teachers introduce global education and concepts of peace from other cultures. Students learn to work cooperatively, to research and analyse media, to track the political and social trends of a global economy in the light of some national objectives. *Secondary school* students examine some realities of global interdependence, e.g. environment, economics, law. They critique national and global organisations and their own expectations for peace and development.

• ***Some things to do***

FOR PARENTS AND OTHERS

Peace education is a good description for the skills, values and expectations that most people hope schools will develop in our children: responsibility and cooperation, critical thinking, tolerance, emotional and social understanding, curiosity. Here are some ideas to help it happen where you live:

- Talk with your child and your child's teachers about what peace education is and where she/he can find resources and support.
- Join your school council. Start a discussion about peace education. Collect some peace education resources – storybooks and songs, curriculum ideas, UN publications, magazines—and display them in the school library.
- Talk about peace and global education with your school board trustee, attend board meetings and ask questions. Consider running for election to your school board.
- Find out what's happening at your nearest university and faculty of education. What are they doing about peace and global education in the schools?
- Write, phone or e-mail the Ministry of Education to ask its views on peace education and what it is doing

> to fulfill its commitment under the UN to promote peace education. Support local teachers, even after your kids have graduated. They are a lifeline to peace in the future...

It is only possible to overcome a system of organised lack of peace by means of a civilising project. The most important aspects associated with the peace civilising project are revealed by taking a look at the conditions which make *internal peace* possible in modern Western industrialised societies. *According to Senghass* he wanted to develop a wide peace concept without getting bogged down in the involved concepts associated with the terms *"negative peace"(=absence of war)* and *"positive peace" (=absence of structural aggression)* and it was for this reason that he developed the *civilising hexagon*. According to this point of view, peace is given when a constellation of conditions is present that provide mutual support for each other (...).

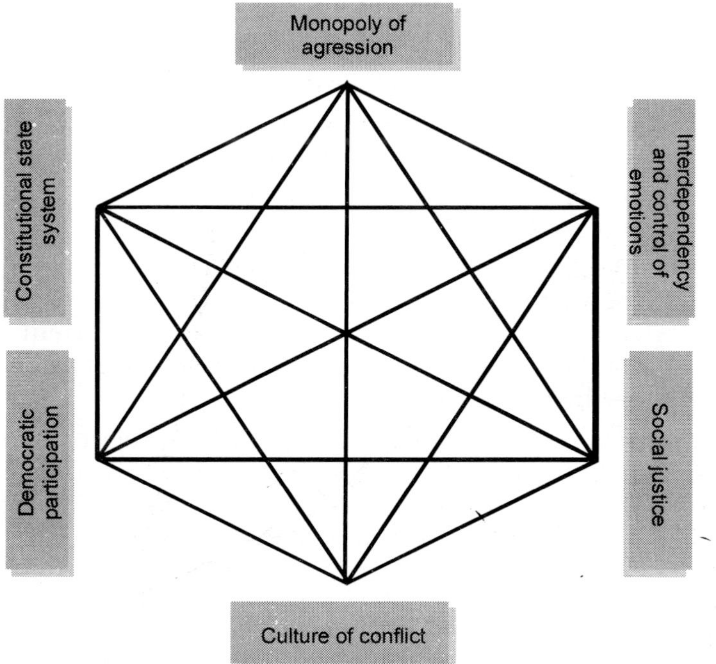

A civilising hexagon of this kind has six cornerstones which can be described as follows :

1. The *de-privatisation of aggression and the establishment of a legitimate state monopoly of aggression is essential for the civilising project.* There can be no lasting peace without "the disarmament of the citizens" (...).
2. On the other hand, however, *control of the state monopoly on aggression and the establishment of a constitutional state* are needed to make sure that state monopoly of aggression is not abused in a despotic way.
3. Increasing *control over emotional states thorough mutual interaction* is established by growing interdependency and by the de-privatisation of aggression; this is referred to by Norbert Elias impressively as the "process of civilisation". The consequences of this might also lead to the establishment of "emotional spheres", which transcend local boundaries and lead to a "national identity".
4. This also serves in laying the foundations for *democratic participation* in the public decision-making process.
5. Another aspect is *social justice.* The physical fortification of the rule of law is a constitutive condition for the ability of constitutional state orders to be sustained and, as a consequence, inner peace to exist.
6. And, finally, a *constructive conflict culture* provides the foundations for disagreements to be resolved in a constructive way and for compromise-orientated conflict skills, and makes up the last cornerstone in the hexagon.

To this end, then, peace as a civilising project becomes the desire for a legitimate and just state order. This also means that effective civilising and peace are in a sense 'identical'. When peace is understood in this way, it becomes clear that it's not a natural state. 'Peace has to be created.' Or to put it another way: "If the aim is to achieve peace in the sense of civilizing politics (...), the ground for peace has to be prepared(*Si vis pacem, para pacem).*

REFERENCES

1. Covell, Dr. (Prof.)., Katherine, Psychology, University College of Cape Breton.
2. www.peaceorganisatio.org.uk.
3. Third Foundation Day Address delivered under the auspices of Higher Secondary Education Council, Guwahati, Assam, on June 1, 2000.
4. See: www.campaignforeducation.org.
5. "Access to Education and Privatisation of Education" : Authors: Leah Ashley and Kirsten Mackay, Partner Organisation: Global Campaign for Education.
6. See: www.peaceeducationbasiccourse2-Thecivilisinghexagon.htm
7. www.mideastweb.org
8. www.quasar.ualberta.ca/css.
9. Canadian Social Studies, Vol. 38, No. 3, Special Issue: *Graduate Work in Social Studies Education*, Spring 2004.
10. en.wikipedia.org/wiki/Globalisation.
11. Montessori, Maria, "Education and Peace", 1949.
12. www.cpnn-usa.org.
13. www.global-ed.org/e4p.
14. www.unitednationscyberschoolbus.home.
15. Page, James S. (2008) 'Chapter 9: The United Nations and Peace Education'. In: Monisha Bajaj (ed.)*Encyclopaedia of Peace Education*. (75-83). Charlotte: Information Age Publishing. ISBN 978-1-59311-898-3. Further information.
16. Page, James S. (2008) *Peace Education: Exploring Ethical and Philosophical Foundations*. Charlotte: Information Age Publishing. ISBN 978-1-59311-889-1. Chapter details.
17. Galtung, Johan (1975) *Essays in Peace Research, Volume 1*. Copenhagen: Eljers. pp. 334-339.
18. Harris, Ian and Synott, John. (2002) 'Peace Education for a New Century' *Social Alternatives* 21(1):3-6.
19. United Nations General Assembly. (1993) *Vienna Declaration and Programme of Action (World Conference on Human Rights)*. New York: United Nations. (A/CONF. 157/23 on June 25, 1993). Part 2, Paragraphs 78-82.

20. Johnson, Marcia L. , *"Trends in Peace Education", ERIC Digest.*
21. *World Peace Newsletter.* 1996-2009 WPE.
22. Fountain, S., 1998. 'Peace Education/Conflict Resolution Evaluation Methods.' New York, UNICEF (Unpublished Paper, Available From the Author).
23. Declaration of the 44th Session of the International Conference on Education (Geneva, October 1994) endorsed by the General Conference of UNESCO at Its Twenty-eighth Session.
24. www.fgc.edu.in
25. www.kouniv.ac.in
26. www.peacedirect.org

CHAPTER 8

Relevance of Peace Education in this Era of LPG (Liberalisation, Privatisation and Globalisations for Combating Social Evils

*Mohit Puri

Peace education may be defined as the process of acquiring the values, the knowledge and developing the attitudes, skills, and behaviours to live in harmony with oneself, with others, and with the natural environment. Ian Harris and John Synott (2002) have described peace education as a series of teaching encounters that draw from people, their desire for peace, non-violent alternatives for managing conflict, and skills for critical analysis of structural arrangements that produce and legitimate injustice and inequality. Peace education can also be thought of as encouraging a commitment to peace as a settled disposition and enhancing the confidence of the individual as an individual agent of peace; as informing the student on the consequences of war and social injustice; as informing the student on the value of peaceful and just social structures and working to uphold or develop such social structures; as encouraging the student to leave the world and to imagine a peaceful future; and as caring for the student and encouraging the student to care for others.

In 1945, the United Nations was established to "save succeeding generations from the scourge of war", "to reaffirm faith in the dignity and worth of the human person [and] in the equal rights of men and women", "to establish conditions under which justice and respect for the obligations arising from treaties and other sources of international law can be maintained", and "to promote social progress and better

*JRF (Education), Punjabi University, Patiala, Punjab.

standards of life in larger freedom". (*Preamble to the UN Charter*). Peace education has developed as a means to achieve these goals. It is education that is "directed to the full development of the human personality and to the strengthening of respect for human rights and fundamental freedoms". It promotes "understanding, tolerance and friendship among all nations, racial or religious groups" and furthers "the activities of the United Nations for the maintenance of peace." (*Article 26, Universal Declaration of Human Rights*).

As far as the requirement of peace education is concerned, there is need for spread of peace education for the students so that they can become efficient members of society. There is need for involving all teachers in the society into the crusade against lack of peace education among the students. Once peace education is assured of its pride of place, social productivity will consequently increase. Often the theory or philosophy of peace education has been assumed and not articulated. Johan Galtung (1975) suggested that no theory for peace education existed and that there was clearly an urgent need for such theory. More recently there have been attempts to establish such a theory.

Joachim James Calleja has suggested that a philosophical basis for peace education might be located in the Kantian notion of duty. James Page (2008) has suggested that a rationale for peace education might be located in virtue ethics, consequentialist ethics, conservative political ethics, aesthetic ethics and the ethics of care.

Liberalisation

Although liberalisation in this era has benefited the shift in the pattern of exports from traditional items like clothes, tea and spices to automobiles, steel, IT etc. The 'made in India' brand, which did not evoke any sort of loyalty has now become a brand name by itself and is now known all over the world for its quality. Many policies and reforms have transformed the education sector with a huge talent pool of qualified professionals now available, waiting to conquer the world with their domain knowledge. But this great amount of professionals are still lacking in the knowledge of peace education. India, after all these years of economic reforms, is at the crossroads. While one road leads India to economic prosperity and glory, the other road leads it to social inequality. Peace education can assist a lot in tackling this social inequality.

Presently, as India is one of the fastest growing economies in the world, the social aspects have been ridden roughshod by the economic benefits. What has been conveniently forgotten or suppressed till date have been the disparities, mainly the socio-economical issues. This has led to growing discontent among the population and it has gathered momentum since the reforms began 15 years ago. It will very soon reach a critical point wherein the very purpose for which the reforms were started, will start to lose their significance rapidly and throw the country back into the 'licence raj' and 'unionist' era. These issues demand adequate peace education so that a new perspective and approach can be found out for handling these socio-economical issues. The chasm between the rich and the poor has increased so vastly that the rich are just getting richer and the poor are just getting poorer. The real benefits of the economic reforms have rarely percolated to the lowest strata of society. Just to illustrate the same with an example, most of the states today vie with one another to grab a project of any significance, be it chemical, auto or even IT. In doing so, the benefits they are offering, right from free land to tax sops are being given on a platter. But the benefits or savings that a company gains from this does not affect the lower strata of management, but remains in the hands of the top management, thus depriving the former of the economic benefits. Also, most of the labor laws in the country are outdated and have not kept pace with economic reforms. Thus, the exploitation of the working class becomes much easier. A classic example is the BPO industry in our country. While most of them work in the nights, the pressure each employee faces to deliver results and the working conditions are appalling, to say the least. The agricultural sector has also seen this disproportionate growth, as it is a field that has been left high and dry in the pursuit of agricultural reforms. The sector has been opened up to the multi-nationals, without having evolved a comprehensive cover for our farmers, most of who are poor and own very little land of their own. A case in point is the spate of farmer suicides that our country has witnessed in the past few years. The developed countries, which clamor for open-ended policies, have, in fact, some of the fiercest protection policies when it comes to their agricultural sector. The Government of India started the economic liberalisation policy in 1991. Even though the power at the center has changed hands, the pace of the reforms has never slackened till date. Before 1991, changes within the industrial sector in the country were modest to say the least. The sector accounted for just one-fifth of the total economic activity within the country. The sectoral structure of the industry has changed, albeit gradually. Most of the industrial sector was dominated by a select band of family-based conglomerates that had been dominant historically. Post 1991, a major restructuring has taken place with the emergence of more technologically advanced segments among industrial companies. Nowadays, more small and medium scale enterprises contribute significantly to the economy. By the mid-90s, the private capital had surpassed the public capital. The management system had shifted from the traditional family based system to a system of qualified and professional managers. Small Scale Industries (SSIs), the heart and soul of many towns and villages, have been virtually ignored. More than half of them have closed down in the last few years in the face of intense competition from multinationals who have unmatched financial and political muscle. Hence the need of peace education arise.On a parting note, what are essential for India are economic reforms taking into consideration peace as a priority in the society. The economic policies and their subsequent reforms must be accompanied by proper peace education and appropriate clauses to advantage the reasonably weaker sections. Various policies for liberalisation must be thoroughly examined and efforts must be made to see that the rewards must reach everyone.

Privatisation

Indian Government is emphasising upon process of the privatisation of the largest number of state-owned enterprises. It develops programmes and carries out so-called 'cash privatisation'—i.e. sale against cash or other means of payment, as opposed to the investment bonds used for 'mass privatisation'. Different State governments in India controls the fulfilment of privatisation contracts and monitors potential violations of the privatisation legislation or the obligations of specific privatisation contracts. It may impose penalties and, in the worst cases of non-performance of obligations, may request that the privatisation deal be broken. Such reversal of privatisation deals is extremely difficult, requiring a court to force the buyer to return the shares it has acquired by the virtue of the privatisation contract. An obstacle to breaking privatisation deals is presented by the changes in the legal status of privatised enterprises, such as capital increases and the presence of new investors. Where privatisation deals turn out unfavourably or the law is breached, the officials who allowed the violation are to be held responsible (with personal responsibility for both sellers and buyers).

The privatisation process in India has been accompanied by political problems and severe conflicts of interests, which have resulted on occasion in public scandals.There is thought to be low public trust in the privatisation process and a general lack of support for it. The reasons have been numerous and have often related to particular privatisation deals. As a whole, the practice of privatisation in India has arguably provoked a negative attitude towards denationalisation and raised doubts about its effects. The basis of this prevailing public opinion is what is regarded as the high social price of privatisation. Delays in the process, including the late start of actual privatisation, but also the way it was implemented—such as the privatisation schemes and procedures used and the lack of solvent local investors—helped produce social tension around every privatisation deal. Commentators argue that a responsible attitude by the social partners towards privatisation is an important prerequisite for public political consensus on how privatisation is to be be implemented. If the social partners, and especially, trade unions, pursue their own specific interests and are not aware of and do not exercise their role as a 'corrective' in the political process, including denationalisation, it is argued that the result will be a misuse of the social aspects of privatisation and its use in favour of certain groups and individuals. More recently, an increased influence of trade unions has, critics allege, had a negative impact on economic development, again because of an 'incorrect' interpretation of the social aspects of privatisation—for example, critics cite cases where managers and employees of an enterprise are entitled to obtain ownership and/or participate in management, without taking responsibility for the company's condition. The state's efforts to compensate for the negative social effects of privatisation have mainly involved imposing on the new owners contractual social commitments, such as a commitment to retain a certain number of jobs for a certain period, or to pay compensation and provide social support in cases of redundancies. Privatisation should be done keeping in view peace related issues.

Globalisation

The term 'globalisation' means assimilation of economies and societies through cross country flows of information, ideas, technologies, goods, services, capital, finance and people. Globalisation in India has permitted companies to enhance their base of operations, develop their employees with least investments, and present new services to a wide range of customers. Cross border assimilation can have numerous dimensions—cultural, social, political and economic. In fact, some natives fear cultural and social assimilation even more than economic assimilation. There is always a fear of cultural domination which haunts many people. Globalisation has affected a lot less developed nations. One of the adverse implications of this Global Integration is the emergence of 'Neo Imperialism' where power relationships have come to determine economic transactions.

Although the process of globalisation has been an important part of the current economic advancement made by India, but it has resulted in community troubles also. One of the major forces of globalisation in India has been in the growth of outsourced IT and business process outsourcing (BPO) services. The last few years have seen an increase in the number of skilled professionals in India employed by both local and foreign companies to service customers in the US and Europe in particular. Taking advantage of India's lower cost but educated and English-speaking work force, and utilising global communications technologies such as voice-over IP (VOIP), e-mail and the Internet, international enterprises have been able to lower their cost base by establishing outsourced knowledge-worker operations in India. But it has led to many social evils also which need proper remediation and it is possible through peace education only. A special case in point is the 'Indian Encounter with globalisation' and how it has led to imbalances, injustice, discrimination, biases, indebtedness, poverty, unemployment and rise of several social evils.

The recent farmer suicides that have occurred in various parts of India clearly point out the evils associated with this phenomenon. In addition to this the nation state seems to be losing out a great degree of power and influence in today's world. There is uncertainty of problems in the society which can be combated with proper peace education. Bursting suddenly on the world scene in the last quarter of the 20th century after the collapse of the Soviet Bloc and the disintegration of Soviet Union around 1990, the concept of globalisation has fast come to dominate the contemporary discourse of human affairs. At the same time, the social phenomenon itself that the concept represents has increasingly acquired a persistent presence in the lives of the public across the planet. Economic globalisation which is a part of the broader concept of globalisation is now considered to be determinative of humanity's future, relentlessly propelling the different societies of the world to a common destination—that of convergence in regard to income levels, social structure and behaviour. Peace has suffered a lot in this process of globalisation. As a new Indian middle class has developed around the wealth that the IT and BPO industries have brought to the country, a new consumer base has developed. On one hand, International companies are expanding their operations in India to service this massive growth opportunity, on the other hand it has also led to social dissatisfaction among Indian middle class also. Globalisation in India has been advantageous for companies that have ventured in the Indian market. By simply increasing their base of operations, expanding their workforce with minimal investments, and providing services to a broad range of consumers, large companies entering the Indian market have opened up many profitable opportunities. Although Indian companies are rapidly gaining confidence and are themselves now major players in globalisation through international expansion, these Indian companies are also fully responsible for increase of social evils in the society. From steel to Bollywood, from cars to IT, on one hand Indian companies are setting themselves up as powerhouses of tomorrow's global economy, on the other hand, it has led to cut throat competition also as well as exploitation of employees and poor working conditions.

Measures to Combat Social Evils Produced by LPG

One of the most important measure is to pay special attention to improving curricula, the content of textbooks, and other educational materials including new technologies, with a view to educating caring and responsible citizens, open to other cultures, able to appreciate the value of freedom, respectful of human dignity and differences, and able to prevent conflicts or resolve them by non-violent means. Education on principles and methods that contribute to the development of the personality of pupils, students and adults who are respectful of their fellow human beings and determined to promote peace, human rights and democracy. The nations of the world should seek the co-operation of all possible partners who would be able to help teachers to link the education process more closely to real social life and transform it into the practice of tolerance and solidarity, respect for human rights, democracy and peace; develop further, at the national and international levels, exchanges of educational experiences and research, direct contacts between students, teachers and researchers, school twinning arrangements and visits, with special attention to experimental schools such as UNESCO Associated Schools, to UNESCO Chairs, educational innovation networks and UNESCO Clubs and Associations. It is imperative to take suitable steps to establish in educational institutions an atmosphere contributing to the success of education for international understanding, so that they become ideal places for the exercise of tolerance, respect for human rights, the practice of democracy and learning about the diversity and wealth of cultural identities. Actions should be taken to eliminate all direct and indirect discrimination against girls and women in education systems and to take specific measures to ensure that they achieve their full potential.

It is important to encourage the development of innovative strategies adapted to the new challenges of educating responsible citizens committed to peace, human rights, democracy and sustainable development, and to apply appropriate measures of evaluation and assessment of these strategies. Measures should be adopted to enhance the role and status of educators in formal and non-formal education and to give priority to pre-service and in-service training as well as the retraining of educational personnel, including planners and managers, oriented notably towards professional ethics, civic and moral education, cultural diversity, national codes and internationally recognised standards of human rights and fundamental freedoms. It is essential to prepare, as quickly as possible and taking into account the constitutional structures of each State and policies for spread of peace education, programmes of action for the implementation of these policies.

A major priority should be given in education to children and young people, who are particularly vulnerable to incitements to intolerance, racism and xenophobia. Peace education has also been recognised as an integral part of the work of the United Nations. Through a humanising process of teaching and learning, peace educators facilitate human development. They strive to counteract the dehumanisation of poverty, prejudice, unemployment, discrimination, exploitation of employees, rape, violence, and war. Originally aimed at eliminating the possibility of global extinction through nuclear war, peace education currently addresses the broader objective of building a culture of peace. In this global effort, progressive educators worldwide are teaching the values, standards and principles articulated in fundamental UN instruments such as the UN Charter, Human Rights documents, the Convention on the Elimination of All forms of Discrimination Against Women (CEDAW), the Convention on the Rights of the Child (CRC), the World Declaration on Education for All, and many others. UNICEF and UNESCO are particularly active advocates of education for peace. UNICEF describes peace education as schooling and other educational initiatives that function as 'zones of peace', where children are safe from violent conflict, uphold children's basic rights as outlined in the CRC, develop a climate that models peaceful and respectful behaviour among all members of the learning community, demonstrate the principles of equality and non-discrimination in administrative policies and practices, draw on the knowledge of peace-building that exists in the community, including means of dealing with conflict that are effective, non-violent, and rooted in the local culture, handle conflicts in ways that respect the rights and dignity of all involved, integrate an understanding of peace, human rights, social justice and global issues throughout the curriculum whenever possible, provide a forum for the explicit discussion of values of peace and social justice, use teaching and learning methods that stress participation, cooperation, problem-solving and respect for differences and enable children to put peace-making into practice in the educational setting as well as in the wider community

Conclusion

It can be concluded that various Conferences at state, national and international level on Peace Education should be organised so as to discuss various issues regarding its relevance and implementation. All the countries need to adopt the various declarations on peace education made by UNESCO. That is, there is need of raising the social awareness about peace education to keep welfare of people at the top of the priority in this era of LPG. A coherent policy of education for peace, in the perspective of LPG should be made and implemented. It is time to realise that a peace education is also a necessity for social welfare. Also there is an extreme need to integrate peace education within educational curriculum of students. Therefore, it is imperative to build up the strategy for social security to cover health, peace education to the all students as well as all the members of society so that the challenges in the era of LPG can be met. What we require to address squarely is expanding and strengthening the awareness creating structure of peace education in the most challenging era of LPG.

REFERENCES

1. Calleja, Joachim James (1991) 'A Kantian Epistemology of Education and Peace : An Examination of Concepts and Values'. Unpublished PhD Thesis. Bradford University.
2. Examples include:
   - Constitution of UNESCO, adopted 16 November, 1945.

- Universal Declaration of Human Rights, Section 26.
- Convention on the Rights of the Child, Article 29.1(d).

3. Galtung, Johan (1975) Essays in Peace Research, Volume 1. Copenhagen: Eljers, pp. 334-339.
4. Harris, Ian and Synott, John. (2002) 'Peace Education for a New Century' *Social Alternatives* 21(1):3-6
5. James S. (2008) Peace Education: Exploring Ethical and Philosophical Foundations. Charlotte: Information Age Publishing, p. 189.
6. Matsuura, Koichiro. (2008) 'Foreword'. In: J.S.Page *Peace Education: Exploring Ethical and Philosophical Foundations.* Charlotte: Information Age Publishing, p. xix.
7. Reardon, Betty. (1997). 'Human Rights as Education for Peace'. In: G.J. Andrepoulos and R.P. Claude (eds.) *Human Rights Education for the Twenty-first Century.* (255-261). Philadelphia: University of Pennsylvania Press.
8. Roche, Douglas. (1993). *The Human Right to Peace.* Toronto: Novalis.
9. United Nations General Assembly. (1993) *Vienna Declaration and Programme of Action (World Conference on Human Rights).* New York: United Nations. (A/CONF. 157/23 on June 25, 1993). Part 2, Paragraphs 78-82.
10. UNESCO (1994) *"Declaration and Integrated Framework of Action on Education for Peace, Human Rights and Democracy"* 44th session of the International Conference on Education (Geneva, October 1994)

CHAPTER 9

Methods for Imparting Peace Education in Schools

*Prof. Sunil Kumar

The Focus and Uniqueness of Peace Education

Peace is both an external phenomenon and an inner factor, but it is 'Inner Peace' that will lead to 'Social Peace' and 'Peace with Nature'. Indian culture is based on the philosophy that life has a higher purpose and unless we lead a value-based life, committed to our duties, *kartavya-palan'*, while striving for *Artha* and *Kaama,* money and desire-fulfillment, we are missing the boat of *poorna-ananda,* ultimate peace and freedom!

While designing the strategy for imparting Peace Education in schools an important point to be considered is that it should not be treated as an academic subject, where we evaluate students based on written or practical examination to test their memory and skills.

We need to evaluate whether the students are sincerely striving to acquire certain attitudes, virtues, characteristics, which will keep them on the critical path to the higher. Peace education will have to teach students the purpose of human life, the role of daily "actions", the critical path of human-values towards it, and the self-development processes to awaken Viveka, develop strength, fearlessness and powers of mind to walk the critical path to perfection, peace and bliss. It is on these aspects that this article will focus.

---

* B.Sc. (Engineering), Member, Managing Committee, Ramakrishna Mission, New Delhi; Former G.M., The PEC of India Ltd. and Founder Trustee and Professor, SriSim (PGDBM, New Delhi)

At the outset let us lay down these basic virtues, which both the teachers and the students must strive to inculcate, and be evaluated upon, through continuous, sincere struggle over a long period of time—students are with us in schools for ten to twelve years:

(*i*) *Viveka:* Knowing the highest and striving to choose that which leads to it

(*ii*) *Focus:* On the higher and withdrawl from lower

(*iii*) *Burning desire:* Vision of highest perfection; to excel, to deliver quality, be better

(*iv*) *Struggle to Control Mind:* bring it back each time it goes away to focus on task

(*v*) *Control/restrain Sense-organs:* Unwanted-thoughts enter from eyes/ears

(*vi*) *Forbearance:* Withstand disturbances-likes/dislikes, sufferings; learn to be cool!

(*vii*) *Balanced life:* Even-mindedness, but directed towards vision

(*viii*) *Self-Contentment:* But focussed on vision

(*ix*) *Sraddha or Faith:* Self-confidence that by practice I can be the best, conviction in power of goodness, spirit of helping all who are trying to be and do good.

What can be a Source of Knowledge and Inspiration to Plan for Peace Education?

We suggest UNESCO and Vivekananda:

Vivekananda: Way back in October 1984, Smt. Indira Gandhi has declared 12th January as the National Youth Day, to commemorate the birthday of Vivekananda, referred as *"the great philosopher, thinker and the greatest patron of the youth in India"* in the government notice, and instructions are issued every year, by the Government, exhorting the youth to draw inspiration from his works, which are a great source of knowledge, strength, self-confidence and inspiration. Leaders like Mahatma Gandhi, Pandit Nehru, Subhas Bose have publicly acknowledged that they drew inspiration for India's freedom movement and love for India through his inspiring words.

He says:

- Each soul is potentially divine (the source of all peace, power, knowledge and bliss).
- The goal of life is to manifest the divinity within by controlling nature, external and internal (our inner instrument, the mind).
- Education is the manifestation of the perfection already within us.
- All power is within you; you can do anything and everything. Believe in that; do not believe that you are weak. Stand up and express the divinity within you.
- All glory, power and purity are within us already... potential or manifest, it is there—and the sooner you believe that, the better for you.
- Teach yourselves, teach everyone his real nature, call upon the sleeping soul and see how it awakes. Power will come, glory will come, goodness will come, purity will come, all that is excellent will come when the sleeping soul is roused to self-conscious activity.

If all power and excellence is already within us, then to bring it out ought to be of utmost value to us. Peace education can therefore be understood as that process of self-development, which helps to *'bring forth from within'* (the meaning of Educare, the Latin of Education) all peace and perfection already within us.

Extracts from UNESCO's book on Peace Education: Wars begin in the *minds* of men and peace can be installed by *cleansing* of the *minds* of men. It asks: Are we giving adequate attention to teach peace? Are our schools really interested in producing a peaceful young generation? And remarks: Those who want *war* prepare the young for war; but those who want peace have neglected training the young for peace. (In 'war' we may include consumerism, sex, violence, drugs, lower pleasures and entertainment). It goes on to say: Peace can be cultivated only through training of the mind to control desire, balancing between deserving and desiring, developing tolerance and respect for differences, concern and love for others, and moving from competition to cooperation

Obviously one who cannot live in peace with oneself cannot live in peace with others. Peace in one's life arises from the deep human *spirit* that underlies all faiths. Peace education deals with the depth of the human mind. Touching the seat of spirituality is necessary. Here *by spirituality we mean that essence rooted in man,* which seeks for fulfillment through expressing and experiencing goodness in the highest degree. It drives us to do good, be kind, search for the true meaning and values lying deep within us. All religions teach that there is still deep peace within us. As a matter of fact all of us know that when the mind calms down a serene feeling of joy and peace begins to unfold within us. One of the effective ways of realizing the peace within is meditation as taught in all religions.

Understanding the Nature of Man and Mind

From the above it is clear that Peace education should cover the concepts of Spirituality and the understanding of the nature of mind, learning how to cleanse it and make it peaceful, learning to control desires, and have care and concern for others so that we can 'Learn to Live Together' in peace and harmony.

Man is 'body', which is matter plus 'life or spirit'. Identified with body we are bound to be petty minded, agitating and self-centered. Matter cannot be the source of peace, values and consciousness. In spirit alone we are at peace and can enjoy poorna-ananda, full-peace and bliss.

Our Problem : Why are we not able to experience and enjoy full-peace and bliss? The villain is our mind. Mind is our instrument of perception but it also acts as a veil, which does not allow us to experience full-peace and bliss.

Attached to our bodies, we identify with its limited happiness but we keep on looking for more and more fulfillment, peace and bliss. In our strivings to seek fulfillment, we create many desires and goals and for fulfilling them we keep on forming, deforming, and reforming our mind every moment, by the permanent impressions that are left on it, by our 'actions or karma', which include—all our thoughts, choices, motives, words, duties, beliefs, values, desires, work and goals (Long-term, Short-term, Weekly, Daily Actions). These impressions create our 'svabhaava', nature and tendencies, our personality and character. The good impressions we gather make us calm, cheerful and peaceful, and can take us towards the highest. The active impressions give us the power and energy to fulfill our goals. Wrong actions make us dull and inactive and give us miseries.

The Solution : So, we need to understand: What are the methods and skills to be acquired to cleanse the mind, control desires and enjoy the peace, which is our inherent nature?

Our education should make us aware of the higher dimensions of education, work and life—'know the truth and the truth shall make us free'. It should establish us in the habit of continuous *practice* and *focus* on the higher. It should help us to practice identification more and more with the 'spirit' within. Only then, we will be better placed to appreciate that every 'action', is our opportunity to either walk towards peace or away from it. What do I choose? To awaken our *Viveka,* the power of making right choices and develop the strength to walk the path that leads to peace and perfection is Peace Education and self-development.

Understanding and Managing our Mind : Mind is the subtlest form of all-pervasive matter and borrows consciousness from the spirit, like the iron rod gets hot and red in contact with fire. It is like a bridge between matter and spirit and is the seat of continuous flow of thoughts—wanted/unwanted. It is built to look outside through the five sense organs. By its very nature mind has a tendency to 'flow down'—be tempted, enjoying the experience of the senses. It is one-track in nature; gets attached easily, but detaches with difficulty It is difficult to lift up and control–like reversing the flow of river. Weak people don't have self-control and their mind propels them to do wrong, because of the past habits and tendencies acquired by us. Doing what 'we' want to do implies doing what the mind wants to do. Freedom is in *not* having to do what the *mind* wants to do.

The motive power for all actions is our desires. Education must teach us to check desires to do wrong actions. Those actions, which take us towards peace, are good or right actions and those that take us away are wrong actions. Through daily self-development processes we can awaken our *Viveka* and develop powers of will to walk the critical path. Not allowing the Mind to take us towards lower desires is to be constantly practiced. Good actions calm the mind and only a calm mind can really be effective and peaceful and allow us to experience our full potential perfection and bliss. Awareness that "I am not the mind" helps in control.

Continuous, daily, regular, repetitive practice is needed to absorb and inculcate the higher values and ideals and develop powers of mind.

Action Plan for Imparting Peace Education in Schools

Based on the above ideals and strategies to manage the mind, the following strategy is suggested:

(*i*) **Vision :** Make students aware of the higher, through daily study and reflection so that they can map out their life accordingly.

- 'Learning: The Treasure Within'—UNESCO
- 'The Kingdom of God is within you'—The Bible
- *'An-al-haqq'* or 'I am the truth'—A Sufi saint (The inner spirit is of utmost importance in building of Islamic personality, ma'rifah, realisation of truth)

(*ii*) **Mission :** Inspire, convince and establish students in the mission to realize the vision.

- *'Atmano-Moksartham-jagad-hitaye-cha'*, striving to manifest our peace and perfection by working for the good of society.
- 'Seek you first the kingdom of God and his righteousness and everything else will be added unto you'; 'Be you Perfect'—The Bible.
- The inner spirit is of utmost importance in building of Islamic personality, *ma'rifah,* realisation of truth.

(*iii*) **Methodologies :** The process to control our mind, awaken *viveka* and acquire the ability to choose the long-term good over the immediate pleasures, is strengthened through the 4-fold daily and regular *self-development practice* of : Prayers; Meditation; Fulfillment of all duties and quality in work, done as worship for the good of society; and Study of the Self to get conviction in the purpose of life and importance of following Human Values.

(*iv*) **Action Plan :** Students are with us in school for more than a decade during which we must teach them how to harmonise their thoughts-motives-choices-short and long-term goals with the ultimate goal of life. We must establish them in the habit of drawing-up their daily and weekly time-table, supported by monthly plans, 3 and 6 month goals, and backed by their long-term goals and constantly review these and harmonise them with the universal values and our common and ultimate goal of perfection, peace and joy.

Strategy for Continuous Studies—Study Circles

We can create study-circles of 4-6 students, meeting once a week, for one hour to study any inspiring book in consultation with their elders and reflect, discuss, debate and question with respect to the higher dimensions of life.

Self-introspection to Know Oneself and Awaken Intellect to Make Right Choices : What do I want? During the long years that students are with us we can establish them in the habit of sitting alone, at least once in a week, for one hour to interview themselves. Let them practice asking various questions relevant to their life.

- What do I want out of my life?
- What do I want to make of myself?
- What are my Governing Values?
- What are my beliefs?
- Are my goals, values, beliefs, worldview in harmony with universal values?

Let them keep a confidential book for the purpose and be perfectly sincere. Let them write whatever answer comes; without any restrain or restriction. Let their mind give as many answers as it wants to give; simply go on noting them. Let it be exhaustive. Do not finish it in one sitting. Give as many sittings till the answers are exhausted. Let this exercise be repeated at regular intervals.

What do I want? : Now we have solid matter to examine and find out the thing that will improve the quality of our life. Now examine every answer given by the mind one by one and see what you really want. Ask yourself why you want to be what you want. Is the ideal that you want in harmony with your inner needs of peace and bliss? Is your daily life in harmony with your short-term and long-term goals? Are your activities and goals in harmony with your inner needs? Do you have the conviction that any activities or goal that does not take you towards your inner needs is not worthwhile? Do you have the conviction that good values alone can fulfill your inner needs?

How Can I become Better? : First point to be noted is that whatever may be the desires and goals of life it should not be based on selfishness and lower desires of enjoyment. Inculcation of values, control of mind and cultivation of good thoughts, are the chief means for reaching any goal in life and also for attaining inner peace.

Intelligence : Intelligence is the master which controls the mind, as is observed from our daily experience. Whenever a bad thought comes into our mind, simultaneously the thinking part of the mind-our higher or awakened intellect says no, we should not do it. Often we are unable to discriminate between right and wrong or to control the mind. Herein comes the higher and better quality of intellect, which we may call wisdom. This power is not always active in us and we need to make it active.

Activating the Intellect, Viveka or Wisdom : The best process is to keep good company—learn from lives and teachings of saints, sages, seers, read inspiring books, which show the difference between good and bad and the benefits of using wisdom, keep good company, learn from people who are actively using it and doing good actions. In the beginning our mind is not only disobedient but is rebellious also. Therefore we need not dictate to it or order it about. We should goad and persuade it to follow wisdom. Tell your mind—just for today—I should not do this but do that. Every now and then let us tell ourselves—wait a minute please—and in that minute let us examine our motives, desires and other thoughts of the mind. This practice will keep a good watch over the mind and it will not go astray.

Remember: Mind is Very Much Susceptible to Suggestion : We should suggest to our mind: I am good; I have to become better. Whatever we suggest to our mind when it is receptive and calm it accepts and sends it to our sub-conscious mind, which in turn amends our character accordingly. A series of positive thoughts and words of wisdom are available which can be used for introspection. The best time to practice is before going to sleep and immediately after getting up. Prayers, meditation, Repetition of holy names, etc. are all time-tested ways to pour good thoughts in the mind to overcome the past self-centered impressions.

It is up to each one of us to acquire the wisdom, strength, and fearlessness to walk the critical path, which guarantees success with peace, joy and prosperity. Only those who are striving on the path and are convinced of it are fit to be our teachers, our executives and leaders.

Repetition of holy name, brief prayer, Visualisation and meditation on a form or symbol of God, or qualities of holy saint and their life and teachings, etc. are the best way to refine and reform the past impressions.

Mind Management

Processes for purifying our mind-set. There are two fundamental methods for self-development and management of flow of thoughts, mind:

- Repetitive thoughts, words and actions, *constant practice;* and
- Learning to *focus on the essentials* and with drawl from the non-essentials.

There are three fundamental processes to impress new thoughts and ideals into the mind:

- Hearing (Reading)
- Reflecting upon the new ideas

- Deep thinking—Meditating upon the new ideas, practising them and ultimately making them your own

  "Sow a thought, reap an action

  Sow an action, reap a habit

  Sow a habit reap, a character

  Sow a character, reap a destiny"

  'We are what our thoughts are'

  "On the quality of our thoughts, depends the quality of our life"

The above processes for managing our mind have to be undertaken regularly, daily, continuously, at all times, in every moment, in every choice that we make, and for our whole life.

There are 4 broad methods for improving our mind-set, for self-development:

- Work as worship or work as meditation with eyes open
- Prayers and worship
- Meditation
- Study of inspiring thoughts giving knowledge of our infinite potential and oneness with all creation

Education Tips from Ancient India

During the Round-Table Conference in the UK in 1931, Mahatma Gandhi, speaking to the Press, had said that when the British came to India, instead of building up on the existing systems, they uprooted the beautiful tree of Indian systems and allowed the roots to decay and die, and he referred to education and health, *vidya* and *vaidya*. Both these were imparted by men of wisdom, men of '*tyaga* and *seva*', the twin ideals of India. The total commercialisation of both education and health today show the wisdom of the Mahatma. Let us therefore, look into Indian system of education, *viz:* the 'gurukul'.

Without the personal life of the teacher working as a role model, no inspiration for peace education or self-development can take place. In India therefore education was always given through men of wisdom. The students did not pay for education. It was thought that knowledge is too sacred, to be sold, it should be given free. To support the teachers, the kings and the rich men made large donations. The *Upanishads* give an inkling of the methods used. The pupils were encouraged to ask questions. Teachers used stories, parables, discussions and assignments. Logic was taught as a subject and thinking, introspection and contemplation were emphasised and were made a part of daily routine and an obligatory duty. It meant study of the self, the infinite potential and the divinity within. The kingdom of God is within you. Seek you first the kingdom of God and his righteousness and everything else will be added unto you, as the Bible says.

It was obligatory for the pupils to have a fixed daily routine of prayers, meditation and self-study. It was known that exposure to noble ideals and constant repetition was the way to impress new ideals in the mind. Daily life therefore provided the time, space, inspiration, and processes suited to individuals. Discipline included control of the senses, practice of austerity, and living a life of dedication and service to elders. A student was to rise before sunrise, bathe early, perform his morning devotional practices without fail and meditate. He was to avoid idle disputes, gossip, backbiting, lying, luxuries, sleeping in the day. He had to be free from sexual desires, anger, envy and covetousness. He was to be forgiving, untiring in fulfilling his duties, modest, self-confident and devoid of pride.

Selflessness, self-control, endurance, desire for freedom and faith in the teacher was the requisite of a good pupil. The ideal of education was the development of personality through inculcation of values. It was recognised that as long as our heart is not pure it is difficult to inculcate good values and character; and that one who hankers after petty joys and sense pleasures, can rarely cultivate the powers of concentration necessary for greatness. By constant practice they were trained to inculcate values and develop their character.

REFERENCES

1. Extracts and Insights from:

   (*i*) "Learning The Way of Peace—A Teachers Guide to Peace Education"–UNESCO

   (*ii*) The Complete Works of Swami Vivekananda

   (*iii*) My Books and article (in my bio-data attached earlier)

CHAPTER 10

Peace Education in Schools : A Need

*Dharmendra Kumar Pandey
**Suman Pandey

"Since wars begin in the minds of men, it is in the mind of men that the defences of peace must be constructed."

(Preamble of the UNESCO Constitution)

Today the world is beset with enormous problems, though modern amenities prevail everywhere. Humane kind has reached the highest peak of success, but human beings are passing their days with anxiety because of the tumultuous situation of the world. These problems include hunger, poverty, illiteracy, unemployment, discrimination against women, moral degradation, lack of healthcare and so on. India as a developing country is not immune to these problems. Poverty, illiteracy and unemployment are the burning questions in our country that contribute to peacelessness in the family, in society as well as in the country. The Government and different NGOs are working to remove these problems from the country but they are having trouble reaching there expectations. Presently Peace education is a very important issue all over the world for sustainable development and successful democracy.

Peace Education is very important for bringing peace and stability in our country and all over the world. It is really difficult to define as universal definition of Peace Education.

* Lecturer (B.Ed) Department Govt. Drgree College Dakpather, Dehradun

** Research Scholar, Allahabad University, Allahabad

Peace is not just a society without weapons or just an absence of war, peace is something far beyond that; an environment in which all humans can enjoy the highest level of inner peace. Peace Education "... is not only rooted in building peace with one self, but it also inter connects and interrelates with every issue of life" (Bull, 2000, p 17). Peace Education teaches a culture of peace that includes six important components (Toh, 2004). These components are: 1. Educating for human rights and responsibilities; 2. Educating for personal peace; 3. Educating for environmental care; 4. Educating for inter-cultural solidarity; 5. Educating for living with justice and compassion; 6. Educating for dismantling a cultural of war. Peace Education is not only concerned with the content of teaching but also the form and structure within which teaching takes place.

This approach of education is known as "Peace Education", which will address all existing concerns of positive and negative peace in society. Peace Education is defined as education for transforming consciousness and worldviews towards a culture of peace and non-violence. It rests on developing a critical understanding of root causes of conflicts and violence, and empowering learners to dismantle a culture of violence and to build a peaceful self and world; takes place across all modes (formal, non-formal, informal) and levels, relying on participatory, creative, and critical pedagogies (Groff and Smoker, 1996).

Peace is the most vital thing in human life. It is the need of the hour to sow the seeds of peace among students. And Peace Education is very important for bringing peace and stability to our country as well as to the world. The role of school is of particular importance because they are one of the few places where young people of diverse backgrounds may be found daily in large numbers. Our schools then, have a unique opportunity to provide understanding of the world's cultures and the point of agreement between the religions of world, recognising that every person male and female is a precious member of the human family. In, general, can schools do to promote culture harmony through peace education? First be guided by the principal of unity in diversity. Recognise that our similarities are more basic than our differences. If schools fails to help to harmonise the society what will be the consequences? Only school is the center which can play a crucial role for brining peace in the society as well as in the country. Following points show the need of Peace Education in school:

- Peace Education can help to a great extent to empower the children who are the future generation of the country.
- Peace education is very important as it makes them more patriotic and respectful to their own culture. From peace education they will understand the human rights and responsibilities, consumerism, poverty, unemployment etc.
- Students and teachers are losing their ethics of education, values of education, greed of power; money and self interest are turning them towards the dirty politics in the country. So peace education is needed for those more educated people in the country that will help to awaken consciousness, responsibilities as well as moral values.
- It can help for the full development of human personality and to the strengthening of respect for human rights and fundamental freedoms.
- Peace education shall promote understanding, tolerance, and friendship among all nations, social or religious groups.
- Our country is facing many important challenges like the hindrance of successful democracy; poverty, unemployment, child labour, corruption and political violence. These challenges contribute greatly to a negative impact in the education sectors in the country as well as create obstacles for peace and sustainable development in the country. Peace education can help to overcome the root causes of the problems in the country.

- Nurturing in students the social skills and outlook needed to live together in harmony.
- Peace education is essential for promoting the knowledge, skills, attitudes and values needed to bring about behaviour changes that will enable children, youth and adults to prevent conflict and violence, both overt and structural; to resolve conflict peacefully: and to create the conditions conducive to peace.
- It is peace education which inculcates and builds love, friendship and creates the conditions conducive to peace.
- It teaches about the danger of violence, develop their capacities to counter violence and builds sustainable peace in their communities.
- Peace education is intended to prepare students for democratic participation in schools and society.
- It talks about poverty, malnutrition, street children and the causes of these on local, national, and global levels. It also discusses how to empower people through cooperation and collaboration.
- It helps in developing a critical understanding of root causes of conflicts and violence, and empowering learners to dismantle a culture of violence.
- It reduces antisocial behaviour in school aged children (Garrard, 2007).
- It increases awareness of violence and appropriate reactions to it by teachers, schoolchildren and parents. It also decreases violence among school children (International Network on School Bullying and Violence, August 2005).
- It decreases problem behaviour at school observed by teachers (International Network on School Bullying and Violence, May 2005).
- It decreases the attractiveness of gangs and help vulnerable students resist them by creating a school

climate that makes every student feel valued and establishing Peace education as part of the school curriculum.

No doubt that the global peace has become a major concern these days. There is a general restlessness in the entire world which is leading to widespread violence. Empathy for others, democratic living, secular values have been relegated to the background. In their place fundamentalism and terrorism have taken control of the world. Educational process seems to have lost track of the original purpose of bringing out the best in each individual. Instead, even schooling is seen as a part of the rat race for which we are preparing the posterity. Under these circumstances, there is a great need to reconsider our own objectives of education and ensure that the principles of right living and non-violence are incorporated into the process of Education. One such effort is reflected in the efforts to think of Peace Education as a part of the school curriculum.

REFERENCES

1. Allen, Douglas. 2007. *Mahatma Gandhi on Violence and Peace education.* Philosophy East and West, Vol. 57, No. 3, University of Hawai'i Press.
2. Bajaj, M. 2008. *'Critical' Peace Education.* Encyclopaedia of Peace Education. Teacher's College, Columbia University. http://www.tc.edu/centers/epe/PDF%20articles/Bajaj_ch16_22feb08.pdf Accessed 3 March 2009.
3. National Council of Educational Research and Training. Education for Peace. New Delhi : National Council of Educational Research and Training, 2002.
4. Prasad. D.(1984). Peace Education or Education for Peace. New Delhi: Gandhi Peace Foundation.
5. Pasad, S.N. (1972). Education: Mental Health and World Peace. Varanasi (India): Author.
6. Sahi, Jane. 2000. *Education for Peace.* Akshar Mudra. Pune, India.
7. Timpson, William M. Teaching and Learning Peace. Madison, Wisconsin: Atwood Publishing, 2002.
8. The Universal House of Justice. The Promise of World Peace. New Delhi: Baha'i Publishing Trust, 1985.

CHAPTER 11

The Role of Peace Education in Preventing Conflict

*Anjana Kaul
**Dr. Shireesh Pal Singh
***Dr. Daljeet Kaur Singh

War has been a constant threat to mankind since the dawn of civilisation. This threat ranges from the everyday violence to the vast devastation left by the great world wars. Now in the 21st century, our world needs to come closer together by a mutual respect and understanding of other cultures. We need to build a world in which people choose to cooperate for the benefit of all mankind, act with selflessness, recognising the values of non-violence and respect for human rights, tolerance and diversity.

The consequences of war are very devastating. People are displaced within their own state, are deprived of security and stability, and prevented them from achieving self-fulfillment and self-realisation. The resulting insecurity and instability that follows from these circumstances like lack of basic needs, harsh surroundings, and oppressive governments. This forces may turn to aggression, violence, hostility, assault and antagonism in defence of their right to survive. These problems have created the need to understand and prevent the conditions leading to violence.

The violence can be reduced through the practice of dialogue and negotiation through an active programme of peace education. Many charitable organisations and individuals are working for the spread of peace education

* Himgiri Nabh Vishvavidhyalaya, Dehradun.
** Sri Guru Ram Rai (P.G.) College, Dehradun.
*** Former Principal, D.W.T. (P.G.) College, Dehradun.

throughout the world. Their valuable efforts are essential for the security of mankind.

THE ROOTS OF CONFLICT

Changing Minds

Wars and conflicts threaten peace and security to all. There is need to reduce violence through peace education. Times have changed, and this requires a more practical outlook. The Seville Statement on Violence affirms: War is not a fatality determined by genes, violent brains, human nature or instincts, but is rather a social invention. (UNESCO. The Seville Statement for Peace 1986.) The recent developments in today's world, including the tragic events of September 11, 2001, 26th November, 2008 Mumbai attack and the current international concern on Iraq's necessity to comply with the demands of the international community, have forced many people to believe that peace is an impossible dream.

Peace education will transform and modify people towards dealing with conflicts. The impact of violence affects all countries. It is a global concern, requiring a global approach to a solution. The usual method countries use to deal with conflict and wars is through oppressive military measures which is not enough. It merely hampers the growth. A preventive approach needs to be recognised and provisions should be made to promote a culture of peace and non-violence. Governments must shift their central priorities from accumulating political and military power towards building a stronger educational infrastructure for peace. Security and stability are all dependent upon a sound education. It is time to adapt a renewed mindset that promotes peace education.

We need to change our mindsets and must strive to build a culture which consists of values, attitudes and behaviours that reject violence. There should be continuous dialogue and negotiation between individuals, groups and nations.

In modern times, the maintenance of peace depends on attitudes and actions undertaken by the community as a whole. Nelson Mandela emphasised the importance of group participation.

Institutions such as the United Nations system, governments, politicians, scientists, NGOs, the media, civil society, and especially teachers and parents should work together to create a culture of peace. Peace education should not only be confined to schools but should involve the entire community. Parents should encourage strong family values that foster a culture of peace.

People need to be made aware that they, too, can work towards the creation of a more peaceful world. People need to be reminded that an individual who acts with pure intentions can make a profound difference, can influence events that are important to the continued existence of mankind. The threat to peace stems from poverty, environmental deterioration and social injustice. There are a variety of factors including economic, political, social, cultural and environmental grounds from which these causes are founded. When we discuss about the need of change in mindset we need to understand the various dimensions like economic, political, social, cultural and environmental dimensions.

Economic Dimensions

As a result of globalisation, the countries are becoming more closely connected and interdependent. Economic stability is an essential requirement in order to build peace within a society the uneven distribution of benefits: economic growth, modernisation and employment, has resulted in an increased gap between members of society. People are not able to come out of the cycle of poverty due to the Inequality in economic opportunities and unemployment. Unequal access to education prevents them from development and attainment of self-sufficiency.

Without improvement to the current situation of developing countries, which constitute the majority of the world's people, global security will become increasingly threatened by acts of terrorism and political instability.

Political Dimensions

Many political systems violate human rights, curb democratic practices, and increase their own power at the expense of the public. This stimulates corruption, injustice and abuse within the society. Such political systems force their own values and beliefs upon members of the society through the use of state-controlled media. This abuse of human rights is correlated with low life expectancies and high mortality rates, deterioration of the environment and the drain of labour and capital resources. Political stability is closely linked to the prevention of conflict and the promotion of peace.

Peace cannot be maintained if there is injustice and disparity in the society.

States should promote the values of democracy, develop democratic attitude, empowerment to the people, the ability to influence policy, protect human rights. Promotion of democracy prevents conflict, strengthens governance, improves the rule of law and creates stability.

Social Dimensions

Advances in technology have enabled millions of people to develop their mobility anywhere in the world. It results in exposure to various cultures and makes societies increasingly multicultural. But this process has brought drawbacks with its many benefits. It can provoke fear, misunderstanding and intolerance of other cultures.

Social dimensions have important role to play. Social structure has seen a tremendous change, life styles of people have changed, and nuclear families have come up, disintegration of joint families, loss of traditional values, and the exposure to violence in the media as well as in daily life and the exposure to different cultures. Due to cultural differences people have turned towards violence. Peace education is vital to teach people to incorporate the skills of dialogue, peace, tolerance, understanding and respect for human rights. This abuse of human rights is correlated with low life expectancies and high mortality rates, deterioration of the environment and the drain of labor and capital resources. (*Ebrahimian* 2002.)

Cultural Dimensions

There is at times marginalisation in the decision-making process due to cultural differences, ethnicity, religion, race, language and age. Women, youth, elderly people, and minorities are more vulnerable to such discriminations. They feel disgrace, isolation, rejection of Human Rights. So they engage themselves in violent actions. This cultural marginalisation major threat to social stability. We must remove is discrimination, encourage the promotion and respect of human rights, and teach the value of tolerance for those of different backgrounds through peace education.

Exclusion of individuals and certain groups from participation in the fields of social, economic and political issues is another major cause of conflict.

Marginalisation in the decision-making process occurs because of discrimination in terms of cultural differences, ethnicity, religion, race, language and age: groups susceptible to discrimination are women, youth, elderly people, and minorities. The impact of marginalization these groups experience causes feelings of humiliation, alienation and denial of human rights and resources.

This creates grounds for them to engage in violent actions, endangering both themselves and others. (*Balanandan* 1998)

Environmental Dimensions

In our country millions of people do not get the basic amenities like drinking water and sanitation. The lack of proper health-care, water care and sanitation infrastructures leads to high mortality and disease rates. Minority groups are frequently deprived of right to use to own property, denying them independence and provoking feelings of bitterness, anger and dislike. Feelings of insecurity and instability as a result of unemployment, poverty, lack of education, good government, healthcare infrastructure and the increase of drug abuse provide further grounds for resorting to the use of violence.

So there are threats from various dimensions. Peace can be attained if individuals are trained, communities are made aware and nations cooperate to attain global equity.

WAYS TO REDUCE THE CONFLICT

Democracy and Equality

The protection of public well-being involves guidance provided by governments as well as the members of the society. For Promoting peace there are many other issues directly linked with maintaining peace.

The first and fundamental commitment of the government is to provide all members of society with a peaceful environment, one that is conducive to freedom and opportunity.

Unlike an harsh government, a democratic government offers equal opportunities for all through economic, political, social and cultural aspects of people's lives. A truly democratic government aims for the benefits of all, and ensures the elimination of poverty by creating employment opportunities. It also offers equal opportunities for education; education for all groups at all levels, both formal and non-formal. Education is essential for fulfillment, essential for providing literacy and numeracy skills, essential for continued development and quality of life. An equal and democratic society is essential for the creation of sustainable peace.

Democratic government stimulates participation of all members, particularly minority groups such as women, children, indigenous and elderly people. It will also maintain the values of peace and compassion.

It is extremely important for democratic societies to develop a sound infrastructure. There should be provision of health and water care and equal access to natural resources to produce a healthy population. A democratic government fights the trade in narcotics and other drug abuses, which are a threat to security and peace. In this way a society will be full of the individuals who are contented, peaceful by nature and will contribute towards the development and prosperity of the nation. A democratic outlook promotes education of tolerance; mutual understanding and the celebration of diversity will be instilled.

Government Programmes

The government can act to establish projects and programmes to promote education for all. Through infrastructure development, ensuring equal access to all for basic and secondary education, and through the provision of learning materials and resources, the government can act as a major catalyst in changing the values of the society as a whole.

Educational Programmes

A strategy should be established to promote peace through education. It should be done through the incorporation of the universal values of peace, non-violence, tolerance and respect for human rights into all education curricula and methods.

Schools must work towards educating students in the benefits of literacy and numeracy, teaching skills and knowledge needed to fulfill self-development, in addition to teaching participation in society and how to collectively improve quality of life.

Governments can take active participation in UNESCO's Associated Schools Project in primary, as well as secondary, levels of education.

To promote peace through education can be accomplished through the incorporation of the universal values of peace, non-violence, tolerance and respect for human rights into all education curricula and methods.

Schools must work towards educating students in the benefits of literacy and numeracy, teaching skills and knowledge needed to fulfill self-development, in addition to teaching participation in society and how to collectively improve quality of life.

Governments can take active participation in UNESCO's Associated Schools Project in primary, as well as secondary, levels of education. The Associated Schools Project provides learning materials to schools and focuses on four main themes, including World Concerns and the United Nations system, Human Rights and Democracy, Intercultural Learning, and Environmental Issues, to enhance the education for a culture of peace, demonstrating the viability of intergovernmental and non-governmental cooperation in the assistance of peace education. There are currently only a few hundred schools in the entire world that actively participate in UNESCO's Associated Schools Project. Much greater participation is needed to make this effort succeed.

Social Programmes

Parents and teachers can play a major role in the reduction of conflict. Children and youth are desperately in need of mentors that can teach them the values of tolerance and compassion.

The role of the media is ever more important as our world develops its Infrastructures and becomes ever more global. The media must place emphasis on moral values, actively cooperate with organisations, utilise all available resources to disseminate the message of peace, tolerance, non-violence, respect for human rights and the promotion of democracy.

Cultural activities and Sporting events create social bonds between different segments of society, which brings them closer. Art activities stimulate members of the society to express themselves in a similar way. The transition to a technology and information-oriented society must not be isolated to the select few. Projects must be aimed to eliminate the unequal distribution of wealth and resources throughout the world.

Conclusion

The creation of peace is a long, ongoing process that will take years to accomplish, but at least the generations to come will have the chance to experience its benefits. It must become our united goal as human beings to live with one another in peace and harmony. Peace education raises awareness of the roots and causes of conflict, and it provides people with the necessary skills and knowledge how to respond to conflict environments, developing educational curricula, including the provision of learning materials containing themes on peace, and training teachers. Outside schools, UNICEF offices have developed programmes including after-school sports and recreation programmes, youth clubs, and summer camps. Workshops and training programs for parents and community leaders show how to utilise media and other channels of communication for the promotion of peace, encouraging participation in cultural activities and art programmes.

REFERENCES

1. Balanandan, E. *Social Development, Including Questions Relating to the World Social Situation and to Youth, Ageing, Disabled Persons and the Family.* Statement by Member of Parliament of the Third Committee on Social, Humanitarian and Cultural Issues, United Nations. October 1998.
2. Ebrahimian, D. L. *Conflict Prevention.* Commission for Social Development in February 2003. November 2002.
3. UNESCO. *The Seville Statement (1986)—Building A Culture of Peace.*
4. UNESCO. *Unit for Peace and New Dimensions of Security.* World Wide Web: http://www.unesco.org/cpp/uk/peace/.November 2002.
5. World Health Organisation. *World Report on Violence and Health.* November 2002.
6. UNESCO. *Plan of Action to follow up the United Nations Year for Tolerance (1995).* http://www.unesco.org/tolerance/planeng.htm.

CHAPTER

12

Choosing the Way of Peace Rather than Violence

*Dr. Jaya Sharma

"Na hinsyat sarva bhutaani" Rigveda. 'No one should be involved in violence' this has been said in our oldest veda Rigveda, which banned killing of animals during the Yajna.

History is said to be a great teacher and there are several episodes in the recent past which have drawn the attention of all the countries towards the peace and the ill-effects of violence as well as of peace with its fruitfullness. In other words we can say that under the situation of violence, conflicts, foreign attacks and their rules every country has to suffer politically, socially, economically and her cultural, ethical and eternal values are affected badly.

Conflicts and Disaster

Conflicts and disasters are always at two levels, one at international level which later on turns into globalisation and domestic conflicts within the country. Economic conflicts can be managed within a specific time period but cultural, social, ethnic, religious and sub-national domestic conflicts are last long and rooted deeply in the society.

When there is conflict between two countries they have geopolitical consequences. If both of them are to give political economic and military or intelligence support to friendly regimes, then some of these regimes may oppress their citizens, violate human rights and reap the fruit of progress of their own benefit.

---

* Lecturer, Mussoorie Institute of Education, Mussoorie.

Conflicts are always serious blow to the chances for economic development and many of these conflicts are, not purely political, they have social and economic roots as well. Peace and development are not linked only at international level but also with in the countries. In a way the whole life is disturbed.

There are domestic conflicts with in the countries which are always quite complex. In many nations, people are emphasizing more on the cultural dimension of their identity as compared to social and economic dimension. These led to new poverties, more complexities and more exploitation. Some conflicts are not new but re-emerged. Those are of both economic and cultural dimensions. Economic conflicts can be managed early but not the cultural ones, they are long lasting.

Violence due to mental obtuseness with respect to cultural identity are based on a tribal group, an ethnic group, religious denomination, social class, sex, tongue, colour, caste, nationalistic clan or any group defining its identity. Frequent attacks on border forced our country to invest a big amount of national income on our security. Serial bomb blasts are the serious causes of causality and results into negative effects on every aspects of life. Riots based on casts and religion creates violence in the whole country and disturbed the peace of the people. Not only in our country but in other countries like Uganda, Australia, England, attacks and threat to Indian scholars and students based on colour are the blows on our identity. However, identity of people should not be threatened but should be respected through communication with other groups. As violence is not confined to the original location of the conflict, it is spread to other countries by the same elements.

Four Crises

This crisis which relate to the conflicts is four fold:

1. Policies are not framed adequately and are too weak to counter imbalances which create crisis in policy making.

Crisis in the world system.the dificeincies mentioned in the international institutions render it alarmingly inadequate to address the global challenges of today. After World War II the new system of the unites nations had been created in order to contain the use and abuse of power by individual countries by establishing a power sharing system on the basis of consensus, meant to address common insecurities and other challenges to the world as a whole.

3. Underneath the crisis in global policy making and in the world systems there is a crisis ridden process, characterised by more poverty, not as an unintended corollary of progress but as a result of intended exclusion, economically as well as politically. The global economy becomes more and more dualistic.

All this reflects a basic crisis in ideas and values, in political theory about the relation between man and society, in the economic theory about what constitutes welfare, in the thinking of people all around the world about the relation between man and nature and earth's resources, in ideas about the legitimacy of violence in order to reach one's objectives. Throughout history such basic questions have been answered differently in different countries. Presently paradigmatic differences have globalised themselves, due to world wide migration, more intense communication, mass information and fast economic as well as technological modernisation. This is bound to lead culutural and political conflicts, everywhere.

These reflect a basic crisis in ideas and values in political theory about the relation between man and society, between man and nature in ideas about the legitimacy of violence in order to reach one's objectives.

Conflict and Globalisation

Since the end of the Cold War conflicts rose mostly within nations, not between them. Some of those conflicts were not new at all. They did not emerge, but re-emerge, often decades of silence. Most of these conflicts had both economic and cultural dimensions. Economic conflicts can be managed within a reasonable period of time, by a good combination of economic growth and (re) distribution of assets and income, creating a perspective of progress for everybody, both future and present generations. On the other hand, cultural, social, ethnic, religious or sub-national domestic conflicts last long. They are roots deeply in society. Cultural conflicts, whether or not accompanied or sharpened by economic inequalities, outlive generations. They are less manageable than economic conflict, because there is no way out by means of sharing or redistribution.

Cultural identity conflicts are different. People and their identity groups-be it a tribe, an ethnic group, a religious denomination, a social class, a sex, a tongue, a colour, a caste, an elite , a nationalistic clan, or any group defining its identity in other than purely economic terms—are inclined to define their identity not as a share of total potential welfare in a society, but as absolute positions, demonstrably different for the groups. From this perspective a stronger position of one group in a society always means that another group will lose. However, when individual people and the groups to which they belong consider their identity not threatened—and thus potentially diminished—but enriched through communication with other identity groups, conflicts can be avoided. For example: Identity of Indian students is threatening by the native people of various countries which is in human and should be banned.

Violence was not contained to the original location of the conflict. It was brought to other countries by the same forces which brought about globalisation. That was the second major new phenomenon in the ninety nineties. Globalisation was not a new process; we had seen it for centuries, and had witnessed a stronger pace in the four decades since World was Two. It got a momentum of its own, became less a consequence of demonstrable human decisions, more self-contained and self supporting. The driving force was twofold. First: technological advance, enabling full and fast information and communication everywhere, physically and virtually. Second: economic, the global market, linking production, investment, transportation, trade, advertisement and consumption anywhere in the world to any other place. The result was a disregard for national frontiers, a strengthening of global corporations and an erosion of nation states.

After September 11, 2001, world leadership has the task to disarm the fanatics without alienating those who doubt. That requires, as was pleaded by Secretary General Kofi Annan when he received the Nobel Peace Prize, building a sustainable, democratic and peaceful world society, within which humanity is seen as indivisible. That concept of sustainability, kofi Annan added, ought to be based upon the dignity and inviolability of all human life, irrespective of origin, race or creed.

In Conventional Truths

In his book AL Gore depicted that six D's which shows the state of mind resulting in:

- Denial of the actual position
- Doubt and disinformation about the situation.
- Deliberate disinformation purposely to creating the velocity of the violence slow.
- Delay of precautionary and remedial action.
- State of despair which is brought by total lack of action.
- Distrust on the department and the leadership concern.

These Six D's results in:

Deeper conflicts and less peace, political alienation, people's distrust on their leader, people become suspicious about values, models and doctrines, group sharpening their identity, fencing themselves in and keeping others out.

Violence creates the choice between two paradigms:

- Security and sustainability, where security is exclusive to the society and nations get threatened by outsiders, foreigners and potential enemies.
- On the other hand sustainability is inclusive of a safe and secure habitat, where job, access to food, water, healthcare, and entitlements to resources are available.

Lesson from the Past

Lesson from the past and evidences strengthen our view of choosing the way of peace rather than violence. When we go back in our history we find both the elements in our life violence as well as non-violence are prevalent. We start from Vedas till today. In the time before Vedas kings were used to kill animals on the occasion of Yajna and were banned to kill them by Rigveda, depicted that *Na Hinsyat Sarvabhutaani.*

During the mahakavya Kaal Ravana had banned the killing and eating of cows on Yajna.

That was Non-violence against animals.

The attacks by one king on the other to capture the kingdoms and quench the materialistic lust made the country weak which led to the foreign rule in India. The invaders looted our country and made the golden bird a poor country.

Jainism favours non-violence in its philosophy. In its theory of banned factor (*Bandh Tatva*) it depicted that a person should follow the path and take an oath of non-violence. In this *Ahimsa,* non-violence is also one *Vrat* for gaining the ultimate goal of life—the *Moksha.*

Buddhism emphasis on non-violence four Arya stays in the fourth truth eight fold path is there to follow, in the path of *Samyak Sankalp, Smayak Vakk, Samyat Karmaant* and *Samyak Aajivika* stress and importance is given to non- violence and effects of non-violence.

After the war of Kalinga, Emperor Ashoka was deeply hurt and chose the path of *ahimsa* and joined Buddhism. His son Mahendra and daughter Sanghmitra preached Buddhism in various countries.

During the struggle for independence we got a common national leader Mahatama Gandhi who supported the struggle and gave the mantra on non-violence and boycott. These two arms helped us in getting Swarajya. Nelson Mandela and Koffi Annan worked in the same way, which made Nelson the Gandhi of South Africa and Koffi Annan get the Nobel of Peace.

Conclusion

There are few lessons of the past which are the evidence of the benefits of peace or non-violence as well the ill-effects of choosing violence. Our Vedas especially Rig-Veda, Jainism, Buddhism, Samrat Ashoka, Mahatma Gandhi all favoured Non-violence and proved that they have selected and given the right way of peace and non-violence. Still there are few hymn of peace which we recite on the occasion of Sandhya, in few schools at the time of Hawan, which only request the God to give the peace not only for human beings but for the entire nature, we feel that we come far away with the violence and conflict but still there is time to return back to peace and harmony. Only we can do so as, 'one should not give up the hope that problems are created by men can also be solved by men'.

It is our duty to maintain the peace and non-violence as in the riots whether communal, cultural and based on religion affect our lives and its all aspects badly. Therefore, there is a serious demand of peace today. We can see this in the hymn recited at the time of yajna known as *Sahnti Mantra*:

Om dyoh Shantirantariksham Shantihi,
Prithivi Shantiraapah Shantiroshadhayah Shantihi
Vanaspatayah Shantirvishve Devah
Sahntirbrahm Shantihi,
Sarva Shantihi, Shantirev Shantihi
So maa Shantiredhi.
Om Shantihi, Shantihi, Shantihi.

There is an appeal and request of peace not only for human being but for the entire universe and nature. Mr. Willy Brandt in his report said very well that, "One should not give up the hope, that problems created by men can also be solved by men" and the only mean is peace. Thus we can say it is beneficial and in our favour to choosing the way of peace rather than violence.

REFERENCES

1. Hiriyanna, M. Bhartiya Darshan ji Rooprekha (1970)
2. Rudrastadhyayee (2004)
3. Pronk Jan, Sustainbale Development and Peace (2007)

CHAPTER

13

Educating Ourselves for Peace during the Present Scenario

*Dr. Jyoti Pandey

The twentieth century, characterised by significant process in political, scientific, technological, social and economic spheres, has witnessed the concretisation of great ideas like globalisation and liberalisation. This has brought about several changes in all the walks of life. However some changes are positive but some have been failed to bring equity, peace and harmony in the society, rather it has resulted in serious social, political and economic imbalances along with value deterioration and value crises. The saddest part of the story is that this state of disorder and confusion in the world, society is affecting the children's innocent minds, hence there is an urgent need to nurture peace in the heart of children.

The Concept

Peace means being one with life itself. Having no fear or bitterness, it is simply having a feeling of security, calmness and restfulness. We often tend to think it as an international issue, far from our daily life, but we don't realise that global peace can only be achieved if each country is settled and at peace. Education for peace is a fairly new phenomenon. Peace encompasses the learning of non-violent communication, tolerance, acceptance of diversity and love as the basic law of life. Peace education encompasses the key concepts of education and peace. Peace education refers to the process of

* Faculty of Education and Allied Sciences, MJP Rohilkhand University, Bareilly (U.P.).

promoting the knowledge, skills, attitudes and values needed to bring about behavioural change that will enable children, youth and adults to prevent conflict and violence, both overt and structural; to resolve conflicts peacefully; and to create a condition conducive to peace whether at an intrapersonal, interpersonal, intergroup, national or international level (*unicef,*) While it is possible to define education as a process of systematic institutionalised transmission of knowledge and skill as well as of basic values and norms that are accepted in a certain society, the concept of peace is less clearly defined. A number of educationists, philosophers and politicians tried to make an important distinction between positive and negative peace. The positive peace involves the development of a society in which, except for the absence of direct violence, there is no structural violence or social injustice. Accordingly, peace education can be defined as an interdisciplinary area of education which is concerned about the development of values related to maintain peace. The aim of peace education is to help students to acquire skills for non-violent conflict resolution and to reinforce these skills for active and responsible action in the society for the promotion of the values of peace.

Developmental Aspect of Peace Education

The historical conceptual understanding and present time concept of peace education has been changing throughout history, and so, has its role and importance in the educational system from the very beginning of the institutionalised socialisation of children. While discussing the evolution of peace education, however, there have been a few important points in the history that define its aims and actions. The end of World War (1914-1918) brought powerful support for the need of international cooperation and understanding and instilled a desire to include these ideas in educational systems. The League of Nations and a number of non-governmental organisations worked together on these ideas, especially through the International Institute of Intellectual Cooperation, an organisation that was the predecessor of the United Nations Educational, Scientific and Cultural Organisation (UNESCO)). World War II (1939-1945) ended with millions of victims and the frightening use of atomic weapons against Japan, at Hiroshima and Nagasaki, In 1949, UNESCO was founded as an umbrella institution of the United Nations, and it was charged with planning, developing, and implementing general changes in education according to the international politics of peace and security. The statute of this organisation reinforced the principle of the role of education in the development of peace, and framework was created for including and applying the principles of peace in the general world education systems. The peace movement began concentrating on stopping the threat of nuclear war, halting the arms race, and encouraging disarmament. Somewhat parallel to this, the issues of environmental protection and development found their place in peace education programmes. The contemporary socio-political environment (particularly the events in eastern Europe since the early 1990's the fear of terrorism, and the increasing gap between developed and undeveloped countries) has created new challenges for the understanding of peace and for the development of the underlying principles of responsibility and security.

Present Scenario

The present scenario is really very remarkable. Never before in history has the human family faced more extraordinary dangers and anxieties. We are in remarkable transition, a pivot point in history. Society feels threatened by different problems like pollution, poverty, corruption and unemployment are the threat of nuclear holocaust so there is an urgent need to develop various dimensions of peace education. Here the question arises, "Is peace of mind possible at all in our rushed life". The answer is in our inner attitude. We must come to grips with ourselves. Though the world may be full of problems and distress, we must see the positive aspect of it. We must have to first see the problematic situations, analyse it and accept it and plan how it may be solved because the solution can lead to the removal of that problem permanently. The similar approach must be in the case of peace education.

Need of Peace Education

The Industrial revolution took a wrong turn promoting consumerism and militarism. The militarism encouraged the promotion of armament industry, which indirectly influenced the war. Peace education on the lines of thought and the action, tries to break such values. The reality of war is created by cultural and educational manipulations by reinforcing group identification. The tendency to dehumanise the enemy is due to the denial of the human values resulting in killing of innocent civilians including children and woman. It is peace education which inculcates love, friendship and international understanding. We intend to teach the young minds valuable contribution towards peaceful society. The society which upholds the values of equality, solidarity, freedom, democratic inclination, tolerance, care and respect for others and willingness to change.

There are value conflicts between individuals and groups and conflict between groups so that these discrepancies within one society or from different societies, and the discrepancy of conflict as an imbalance of different interests the need to be resolved without violence. Peoples in every society are social being by nature and it is the basic tendency to human being to evaluate groups they belong to as more valuable than groups they don't belong to. Such biased approach develops the stereotypes, negative feelings towards out groups and creates discrimination and all these factors are transmitted from generation to generation and greatly influences the collective identify. Hence, all these situation/ circumstances leads to the need of peace education.

In the present scenario, there is no peace among individuals in any society. Neither our education nor our educational system has any scope for highlighting the importance of peace and conflict resolution. In every walk of life, our attention is focussed on violence, confrontations, competition, self-interest and the need to win. This history of wars is not longer than peace. This entire situation, which we are facing in the present time are expressing that the world is in turmoil. It requires the healing touch, for we have to prepare all the individuals so that the society will be prepared automatically.

Approaches and Principal Theme for Peace Education

The key problem of peace education is not the interpersonal conflict but the collective conflict between groups, races, nations, or states. Therefore, the issue of transferring the positive attitudes toward members of other groups—attitudes achieved in safe environments such as classrooms, schools, workshops, and the like—to all members of the out-group and all other out groups remains the pivotal issue of peace education. Children learn about peace and the need for peace in safe protected environments and then return to a wider society where there is still injustice, asymmetry of power, a hierarchical structure, discrimination, and xenophobia. Therefore, each programme for peace education must not only strengthen the capacity of an individual for critical thinking but also strengthen the individual's ability to resist the majority, if the majority is one that discriminates. A very successful technique was developed for improving the relations among groups, highly applicable as a general teaching and learning method. It is the cooperating learning technique in which a smaller group of students study in face-to-face interaction, cooperating to complete a common task. This technique was very successful both in lower and higher grades of elementary school, not only as a teaching method but also for creating a positive atmosphere in the classroom, reinforcing students relationships, and creating intergroup friendships. On the other hand, based on the idea that adopting knowledge and developing skills in the basis for gaining positive attitudes and behaviour, intercultural training programmes were also developed. These basically involve a group of techniques that accept the primary notion that differences between cultures are what lead to misunderstandings and conflicts between groups. Such programmes assume that information about the values, customs, and practices of the members of a different culture contributes to better understanding of others, thereby reducing prejudices, negative stereotypes, and tensions between people who belong to different cultures. Educating students about similarities in cultures and cultural pluralism is a significant factor in reducing prejudice.

Educating for peace is concerned to help students develop a rich vision of peace which should form part of his personal life. He should understand the fullness of his own religion and appreciate all other religions. Education for peace is also concerned with developing values and skills to assist the students in striving for the fullness of life that embraces all people. Education for peace is concerned with helping the students to recognise the many forms and causes of violence and to promote values and skills for living in society. Educating for peace helps students about the awareness of peace and to find ways of keeping peace by conflict resolution. Educating for peace is helping students to be aware of interdependence, compassion and sensitivity for the needs of others and to encourage them to help in building a nation and not in destroying it. Education for peace is helping students to enjoy the environment, to value the relationship of man and environment, to work individually and collectively for the betterment of the world. Educating for peace is providing students the vision towards a peaceful, loving and just world. Use children to save the world. Peace Education should be a part of the school syllabus. Peace is a value. Values involve interaction between intellectual and emotional development of a child. In the subconscious of every child is impulse. Attitude and values give direction and quality to an action. The students accept the stimulus in the form of planned activities. He responds and reacts to them, which brings pleasure or displeasure. He learns to value the feelings of peace and harmony and responds accordingly. He develops thoughts. Ideas and images consistent with the value of peace as priority in his personal life. (Nair, 2009)

Within the field of peace education, therefore, one can find a variety of issues, ranging from violence in schools to international security and cooperation, from the conflict between the developed world and the undeveloped world to peace as the ideal for the future, from the question of human rights to the teaching of sustainable development and environmental protection. A critic could say that the field is too wide and that peace education is full of people with good intentions but without a unique theoretical framework, firm methodology, and evaluation of the efficiency of applied programs. The complex systems of society, the circumstances, and the context make the peace education field very active and diverse.

Peace Education: How?

To remove various discrepancies and conflicts from society and in this context, only peace education can bring changes. It addresses the issues of conflicts and conflict resolution by teaching children how to find different possibilities for the conflict resolution. To perform this task, schools and colleges have to play their immense role in developing peace education in students. From the very beginnings of the development of systematic peace education, there has been discussion about whether it should be added as a separate programme in the schools, or if the principles of peace education should be applied through the regular school subjects. The variety of approaches and attitudes on what peace education actually is leads to the introduction of a series of titles, such as multicultural training, education for democracy and human rights, and education for development. Many in the field, however, believe that the implementation of principles of peace education into the institutionalized education system is better approach especially within the subjects encompassing the cultural heritage. Along with it, the theoretical aspects and implication of different values, which are needed in the present time can be included while formulating curriculum for peace education because peace education is what, it is not an another form of values. If we are able to inculcate values in our children and young generation, the concept of peace will be automatically attained.

Today we move into the technology era and a time of downloading information. This is an invitation to educators to finally be able to focus on the personal evolving development of children. Schools have become the main social institution for children as so many parents are forced to be out of the home for most of the day. Teachers are the social service providers and become partially responsible for the development of their value system. Teachers from small societies or daily communities in which children interact with each other, learn about their personal selves, develop interests and start to plan for their futures.

It is possible of education for peace to begin to initiate curriculum that reflects on the deeper meanings of life and fosters children to explore their individual entitled birth potential. Recognizing that information is acquired and only exists as relevant if the individual is able to integrate this into knowledge. Learning becomes predicated on self knowing. Presently character education, moral education, and self esteem development are considered aspects of aiding in the child's reaching this personal inner potential and becoming a valued citizen for peaceful coexistence. Peace can be taught as a conceptual construct. Peace can be emphasised as management too. To do this in mainstream classroom it is necessary to develop a classroom with guidelines that stresses that living ethics offers a meaningful life. Children can project themselves into this future and think backward to begin to understand the importance of living a life of virtue and in service to the others. Nothing is more fulfilling than to know one's life has purpose.

Teachers are role models who exhibit the seeking for becoming more enlightened. Right speech and harmlessness by a teacher offer possibilities for open dialogues about self. A child is offered this learning and teaching model often already knows that inner self. This process must not need be through meditation through considered a faster process but also can be achieved through the the written word, drawings, and examples of great heroes who have chosen to be self-reflective and walk a path of personal conviction. Teachers are the inspiration and model the values they espouse. Inspiring young people who most often feel disenfranchised from society and lost in the sea of troubles when presented with an educational platform that encourages self realisation and an attitude of listening to an inner voice most often can become the peacemakers of the future giving voice to an inner calling.

Teacher Training and Peace Education

In a number of countries, efforts are underway to upgrade the quality of pre-service teacher education. Training may include a focus on such skills as the use of interactive and participatory methods, organising cooperative group work, and facilitating group discussions. These types of teaching methods is essential to quality basic education, and enables teachers to convey values of cooperation, respect for the opinions of the child, and appreciation of difference. Participatory teaching and learning strategies can be used throughout the curriculum, and are an essential component of efforts to promote peace through pre-service and in-services teacher education programmers.

Other Activities

A number programmers of after-school programmes and summer programmes can promote peace education. Workshops, training programmes, and activities for out-of school youth can be created, along with initiatives that focus on the media, publications for youth, and community-based arts programmes. Taken together, such approaches demonstrate that learning takes place in many different contexts, all of which can promote messages of peace which are Camps for youth in bring together young people of different ethnic groups for recreational and community service activities. Sports and recreation programmes that focus on building teamwork, cooperation, sportsmanship, and decision-making skills can be the part of the peace education programme. Training for community leaders and workshops for parents on peace education. media training is one way to influence media producers to reduce violence and to increase peaceful content of radio and television programmes for children. Along with it, magazines for young people with a focus on peace themes, theaters showing , media and dramas, puppetry, Television and radio sports, animation is another medium that can make complex concepts about peace and conflict readily accessible to a rage of audiences, peace campaigns, contests and exhibitions can build awareness of peace and conflict issues.

Conclusion

Educating the young generation for peace education is the responsibility of every individual, society; family, school & University system hence all of them have to do the collaborative efforts for it.

REFERENCES

1. Aspeslagh R. (1996)—"Educating for a Peace Culture. "in three Decades of Peace Education around the World: An Anthology, ed. Robin J. Burns and Robert Aspeslagh. New York: Garland.
2. Fountain, S., (1997)—Education for Conflict Resolution: Training for Trainers Manual. New York, UNICEF.
3. Fountain, S., (1999)—Peace Education in UNICEF.
4. Herath, A., (1995)—'A Critical Evaluation of the Education for Conflict Resolution Project: A Synopsis of the Evaluation Report.' Colombo: UNICEF.
5. Nair, G.—Peace Education and conflict resolution in school Health Administrator Vol. XVII (1), 38-42.

6. Stevahn, L., Johnson, R., and Real, D., (1996)—'The Impact of a Cooperative or Individualistic Context on the Effectiveness of Conflict Resolution Training.' American Educational Research Journal Vol. 33 (3), 801-823.

7. Salomon, Gavriel, and Nevo, Baruch. (2002)— Peace Education: The Concept, Principles and Practices around the World. New York: Erlbaum.

8. Slavin Robert E. (1990)—Cooperative Learning: Theory Research and Practice. Needham, MA: Allyn and Bacon.

9. UNICEF ESARO, (1996)—Peace Education: Review of Concepts and Implementation; Report of the first ESARO Technical Workshop on Peace Education, 3-4 June 1996. Nairobi; UNICEF Esaro Education and Emergency Sections.

CHAPTER 14

Peace Education as a Means of Value-based Society

*Dr. M.B. Singh
**Smt. Sunita Singh

Peace is simply having a feeling of security, calm and restfulness. We often tend to think of peace as being an international issue, far from our daily life, but we do not realise that global peace can only be achieved if each country is settled and at peace. The peace and happiness of each country can only be achieved if every citizen is at peace. This follows therefore that a country can be peaceful and progress if her people live tolerantly. We all want peace of mind.

Present day society is passing through a turbulent period. We have no statesman to guide and rule us, there is an acute shortage of leaders, society to day is divided on the basis of religion, caste, poverty, so today we require value-based society : good citizen, which is possible by Peace Education.

Some lines of Gitanjali—addressed by Gurudev Rabindranath Tagore—inspires us for peace education.

"Where the mind is without fear and the head is held high;
Where knowledge is free;
Where the world has not been broken up into fragments by narrow domestic walls;
Where words come out from the depth of truth;
Where tireless striving stretches its arms towards perfection;

* Principal, Pt. Harishankar Shiksha Mahavidyalaya, Janjgir, District Janjgir, Champa (C.G.).

** Assistant Professor in Education Department, Guru Ghasidas, Central Vishwavidyalaya, Bilaspur (C.G.).

Where the clear stream of reason has not lost its way into the dreary desert sand of dead habit;

Where the mind is fed forward by there into ever-widening thought and action...Into that heaven of freedom, my Father, let my country awake."

Educating for peace is concerned to help students develop a rich vision of peace which should form part of his personal life. He should understand the fullness of his own religion and appreciate all other religions. Educating for peace is also concerned with developing values and skills to assist the students in striving for the fullness of life that embraces all people. Educating for peace is concerned with helping the students to recognise the many forms and causes of violence and to promote values and skills for living in society.

Educating for peace is helping students to the awareness of peace and to find ways of keeping peace by conflict resolution. Educating for peace is helping students to be aware of interdependence, compassion and sensitivity for the needs of others and to encourage them to help in building nation and not in destroying it. Education for peace is helping students to enjoy the environment, to value the relationship of man and environment, to work individually and collectively for the betterment of the world. Educating for peace is providing students the vision towards a peaceful, loving and just world. Use children to save the world. Peace Education should be a part of the school syllabus. Peace is a value. Values involve interaction between intellectual and emotional development of a child. In the subconscious of every child is impulse. Attitude and values give direction and quality to an action.

The students accept the stimulus in the form of planned activities. He responds and reacts to them, which brings pleasure or displeasure. He learns to value the feelings of peace and harmony and responds accordingly.

Peace Education is the process of promoting the knowledge skills, attitude and values needed to bring about behaviour change, that will enable children, youth and adult to prevent conflict and violence both overt and structural; to resolve conflict peacefully; and to create the conditions conducive to peace, whether at an intrapersonal, inter personal, inter group, national or international level.

Today Peace Education is an essential component of quality basis education. The 1990 world declaration on Education for all (The Jomtein Declaration) clearly states that basic living needs comprise not only essential tools such as literacy and numeracy, but also needs the knowledge, skills, attitudes and values required to live and work in dignity and to participate in development. It further writes that the satisfaction of those needs implies a responsibility to promote social justice, acceptance of differences and peace (Inter-Agency Commission, WCEFA, 1990). UNICEF (1990) have confirmed the vision of basic education as a process that encompasses the knowledge, skills, attitudes and values needed to live peacefully in an interdependent world.

UNICEF "Anti-war Agenda", (1996) declares—"Dispute may be inevitable; but violence is not, to prevent continued cycles of conflict education must seek to promote peace and tolerance, not full hearted and suspicion." In respect to this Hick (1985) emphasis that peace does not merely imply the absence of overt violence. It also encompasses the presence of social, economical and political justice which is essential for the Nation. So Peace Education must address the prevention and resolute of all forms of conflict and violence whether overt or strut, from the interpersonal level to the societal and global level. So it is necessary that we promote understanding, peace and tolerance through education as fundamental right of all children.

Peace Education includes human right, gender training, global education, life skills education, landmine awareness and psychosocial rehabilitation. Each of those initiative tries peace can be "main streamed" in basic education.

Human Right Education

Peace Education and Human Right Education are closely linked activates that complements and support each other. Peace is a fundamental precondition without which right cannot be realised, at the same time for ensuring the basic rights it is essential to bring peace. Human Right Education has become another Global Educational phenomena, appears to be developing along equally varied but more substantially focussed and perceptive lines.

As we know the conceptual core of Peace Education is violence, its control, reduction and elimination and like-wise conceptual core of human rights education is human dignity, its recognition, fulfillment and universalisation. So both conceptual core are interrelated and dependent on each other. Human Right Education can be attained by positive peace education. The inextricable relationship between Human rights and Peace is articulated in the very first sentence of the preamble to the Declaration ... recognition of the inherent dignity and of the equal and inalienable rights of all member of the human family is the foundation of freedom, justice and peace in the world.

Since peace resembles, human right scholars and advocates can agree that violence in all its forms is assault on human dignity. So Peace Education need's Human Right Education.

Education for Development

Peace Education also known as Education for Development, it builds global solidarity, peace, acceptance of difference, social justice, environment awareness (foundation 1995) above all also the basic concept of Education for development and we learn this fact by formal and non-formal activeness.

Gender Training

Gender conflict is found in societies around the globe and gender discrimination and conflict is a leading came of violence (UNICEF, Rosa, 1998). So a number of gender training institute have begun to address the prevention of violence against women, and provide alternative ways in which gender conflict may be handled. So gender training is an initiative that promotes Peace Education by developing positive attitude towards non-discriminate women empowerment, safety, respect to women. In India NGO called *"Sakshi"* is dedicated to working with youth to end gender violence.

Global Education

Global Education, a term coined in the 1970s, has been adopted in the UNICEF MENA region. It incorporates themes such as environment, ecology, peace, tolerance, conflict avoidance, personal health, cooperative skills, multi culturalism, comparative view on human values and human and child right. Such Global Education gives priority to active, learning based training matures peer-living, problem solving skills, such education provides another broad curricular framework for Peace Education ... actual in Lebanon there are many activity based training modules provided in global Education programme which appreciate Peace Education.

Life Skills Education

Life skills include cooperation, negotiation, communication, decision-making, problem-solving, coping with emotions, self-awareness, empathy, creative thinking, dealing with peer pressure, assertiveness (Baldo and Furniss, 1998) all of these life skills promote the development of knowledge, attitude and values of Peace Education. These negotiation skills may be used to resolve a conflict between peers. Decision making skills can be used in arriving at a mutually agreeable solution to dispute between two people.

Landmine Awareness

Landmine awareness is related to issues of personal health and safety rather than issues relating to the resolution and prevention of conflict.

Psycho-social Rehabilitation

Most of these programmes are therapeutic in focus, aiming to promote self expression, coping skills and psychological healing. So psycho-social rehabilitation programme support Peace education.

Methods which accelerate Peace Education—Peace Education must effectively attain which school environment is improved. (Baldo and Furniss 1998)—By the help of Peace Education, curricula, usually consisting of activate, and themes such as communication, cooperation and problem-solving initiate Peace Education.

Many Peace Education activities as related to relation between needs and feeling. Tolerance of differences etc. also appreciates Peace Education.

Outside of school by the help of camps, sports and recreation programmes, team work, clubs and youth groups works shops for parents on Peace Education accelerate Peace Education. Media also helpful to reduce violence, so media training programme has been carried out in Sri Lanka.

Television programme, movies based on non-violence also accelerate Peace Education. Radio spots, puppetry is also an ideal medium for discussing sensitive issue related to Peace Education. Animation is another medium that can make complex concepts about Peace Education. Concepts and exhibitions also build awareness of peace and conflict issue.

Method for Peace Education

According to the 1990 Jomtien Declaration, Active and participatory approaches are particularly valuable in assuring learning acquisition and allowing learner to reach their fullest potential.

Cooperation and interactive learning method promote the values and behaviour that are conducive to peace.Peer teaching discussion in pairs and small groups, collaborative games, brain storming, priority setting exercises, consensus building exercises, negotiations, role play and simulation is desirable to encourage Peace Education.

Environment clean-up programme, peer mediation programme are also useful for Peace Education. Cooperation group work also improves understanding of complex concepts (Johnson et.al 1981). It increases problem solving skills enabling participants to devise more solution that demonstrate greater creating and practicality.

Children books—Books such as Sadako and the Thousand paper craves (Coerr, 1977) the story of young girl who fell ill due to radiation after the bombing of Hiroshima in World War II, has inspired hundred of school groups to take action for peace.

Tradition folk stories and traditional literature helps to ensure Peace Education. Likewise art work, peacemaking are stories, artifacts also useful for Peace. Language teaching has symbolic significance, especially for minority group and refugees. It reduces linguistic difference and issue and promotes Peace Education.

Conclusion

So at last we want to say that Peace Education is based on a philosophy that teaches non-violence, love, compassion, trust, fairness, cooperation and reverence for the human family and all life on our planet.

It can be attained by including communication, listening, understanding different perspective, cooperation, and critical telling and conflict resolution skill. So basically Peace Education is an essential component of life because Peace Education leads to peaceful living.

REFERENCES

1. Baldo, M., and Furniss, E., 1998. 'Integrating Life Skills into the Primary Curriculum'. New York, UNICEF.
2. Chang, I., 1969, *Tales from Old China*. New York: Random House.
3. Coerr, E., 1977. *Sadako and the Thousand Paper Cranes*. New York : Dell.

4. Cohen, E., 1986. *Designing Groupwork.* New York, Teachers College Press.

5. Hicks, D., 1985. *Education for Peace : Issues, Dilemmas and Alternatives.* Lancaster : St. Martin's College.

6. Johnson, D., Johnson, R., and Maruyama, G. 1983. 'Interdependence and Interpersonal Attraction Among Heterogeneous and Homogeneous Individuals : A Theoretical Formulation and a Meta-analysis of the Research.' *Review of Educational Research,* 53(1), pp. 5-54.

7. Johnson, D., Maruyama, G., Johnson, R., Nelson, D., and Skon, L., 1981. 'The Effects of Cooperative, Competitive and Individualistic Goal Structures on Achievement : A Meta-analysis'. *Psychological Bulletin,* 89, (1), pp. 47-62.

8. Shah, I., 1971. *Thinkers of the East.* London : Penguin Books.

9. UNICEF Burundi, 1994. Batissons la paix : manuel pour l'educateur. Bujumbura : Government of Burundi and UNICEF Burundi.

10. UNICEF Colombia, 1997. 'Programme : Towards Implementing the Citizen's Mandate for Peace, Life and Liberty'.

CHAPTER 15

Current State of Peace Education the Global Scenario

*Dr. Prasanjeet Kumar
**Dr. Parth Sarthi Pandey
***Mrs. Neeta Pandey

Peace means freedom from mental agitation or anxiety or the absence or cessation of war or a state or condition of order or harmony. Peace ensures an education that makes an individual a citizen and creates a learning environment to live in harmony with the adjacent nature and act cooperatively. At Present, the need of the hour is education for peace for peace of mind, peace in the family, peace in society, peace between nations and peace in the universe.

"Education for peace seeks to nature ethical development, inculcating the values attitudes and skills required for living in harmony with oneself and with others, including nature. It embodies the joy of living and personality development with the qualities of love, hope and courage. It enccompasses respect for human rights justice, tolerance, cooperation, social responsibility, and respect for cultural diversity, in addition to a firm commitment to democracy and non-violent conflict resolution. Social justice is an impotent aspect of peace education. The concern for equality and social justice, while refers to practicing non-exploitation towards the have-nots, the poor and the under privileged and creating a non-violent social system, is the hallmark of education for peace(NCF 2005).

* Director Anand College of Education, Agra
** Lecturer Anand College of Education, Agra
*** Lecturer Anand College of Education, Agra

Among the countries, which have made peace education national policy Norway is perhaps the fore most followed by other Scandinavian countries. Johan Galtung is the foremost name among peace researchers and educationists. He founded the International Peace Institute in Osloin 1968. He has become one of the world's leading figures in peace research and scholarship. Another Norwegian who has done a lot to promote peace education is Birgit Brockutne. USA has several universities, which have centers for peace research but their focus is on outer peace: geopolitical aspects of peace. Maria Montessori is the mother of schools named after her, which have made peace education an integral part of the syllabus,

Indian Scene

Mahatma Gandhi was one who combined both long and short-term strategy for peace. He was a great educator for first experimented and then annunciated principles. At the same time he was a great fighter against injustice no matter what form it took. Unfortunately in the land of Gandhi neither peace education nor peace activism has yet taken deep roots. We can count on fingertips the men and women who are peace activists of some substance such as Bahuguna of Chipko fame, and Medha Parker of Sardar Sarovar fame. Peace education in the country through formal schooling system is negligible, among the schools which name made peace education the main thrust of their educational programmes are Montessori school, Lucknow, and schools operated by Aurobind Society. The universities, which are engaged in peace education and research are Gujarat Vidyapeeth, Ahmedabad, and Shantiniketan, West Bengal. Then there are a number of Gandhian scholars and institutions, which have played a leading role in peace education in the past. many of them are active today but they do empire many a youth to follow the Gandhian way.

What is Peace Education

According to Dale Hudson an elementary school teacher, Peace education can be defined as : education that actualise children's Potentialities in helping them learn how to make peace with them selves and with others, to live in harmony and unity with self, human kind with nature, this definition rests on following two principles:

- The cardinal prerequisite for world peace is the unity of Human kind; and
- World order can be founded only on the consciousness of the oneness of human kind which has at least three major aspects:
    1. All human being belong to the same species and all
    2. Humans are related, at least as close an 50th cousins,
    3. A common spiritual capacity and a common home planet earth."

Peace education is based on the belief that world peace is attainable and one of the starting points is the education of children and youth. Each human beings is a victim of the brute force perpetrated by fellow human being. Each one, therefore, dreams of a world that is devoid of brute force and full of love and compassion. When these dreams prompt us act so as to realise them then we see men like Mahatma Gandhi. He was thrown out of train because he was an Indian. He sat for a while on the platform, shivering and frightened. And he then decided to convert the brute into a human being becoming a peace educator. He invented Satyagraha, a non-violent weapon that not only makes the user victorious by also the one against whom it is used. It ends in win-win game. In the promise of World Peace, the Universal House of Justice declares, "Whether peace is to be reached only after unimaginable horrors precipitate by humanity's stubborn clinging to old patterns of behaviour or is to be embraced now by an act of consultative will, is the choice before all who inhabit the earth"

The horrors and suffering man is under going to day can be very reduced if we act resolutely " We must will peace with our whole body and soul, our feelings and instincts our flesh and its affections." Said Sarvapalli Radha Krishnan. The strategies to achieve peace may be different, they may be oriented to outer peace or to inner peace or to both. No matter what the orientation, they are not exclusive of each other, they often complement each other. Peace education is one of the strategies to moulds the minds of the youth who shape the world of tomorrow. To be effective, in must draw on the local resources, tradition, values, and ethos and integrate the universal values with them. Mahatma Gandhi has left behind very rich literature and practical wisdom on ahimsa satyagraha, Truth and Development. He was the greatest peace education of the last Millennium. Peace educations in India must draw on this. With the emergence of weapons of mass destruction like atom bomb main focus of peace education was the nature, causes and consequences of war and the peaceful ways of resolving conflicts among nations Today the scope of peace education is broader to study of violence in all forms. such forms of violence include conflict, threat to life, ethnic hatred discrimination, prejudice, racism, injustice genocide, poverty violence in the home and family, destruction of the environment and so forth at individual, group or society national or international levels. The basic aim of peace education is to save human kind from destroying itself, and the habitat in which lives. The first step in peace education is make man aware of his suicidal behaviour, and then it suggests the alternatives that can gradually slow down and stop this mad rush. Peace Education has its limitations. It alone cannot establish peace nor can it change the man and his behavior in the short-run. It offers a long-term solution to threats to peace.Its resources constitute millions of students being educated, ideally in every country to work to change from violent to peace full behaviour. This takes time and effort fortunately, more and more countries are waking up to the neat to promote peace education. For short-term solution we have to depend on the United Nations, UNESCO and other peace forums that deal with more immediate dangers.

The next important focus of peace education is to promote a feeling oneness with the humanity as a whole. This is possible only if each man is prepared to sacrifice part of his interests for others as it happens in a family. How can a baby survive if the parents do not rear it at the cost of their own comforts. In fact in sacrifice they feel a sense of fulfillment. At the same time the other members of the family should also see that each member is different in many ways. He should be given the privilege to be different. A good family is one, which is based on maximum interdependence with maximum autonomy. The global society is a family for it jointly strives to promote human survival and development. It consists of billions of people who are bounded in groups based on geography, history, religion and culture. Each group must have the right to be different but it must also have the duty to protect the rights of other groups. Each tolerates and respects the differences and each makes some sacrifices to minimise and eliminate the pains of others. The same is the Caze when see the relations amongst the individuals forming a group. This understanding is critical as we strive to build a culture of peace. However, before we can truly understand notions of citizenship and participation (our selves in relation to others), we must first ask the question, " Who am I ? Identity is what distinguishes us from others and joins us to them. Our unique identities and common human dignity provide the foundation for peace education. In article 8 of the convention on the Rights of the child, identity is protected. It states—

1. States/Parties undertake to respect the right of the child to preserve his or her identiy, including nationality name and family relations as recognised by law without unlawful interference.
2. Where a child is illegally deprived of some or all of the elements of his or her identiy, States/Parties shall provide appropriate assistance and protection, with a view to re-establishing speedily his or her identity.

What is the meaning of "identity" in this context? How is it defined and by whom? This unit examines the notion of identity in different contexts. It presents an opportunity for students to think about what identity means to them. While these themes can be integrated effectively into all of learning.

Education and Peace Building

"If we are to teach real peace in the world we shall have to begin with children" (Mahatma Gandhi) "All education is for peace

"(Maria Outsoar)." Living together in harmony must be the ultimate goal of education in the twenty first century (Learning the treasure within: Report of International Commission of education for the 21st century;

Paris, UNESCO, 1996. The young mind should be saturated with the idea that it has been born in a human world which is in harmony with the world around it" (Rabindranath Tagore). These clearly reiterate the importance of peace is education. And show that peace in a center of education and peace building could be an excellent plan/strategy for educating present day society infested with distrust, discrimination, hatred and violence. Even then, it is remarkable that almost all Indian schools are free from violence and crime. What we need is an education for peace where peace is freedom from mental agitation (self created or otherwise) or anxiety. This calls for an education for peace at a very young age to sustain peace such as education has to be miles away from "only preaching and this should have its foundations only in "experience and practice". This clearly follows the vision of Maria Montessori that the early years of one's life to be of great importance for the development of inclination towards peace and justice.

The position paper of the national focus groups on Education for Peace (NCERT-2006) suggests a plan for peace education at different stages of school. The plan is as follows:

- The primary school years could focus on laying the value foundations for personality formation and the development of the social skills necessarily to live together in harmony. Focus could then shift gradually to perspective on peace, especially to enable students to understand the value foundations of peace. The area of special emphasis here is the need to promote skills for the peaceful resolution of conflicts.

- In the upper primary years, students could be enabled to view the culture of peace from the perspective for of Indian history, philosophy and culture.
- Then after, education for Peace could focus more on citizenship education. The emphasis may shift, there after, to peace as a lifestyle movement. The main emphasis here must be on promoting an attitude of respect for diversity and difference. Students also need to be made aware of the various hindrances to unity.
- At the plus two level the foci of education for peace could be (*a*) understanding the logic, modes and expressions of violence; (*b*) skills for an objective understanding of issues; and (*c*) developing a global perspective on peace.

The basic assumption that shape the approach to education for peace. These are: (*a*) schools can be nurseries for peace; (*b*) teachers can be social healers; (*c*) education for peace can humanise education as a whole the skills and orientation of peace promote life long excellence and justice is integral to peace.

The teaches can act as peace builders being themselves examples of social healing engaging their responsibilities from enlarged perspective of peace.

'The task of building a peaceful and warless world is a twin programme. The first is the task to redifine our educational needs, workout a practical programme, inject the perspective into all our activities and aspects of life, and the second is to focus on non-violently resisting the evil that war is and its preparation in direct or direct. It is for learning the art of *satyagraha* with its two essential assets constructive work and resistance to evil. It is a plan to build a new civilisation *civilisation of non-violence* (Devi Prasad, Peace Education or Education for Peace, Gandhi Peace Foundation, 1984).

Peace and Conflict Resolution

Generally conflicts/Conflicting interests arise in situations like economic deprivation discrimination (racial, sexual, religious, economic etc.) greed, caste system and military.

As reported in the book "Fundamentals of Operation Research (by Ackoff and Sasieni, Wiley Eastern, 1978) Repoport (1961) identified three modes of conflict:

- *Fights,* in which the objective is to eliminate the opponent.
- *Games,* in which the objective is to outwit the opponent.
- *Debates* in which the objective is to convince the opponent.

Competitive theory (which provides solution to conflict component of competition) has been preoccupied with fights and games but not with debates. It is perhaps characteristic of our culture that we are more interested in increasing our ability to wage conflict than we are in increasing our ability to cooperate.

Debates are part of peace process and they are the needs of the hour.

It is not true that all conflicts are resolved by politics of war, scientific methods or management techniques. But many of them could be solved by peace process, involving dialogue, cooperation, living together, concern for others, working towards a common objective. Conflict resolutions skills emanate from dialogue cooperation, living together concern for others, avoiding discrimination mixed with suitable management skills like optimisation analysis etc. for example (David A, Hamburg, Education for Conflict resolution, 1994) by teaching young people to adopt the point of view of other ethnic or religious groups to lack of understanding that leads to hatred and violence among adults can be avoided. The teaching of the history of religious and costums can thus serve as a useful benchmark for future behaviour.

School children could be made to learn to act cooperatively and work towards a common objective through participation in sport, cultural activities (enacting a skit etc.), environmental protection, helping the underprivileged etc.

There are conflicts within oneself, These could by resolved through 'yoga', self learning and learning of self, self-realisation.

Education for Peace—A Curriculum Framework

Over the past 50 years global events and human experience in general have given the quest for peace a new urgency. Peace is no longer considered as the absence of war but it is conceptualised to include harmony at all levels of human endeavor. The UN and its agencies have adopted clear statements concerning human rights responsibilities which recognise peace as an essential human construct. The International Educational System Pilot Project (now known as International Schools Association Global Issues Network-ISAGIN) community, see education as the principal vehicle which will develop and inculcate school age children with the habit of peace. Education for peace when is conceptual framework from which school may devise programme comprising the transmission of universal and enduring attitudes and the development of skills which will enable our student to become active global citizens. Value and Attitude included in Curriculum Framework of Peace Education

1. Human Rights and Democracy
2. Cooperation and Solidarity
3. Preservation
4. Self and Others
5. Internationalism
6. Protection of the Environment
7. Spirituality

Skills to be Developed for Peace Education

It is expected that students will develop the skills (as well as attitude) necessary to be proactive and effective peace makers these can be summarised under the heading of—

1. **Thinking Skills** : Critical Thinking Information Handling Creative Thinking Reflection, Dialectical Thinking.
2. **Communication Skills**: Presentation, Active listening, Negotiation, Non-verbal Communication.
3. **Personal Skills:** Co-operation, Adaptability Responsibility, Respect.

Peace Development Across the Curriculum

The formal curriculum : Cross curricular planning and inter-disciplinary planning will see the issues brought forth in an education for peace programme.

The Informal Curriculum : Extra-curricular or co-curricular life of school, Conflict Resolution Programme, Advisory programmes and pastoral care programmes can also be provided.

The Hidden Curriculum : Inherent school-wide goals of improved communication, inclusion, acceptance, encouraged interaction between and divers groups, and the creation of a general climate of tolerance and respect can be enhanced and identified as precepts of peace education.

The Integrated Curriculum : The common school subjects which develop values and skills related to peace include in integrated curriculum which as follows.

English, Science, History and Geography, Language and Expensive Art, Mathematics, Designing and Information Technology, Physical Education, Religion etc.

Conclusion

The given curriculum framework describes those elements which we feel are fundamental to teaching and learning in the area education for peace. Education shall be directed to the full development of the human personality and nature, and strengthening respect for human right and fundamental freedom. It shall promote understanding, tolerance and friendship among all nations racial and religious groups and shall further and activities of the United Nations in the maintenance of peace.

We, teachers, have a great responsibility on our shoulders. We have to play a very special role in the society and work more than what we are paid for. On us lies the responsibility of shaping the future of India and this responsibility we carry out not only by lecturing but also demonstrating what we teach. Gandhi was the greatest teachers because he never asked his followers to do anything that he himself did not follow.

NCERT'S (Initiative)

1. A National focus group on education for peace was setup by NCERT in 2004 views of the focus group form an important element of NCF -2005 the position paper of the focus group on education for peace is available as a publication of NCERT. The NCF-2005 visualises peace as a way of resolving conflicts and as a precondition for national development.
2. Peace education as and area of study is recommended for inclusion in the curriculum for teacher education, already peace education is part of course study in the teacher education programmes of Regional Institutes of Education (NCERT)
3. The department of educational psychology and foundation of education, NCERT has been organising a 6-week Training course on peace education for teachers since May 2005. This programme is conducted annually and programme provides training to teachers to enable them to develop knowledge and understanding of various issues and concerns having bearing on educational for peace such as self development,

identify and prejudice, conflict resolution, democracy justice and human rights sustainable economic development, gender equality etc. the course motivates the teachers to act as peace builders equipping them with peace skills.

The themes of the training course are:

1. concept and concerns
2. empowering self for peace
3. conflict resolution
4. parenting for peace
5. pedagogy for peace
6. assessment of peace proun

Each of the themes is supported by 'Activities/ Assignments' course material is provided to each of the participants. In addition field visits, film shows related to peace are organised.

REFERENCES

1. AVP Education Committee. *Alternatives to Violence Project Manual (Second Level Course)* New York: Alternatives to Violence Project.
2. Balasooriya, A.S. (1994 B) *Management of Conflict in Schools.* Maharagama, Sri Lanka : National Institute of Education.
3. Balasooriya, A.S. (1995 B) *Education for Peace Learning Activities,* Maharagama, Sri Lanka : National Institute of Education.
4. Brown, G. (1971). *Human Teaching for Human Learning.* New York, Viking.
5. Dewy, J. (1916). *Democracy and Education,*London : The Free Press.
6. Galtung, J and D Ikeda (1995). *Choose Peace. London: Pluto Press.*
7. Government of India (1949). *Report of the University Education* Commission (1948-1949). New Delhi.
8. Harris, I.M. (1988). Education for Peace. London: MCFARLAND and Company.
9. National council of Educational Research and Trainging (NCERT) (2000) *National Curriculam for School Education. New Delhi : NCERT.*

CHAPTER 16

Peace Education through Educational Institutions : A Need to Integrate for Fresh Learning Experiences

*Dr. Shireesh Pal Singh
**Anjana Kaul

Introduction

Peace education is an essential component of quality basic education that aims to build the knowledge, skills, attitudes and values that enable young people to prevent violence, resolve conflict peacefully, and promote social conditions conducive to peace and justice. Peace should mean not only absence of war, but also violence in all forms, such as conflicts, threat to life, social degradation, discrimination, oppression, exploitation, poverty, injustice, and so on. The concept of peace ranks among the most among the most controversial in our time. Peace undoubtedly carries a positive commutation; almost nobody admits to opposing peace; world peace is widely seen as one of the noblest goals of humanity. Peace is many things; the meaning of the work peace changes with context peace may referred specifically to an agreement concluded to and a war, or to a lack of external warfare. Peace is more than the absence of certain societal maladies. From this perspective, peace requires not only the absence of violence but also the presence of justice.

Peace is a state of mind. This is beautifully expressed in the Preamble to the UNESCO Constitution:" Since wars begin in the minds of men, it is in the minds of men that the defence of peace must be constructed". Violence emerges out of

* Lecturer, S.G.R.R. (P.G.) College, Dehradun.
** Lecturer, Himgiri Nabh Vishwavidyalaya, Dehradun

intolerance for differences in beliefs, views, and cultures. Peace can be installed through education in cooperation and mutual support, deep-seated concern for others over concern for self. Presence of happiness, health, content and good economy, social justice, and freedom of expression, creative support for personal growth at all levels, are some of the elements of peace. Peace education is the soul of education that can create the shield for human survival on the planet earth. Global education gives priority to active, learner-based teaching methods, peer-learning, problem solving, community participation, and conflict resolution skills. It is values-based and future-oriented (Selby, 1997).

To live peacefully, an individual has to have many skills, like those related to affirmation, positive thinking, empathetic listening and communication, assertive behaviour, decision-making and critical thinking, etc. Schools need to help children to develop such skills so that they become responsible individuals in the society. Peace education is a remedial measure to protect children from falling into the ways of violence in society. It aims at the total development of the child and tries to inculcate higher human and social values in the mind of the child. Therefore, in order to implement the peace education, it is necessary to develop a mechanism and a process through which peace education can be institutionalised.

Peace Education through Educational Institutions

How to cultivate that 'peace-behaviour' among children, youth and adults is the broad concern and challenge of peace education. The success of peace education initiative in educational institutions will also depend significantly upon the teacher preparedness in terms of attitudes, skills, and knowledge yet the teachers and students concentrate primarily on the school subjects limiting the learning to the purpose of examination alone.

In this kind of non-supportive academic ambience, peace education may easily get lost unless teachers are adequately prepared. Further, since peace education is seen to be integrated in different subjects, it will be necessary to involve all the teachers in the peace education programme in the school. Before peace education is actually introduced in the schools, it will be necessary to mount a well-designed programme for teachers in this area. There should not be any need for separate teacher for peace education and that the peace education needs to be introduced at Pre-service teacher education level and inservice teacher education level.

Nevertheless, the concern for developing the 'peace-behaviour' in educational institutions, among school children; and equipping the teachers to facilitate peace education, can only be accomplished if it is nested within the context of the family, peer group, the community and the larger society.

Aims of Peace Education

The aims of peace education are commonly expressed as knowledge, skill and attitudinal aims. The approaches of Peace education are based on the assumptions that peace education is primarily either a knowledge-based subject that can be directly taught in the school curriculum or a set of skills and attitudes that can be explicitly taught or some combination of the two.

Knowledge Aim

The aim is to be aware of own needs and self awareness, understanding nature of conflict and peace, ability to identify causes of conflict and non-violent means of resolution, enhancing knowledge of community and increasing interaction with them, to find mechanisms for building peace and resolving conflict, understanding of rights and responsibilities, to understand interdependence between individuals and societies, to make students aware of cultural heritage.

Skill

Communication: active listening, self-expression, paraphrasing, reframing assertiveness, ability to cooperate, affirmation, critical thinking, ability to think critically about prejudice, ability to deal with stereotypes, dealing with emotions, Problem-solving, ability to generate alternative solutions, constructive conflict resolution, conflict prevention, participation in society on behalf of peace, ability to live with change.

Attitude

Self respect, positive self image, strong self-concept, tolerance, acceptance of others, respect for differences, respect for rights and responsibilities of children and parents, bias awareness, gender equity, respect for females, solidarity, social responsibility, sense of justice and equality joy in living.

Various approaches should be followed in the schools to achieve the aims of peace education.

A school needs to carry out activities in the areas of improving the school environment, curriculum development, pre-service teacher education, and in-service teacher education. Peace education is most effective when the skills of peace and conflict resolution are learned actively and are modelled by the school environment in which they are taught (Baldo and Furniss, 1998).

Peace education is a process of recognising values and clarifying concepts in order to develop skills and added tools necessary to understand and appreciate the inter-relationship among man. A free environment where there is a democratic set-up, a proper teaching and learning takes place.

Pre-service Teacher level

Pre-service teacher education in peace education is an important feature; therefore, efforts need to be made to upgrade the quality of pre service teacher education. Training may include a focus on such skills as the use of interactive and participatory teaching methods, organising cooperative group work, and facilitating group discussions. The use of these types of teaching methods is essential to quality basic education, and enables teachers to convey values of cooperation, respect for the opinions of the child, and appreciation of differences.

According to the 1990 Jomtien Declaration, "Active and participatory approaches are particularly valuable in assuring learning acquisition and allowing learner to reach their fullest potential." Participatory teaching and learning strategies can be used throughout the curriculum, and are an essential component of efforts to promote peace through education.

Teachers must encourage the use of interactive, learner-centered methods as a priority in the promotion of quality basic education. These methods should be used deliberately to support learning aims that relate to the knowledge, skills, and attitudes of peace education. Typical methods used in peace education programmes may include cooperative group work, peer teaching, discussion in pairs and small groups, collaborative games, brainstorming, priority-setting exercises, decision-making and consensus-building exercises, negotiations, role plays and simulations should be used.

In-service Teacher Level

In-service teacher education may focus on participatory teaching and learning methods, as well as content areas such as children's rights. This helps to ensure administrative support for new teachers who are attempting to introduce peace education. This can be significantly increased with a large number of activities like debating, colloquy, fishbowl, buzzing, brainstorming, puzzles, self-expression, creative drama and storytelling and composing poetry, drawing, guided fantasy, ice-breakers, energisers, etc.

Life skills education enables children and young people to translate knowledge, attitudes and values into action. It promotes the development of a wide range of skills that help children and young people cope effectively with the challenges of everyday life, enabling them to become socially and psychologically competent. Life skills can include cooperation, negotiation, communication, decision-making, problem-solving, coping with emotions, self-awareness, empathy, critical and creative thinking, dealing with peer pressure, awareness of risk, assertiveness, and preparation for the world of work. (Baldo and Furniss 1998).

Peace education is a remedial measure to protect children from falling into the ways of violence in society. It tries to inculcate higher human kind and social values in the mind of the child. Peace education is to develop a mechanism and a process through which peace education can be institutionalised. It is necessary to onvolve all the teachers and school administrators in the peace education programme in the school.

Suggestions for Teachers

Teachers integrate the positive contacts with the students and show positive regard for all the students. They will help the students in overcoming ignorance, misinformation and stereotypes and will gain information about the various cultures. The teachers will enable the students to adjust with the different cultural norms and learning styles train students to practice non-violence before and during conflicts. A school-home environment needs to be created where various agendas are created and supported for peace development. Such strategies should be used which support the peaceful interaction with the self and all people. Students should be taught the ecological care of the physical environment including sustainable use of its resources. The students should be encouraged for the discussions of controversy and unresolved problems locally and globally. There should be cultivation of the intellectual and communication skills for comprehending and analysing conflicts. If at all there are conflicts; whether between children or between children and adults; in a non-violent manner.

Partcipatory learning methods should be used in peace education. According to a 1990 Jomtein Declaration, "Active and Participatory approaches are particularly valuable in assuring learning acquisition and allowing learner to reach their fullest potential". Teachers must encourage the use of interactive learner centered methods as a priority in the promotion of quality basic education. The methods used in the peace education programme include cooperative group work, peer teaching, discussion in pair and in small groups, collaborative games, brain storming, priority settling exercises, decision making and role plays should be used.

Suggestions for Teacher Educators

Peace education should be included in the course.

- Opportunities should be provided to the pupil teachers to identify and examine their views.
- The pupil teachers need to develop their civil courage to make their own opinion and public voices.
- Encouragement should be given to develop creative and critical thinking, to obtain information about the international relations and also of capitalism and imperialism.
- Pupil teachers must be aware of the democratic citizenship as to how to get involved in social, economic, environmental and political responsibilities in a democracy.
- Students should be encouraged to prepare the social and environmental action projects.
- Teacher training approaches should be revised.
- A forum should be provided for the explicit discussion of values of peace and social justice.
- Opportunities should be provided for the continuous reflection and professional development of all educators in relation to issues of peace justice and rights.

Suggestions for School Administrators

School administrators must also practice the peace making skills and should encourage in the students. Among all the school participants' cooperation and mutual support and problem solving attitude must be appreciated.

Students' achievement, their aspiration for peace should be encouraged. Provide oppurtunities for peace education whereby the family environment takes its own place. In all the systems and interactions of school, emphasis should be laid upon non-violence. School may act as a seat where there can be peaceful ways to collaborate between parents, students and all school staff.

Some more Activities Outside the School

Peace education should not be limited to activities that take place in schools. Workshops, training programmes, and activities for out-of school youth should be created, along with initiatives that focus on the media, publications for youth, and community-based arts programmes. Taken together, such approaches demonstrate that learning takes place in many different contexts, all of which can promote messages of peace.

Camps for youth should be organised in recreational activities, vocational training, and study of the history and geography of the country. Children of different cultural groups can be arranged in the region for summer camps that should focus on building mutual understanding. Students may be informed about the consequences of war and social injustice.

Sports and recreation programmes that focus on building teamwork, cooperation, sportsmanship, and decision-making skills are part of the peace education programme. Youth groups and clubs and training for community leaders may be carried out. Workshops for parents on peace education should be held. Librarians should be recruited to receive training on education for development, and how to use library activities such as storytelling and discussions to promote tolerance and understanding.

Media training is one way to influence media producers to reduce violence and to increase peaceful content of radio and television programmes for children. Media awareness training for parents and children may be one way to help to lessen the impact of violent media programming. Other methods like puppetry are an ideal medium for discussing sensitive issues. Puppets draw viewers into the drama without causing them to feel threatened by the actions in the drama and can nurture child development and promote values such as fairness, non-violence, and working together to deal with problems. Animation is another medium that can make complex concepts about peace and conflict readily accessible to a range of audiences. The National Film Board of Canada has successfully used animated cartoon films on topics such as dealing with differences and peaceful problem-solving.

Peace campaigns can take many forms, and can be a powerful way to create a broad base of support for peaceful social change. Public opinion surveys on the peace process have taken place in Somalia. In Colombia, the 'Vote for Peace' project invited citizens to express a mandate for an end to violence. Children were also invited to express their opinions on peace and conflict issues. Activities included song, dance and poetry competitions on peace themes, and community discussion forums on peace issues and this initiative is made to continue on a yearly basis. Contests and exhibitions can build awareness of peace and conflict issues. A nation-wide play-writing competition on themes of peace-building and tolerance can inculcate strings of peace education. Liberia used exhibitions of children's drawings about the effects of armed conflict to encourage public discussion about the need for peace.

Technology can be utilised to impart peace education. New technologies provide children and youth around the world with the opportunity to discuss issues of common concern. One of the best Web sites to take advantage of the power of the Internet is UNICEF's own Web site for children,

Voices of Youth (www.unicef.org/voy/). The site provides information like photos, captions, drawings, case studies on children's rights issues, including children and war, the girl child, child labour, and children and cities and through the presence of Voices of Youth at international conferences, young people are able to express their opinions directly to delegates and world leaders. Both the content of the site, and the process of linking children around the world, promote the aims of peace education.

Contemporary children's literature can be used to raise discussion about issues of peace and conflict, even with very young children. Encouraging children to come up with their own solutions to conflicts or problems presented in storybooks helps develop skills of problem solving and anticipating consequences of actions. Children can be encouraged to produce books of their own. These may contain real life stories of how they have dealt with conflict, fictional stories, and children's own poems, songs and drawings on themes of peace.

Any of the subject areas traditionally taught in the school curriculum can be vehicle for peace education, but the teaching of different languages can play a special role. Language has enormous real and symbolic significance, especially for minority groups and refugees. Linguistic differences, and issues around what language should be used in schools in multi-lingual societies, are often sources of conflict. Language teachers can actively challenge stereotypes about people who are members of different linguistic groups.

Peace education need not be taught as an independent subject. It can be integrated in the regular school subject. Also, various extracurricular activities can form part of a well-designed experiential curriculum. Integrated with the content of various subjects taught in school e.g. : Social studies, Science, Home science, Mathematics, Language, Art, Music, Computers, Vocational subjects, Psychology. The content of various subjects taught in Teacher Training Programmes; Sociology and philosophy of education, Educational psychology, History of education, School plant, Teaching methodology, Psychology practical, Science/home science practical, Work experience, Working with community, Teaching practice, Tutorials, Educational technology and in extracurricular activities during assembly, lean periods, or Saturdays. Special lectures in assembly or otherwise—may be once a month, Games, Film shows, Discourses and debates, Presentation of related project report/seminar/exhibition Community campaigns, Club activities break the monotony of the classrooms.

Evaluation Methods

Evaluations of peace education programmes are most commonly carried out in non-experimental contexts. There are a number of different types of evaluation methods that are widely used (Fountain, 1998):

Observations tend to focus on changes in the behaviour of children and young people, and are usually carried out both before and after a programme is implemented. Observation is a mental activity consisting of perception and reflective thinking. Observation is usually systematic, selective and systematic. conclusions are drawn from a comparison of the frequency of observed behaviour. For example: ability to cooperate, methods used to resolve a conflict, incidence of name-calling or other biased behaviour, and use of mediation skills.

Surveys/questionnaires/rating scales are used by students to assess their own learning, by teachers to assess student learning, by teachers to assess their own learning and by parents to assess their children's behaviour. They are a self reporting instruments. A few cautions need to be kept in mind like the questions should be limited to the variables of primary interests. The sensitivity or delicacy of the content of particular questions should be avoided. Surveys, questionnaires and rating scales have been used to assess knowledge of conflict resolution concepts, ways of handling a hypothetical conflict, self-image and school climate.

Interview technique, a face to face interaction is to be used primarily after a peace education programme has been implemented. Interviews may be carried out with students, teachers or parents to assess the impact of the programme. This technique is flexible and a rapport is established. Many different kinds of knowledge, skills and attitudes can be assessed through interviews.

Focus groups are similar to interviews, but are carried out with groups of five to ten people, rather than on an individual basis (Debus, 1988). They are run by a moderator who develops a discussion guideline appropriate to the group, and ensures that each person has the chance to speak. The interaction between the participants can stimulate rich discussion and insights. They have been used to examine the types of concepts and values that children and adults have about peace, ideas about how to deal with violence, and suggestions for how best to promote peace in schools and communities (Fateem, 1993).

School records are reviewed and provide quantitative information on variables that may relate to the effects of a peace education programme such as student grades, attendance, drop-out rates, number of student conflicts, or numbers of school suspensions for fighting. These reviews of school records facilitate the comparison.

Experimental procedures are sometimes used to evaluate peace education programmes. They are primarily used in academic settings where focused educational research is being carried out.

Conclusion

Peace education may not turn out to be a part of the formal course work. There would be no examination and certification. Its foundation is conviction, understanding and appreciating its need in the individual, community, national and global life. In this paper, we have presented the concept of peace and peace education, area of peace education, a brief outline of the curriculum and methods of transaction of peace education. Peace education is most effective when the skills of peace and conflict resolution are learned actively and are modelled by the school environment in which they are taught (Baldo and Furniss, 1998). In a number of countries, emphasis is placed on improving the school environment so that it becomes a microcosm of the more peaceful and just society that is the objective of peace education. This creates a consistency between the messages of the curriculum and the school setting, between the overt and the 'hidden' curriculum. Interventions on the level of the school environment tend to address how children's rights are either upheld or denied in school, discipline methods, how the classroom and school day is organised, and how decisions are made. So peace education should make aware of own needs and awareness of self. It will enable us to understand nature of conflict and peace. Enhancing knowledge of community, mechanisms for building peace and resolving conflict peace education will put emphasis on Mediation process. It will enable to understand rights and responsibilities and understanding interdependence between individuals and societies. It will spread awareness of cultural heritage as well.

REFERENCES

1. Baldo, M., and Furniss, E., 1998. 'Integrating Life Skills into the Primary Curriculum'. New York, UNICEF.
2. Balvinder Kaur; Peace Education, Deep & Deep Publication. New Delhi 2006 (Chapter 10, Peace Education in India), p. 232-233.
3. Blakeway, M., 1997. 'Compilation of Research Materials'. Washington D.C., National Institute for Dispute Resolution.
4. Debus, Mary, 1988. The Handbook for Excellence in Focus Group Research. Washington D.C., Academy for Educational Development/Healthcom.
5. Fateem, Elham, 1993. 'Concepts of Peace and Violence: Focus Group Discussions on a Sample of Children, Parents, Teachers and front-line Workers with Children'. Cairo: The National Center for Children's Culture (Ministry of Culture) and UNICEF.

6. Fountain, S., 1998. 'Peace Education/Conflict Resolution Evaluation Methods.' New York, UNICEF (Unpublished Paper, Available from the Author).

7. Hart, R., 1997. Children's Participation: the Theory and Practice of Involving Young Citizens in Community Development and Environmental Care. London: UNICEF/Earthscan.

8. Inter-Agency Commission, World Conference on Education for All (Jomtien Declaration), 1990. 'World Declaration on Education for All'.

9. Institute for Conflict Analysis and Resolution, 1994. 'Survey of Conflict Resolution Programmes and Attitudes in Virginia's Schools'. Fairfax, Virginia: George Mason University.

10. National Institute of Education, Sri Lanka, undated (a). Education for Conflict Resolution: Teacher's Guide for Primary Grades. Colombo: UNICEF Sri Lanka.

11. National Institute of Education and UNICEF Colombo, undated (c). 'Peace Education Activities from Sri Lanka.'

12. Selby, D., 1997. 'Globalising the Curriculum: Infusion, Integration and Innovations for life Skills and Science Learning. 'Toronto, International Institute for Global Education, University of Toronto.

13. Stevahn, L., Johnson, D., Johnson, R., and Real, D., 1996. 'The impact of a Cooperative or Individualistic Context on the Effectiveness of Conflict Resolution Training.' American Educational Research Journal, Vol. 33 (3), 801-823.

14. Tolan, P., and Guerra, N., 1994. 'What Works in Reducing Adolescent Violence: An Empirical Review of the Field.' Boulder, CO, USA: Center for the Study and Prevention of Violence: Institute for Behavioural Sciences. UNICEF, 1994.

15. World Health Organisation, 1998. 'Violence Prevention: an Important Element of a Health-Promoting School' (WHO Information Series on School Health, Document. Geneva, WHO.

CHAPTER 17

Environmental Ethic and the Culture of Peace : An Integrated Approach to Peace Education

*Dr. Madhumala Sengupta, Reader

Introduction

The culture of peace enshrines all forms of humane values, attitudes and behaviours which are manifested in respect for life, for human dignity. It also implies rejection of violence of all forms and upholding of human rights. Finally it is commitment to principle of freedom, justice, solidarity and tolerance. Culture of peace is about learning to live together, one of the four pillars of learning (Delors 1993) Peace is not absence of war (Spinoza). It has two aspects namely negative and positive. From negative consideration peace is absence of war whereas more positive approach to peace is manifested in following standard of justice, living in balance with nature and meaningful participation in society. Peace, however, does not exclude the concept of conflict as conflict is part and parcel of social interaction. The culture of peace requires that conflict be resolved in non-violent manner without fueling hatred and suspicion. The social conflict can only be minimised when the social fabric is based on justice and power and wealth are used for the benefit of all groups.

Now the question comes where does environmental ethic may be fitted in this scheme of culture of peace. The term ethic is a branch of the broader discipline of philosophy. It is concerned with the moral behaviour of man. Environmental ethic implies man's relationship with nature or environment.

* Department of Education, Calcutta University.

However, the term environment has a broader connotation in the context of man's relation with it. The environment that encompasses man is of three type's namely social environment, psychological environment and of course natural or physical environment. So it is obvious that moral and ethical behaviour of man generally determine the nature of culture of peace. Environmental ethic and culture of peace are inter-related, both seek to eschew violence. Whereas environmental ethic is about extolling right of non-human species and safeguarding nature, the culture of peace emphasises more on human rights. As a matter of fact the two issues when integrated together can ensure the wholistic development of human civilisation.

Environmental Ethic : The Influence of the Western Philosophy

The western philosophy focuses on the tenets of anthropocentrism which eulogises man as the centre of creation. According to Seed (2000), anthropocentrism means human chauvinism or human centrism which implies men are the crown of creation, source of all values and the measures of all things. Its concept was derived from the time of Greek philosopher Aristotle who said that nature has made all things specially for the sake of men. Later on the Bible proclaimed that God created man in his own image. The Book of Genesis (verse 1.26) mentions that God said unto men, be fruitful, multiply, replenish the earth and subdue it, have dominion over fish of sea, over fowl of the air, over every living thing that moveth upon the earth. The Christian philosophy gave birth to the idea of human exceptionalism referring human being's special status in nature. The European philosopher Aquinas (Summa Centra Gentiles) maintained that non-human animals are 'ordered to man's use'. Man can kill and use them in any way he wishes without injustice. In recent times gene scientists also supported this view that gene mutation has been instrumental in developing the intellectual faculty of man. A very interesting research finding was reported by Howard Hughes Medical Institute (2004). Bruce T. Lahn of this Institute found that selection for greater intelligence and hence larger and more complex brains is far more intense during human evolution than during evolution of other mammals. Hence the superiority of human race is proved beyond doubt. What is the reason behind this astounding finding? Lahn says answer to this intensified selection should not come from biological science only but also from social sciences. It was further stated that complex social structure and cultural behaviour unique in human ancestors fuelled rapid evolution of brain. This research should highlight the fact that the attainment of objectives of peace education is so important for the evolution of man which only can provide a society conducive for continuous human growth.

However, anthropocentrism as the basis of environmental ethic was challenged by some eminent thinkers of twentieth century. Aldo Leopold (1949) in his A Sand County Almanac discussed about land ethic and pointed out that the roots of environmental crisis were philosophical. White (1967) in his book 'The Historical Roots of Our Ecological Crisis' criticised the notion of anthropocentrism as the main cause of ecological crisis. Garrat Hardin in his writing 'Tragedy of Commons' (1968) reiterated the same view and cautioned that unless man changes his attitude towards living and non-living non-human being world the ecological crisis is inevitable. Leopold's views on land ethic ushered the concept of ecocentrism.The important principle of Land Ethic is, a thing is right when it tends to preserve the integrity, stability and beauty of the biotic community and it is wrong when it tends otherwise. Man is now considered to be citizen of biotic community no longer a conqueror of nature.

Another view regarding environmentalism is deep ecology, which is considered to be diametrically opposed to anthropocentrism. Naess (1988) is the main proponent of this concept. The basic tenets of deep ecology are as follows:

- *Relational image*—the organisms have no independent existence rather they are all part of nature and human beings are no exception.

- *Biospherical egalitarianism*—all organisms have equal moral worth and they deserve certain amount of respect.
- *Principle of diversity and symbiosis*—Instead of domination, human relation with diverse nature should be symbiotic with emphasis on cooperation.
- *Local autonomy and control*—it means decentralised mode of decision-making and power sharing.

The ideas of Naess should ideally be part of 'ecosophy', combining ecology and philosophy and requires to be part of attitude towards natural world. One of the very important aspects of deep ecology is the recognition of intrinsic or inherent value ascribed to human and non-human life on earth irrespective of their usefulness. It also cautions that the present human interference with non-human world is excessive and the situation is rapidly worsening. (Devall and Sessions 1985).

The Indian View of Environmental Ethic

The Indian philosophy and religion offers a different proposition as far as man nature relationship is concerned. According to the Upanishads after creation God entered into every object created, which ascribes moral worth in every object. The ancient Indian philosophy taught people to live in harmony with nature based on mutual respect and symbiosis. The Vedas eulogised the inter relationship between living species and the important of biodiversity thereby negating the western concept of speciesism. The scriptures advised about the right ways of treating the plants and trees, flora and fauna. The basic principle of the relation between human beings and nature must be based on mutual respect and reciprocity. Thus the nature was held in great reverence and the sanctity of rivers, trees and mountains was upheld. This proves the fact ancient Indian philosophy ascribed inherent and intrinsic values to animate and inanimate objects. The Atharva Veda mentioned sixty verses explaining the dependence of humans on Mother Nature. The Vedic hymns speak of the concept of unique all being Brahma. Everything is part of this amazing whole implying unity of creation and mysterious interconnectedness and co-dependence of everything on everything else. (Billimoria 1995)

The fundamental concepts of Indian philosophy are *R'ta* and *Dharma* which have ecological implication.

- *R'ta* is the sense of fundamental order or balance in the universe. This balance should be observed and sustained. At present the environmental science has realised the importance of maintaining balance of nature.
- The concept of *Dharma* can be attributed to peace education. It is the need to act for the sake of good in the world. The observation of *Dharma* is the highest ethical standard based on the concept of *Sarva Bhuta Hita* i.e. welfare of all being. It is prescribed that people should strive for common good instead of taking private advantages. Within this principle the ideas of peace education and environmental education are fused together as *Dharma* signifies protection of environment, support of poor, needy and oppressed and the children yet to be born. The seed of the modern day concept of sustainable development is germane in the idea of *dharma*.
- The concept of *Karma* has also social and environmental connotation. One's action of present life follows again and again in future lives. So *Karma* requires that man should comply with injunctions of the scriptures so that the *R'ta* is maintained.

Like Vedic philosophy, the Buddhism and Jainism too steeped in those views which have strong environmental connotation. These two philosophies also emphasis on non-injury and advocate the virtues of non-greed, non-hatred and non-delusion in all human pursuits. Contentment and frugality are two virtues eulogised by the Buddhism. We have become more and more greedy and as a result we have adopted violent and aggressive attitudes towards nature. The

Buddhism advocates a simple moderate life style avoiding both self deprivation and self indulgence. One of the sayings of His Holiness XIV Dalai Lama may be mentioned here-Whether they belong to more evolved species like humans or to simpler ones such as animals; all beings primarily seek peace, comfort, and security. Life is as dear to the mute animal as it is to any human being; even the simplest insect strives for protection from dangers that threaten its life. Just as each one of us wants to live and does not wish to die, so it is with all other creatures in the universe, though their power to effect this is a different matter." He also observes that "It is our collective and individual responsibility to protect and nurture the global family, to support its weaker members and to preserve and tend to the environment in which we all live."

Thus it is evident that the Indian and oriental philosophy emphasised on the ecocentric view of environmentalism, which is based on the belief that peace lies in nourishing ecological and economic democracy and nurturing diversity (Shiva)

The science based culture of human civilisation has given birth to technocentrism indicating that technology can solve all human related problems. Biocentrism on the other hand is concerned with the organisms. But ecocentrism maintains that ecosphere is more significant more inclusive more integrated more mysterious in which human beings are inseparable part with no special privilege. The earth is the sustainer as all organisms evolve from her.

Specific Teachings in the Context of Conservation of Nature

The Vedas and other scriptures specifically laid down the dictum of environment related behaviour. As nature is the manifestation of divinity nature worship is an integral part of Upanishadic practices. Environmental awareness is created through praise of the deities. Besides man is considered to be the trustee of earth and the resources and he must use these resources wisely. Abuse of nature is equated with unjust and irreligious behaviour. As a result conservative practices have been interlinked to ways of life. Some of the teachings of the scriptures are worth mentioning.

- Do not cut trees because they remove pollution (*Rig Veda* 6:48:17).
- Do not disturb the sky, do not pollute the atmosphere (*Yajur Veda* 5:43).
- Destruction of forest is taken as destruction state, reforestation is an act of rebuilding the state. Protection of animals is sacred duty (*Charak Samhita*).
- No creature is superior to any other. Human beings should not be above nature. Let no one species encroach over the rights and privileges of other species (*Isha Upanishad*).
- Rig Veda directs man to form friendship with animals and inanimate objects.
- Resources are given to mankind for their living. Knowledge of using them is necessary (First stanza of Isha Upanishad.
- The Bhagavat Gita prescribes a devout and frugal life style and suggests the avoidance wasteful consumption, which is today's most important sustainable behaviour. Wasteful behaviour is an act of sacrilege. It is considered to be the theft from future generation. This actually is the modern notion of sustainable development.

Ecological Values and Sustainable Development

The term sustainable development was used by the Brundtland Commission (1987) to connote a development strategy that meets the needs of the present without compromising the ability of future generations to meet their own needs. (WCED 1987. p. 43). The phrase is often ambiguous and later on when The Earth Summit was held in Rio de Janeiro (1992) more similar terms like 'sustainable consumption pattern', 'life style changes', 'optimisation of resource use', 'minimisation of waste' were coined without defining them properly. (Pearce 2007)

Sustainable development should be understood from three aspects namely environment (controlling pollution and managing waste), society (including issues like unemployment, human rights, gender equity, peace), Economy (poverty alleviation, inclusive economic development). These are the three pillars of human development. In order to follow the path of sustainable development both peace education and the protection of environment are to be taken care of. Actually most of the problems involve all these three aspects, for example HIV, AIDS, climate change, migration, terrorism etc. The process of development should strive for economic growth, get rid of human misery but at the same time prevent overuse of resources. The following equation depicts the relationship among the variables and the process of development.

Development = PAE where P = population, A = affluence, E = Entitlement/Equity. The process of development will usher affluence with concomitant entitlement where material acquisition and social status will lead to more consumption threatening the human culture and environment. (Annual Review of Environment Resource 2006). Thus development is double edged sword. The Earth Charter (2004) rightly stresses that human development is primarily about being more not having more.

So where should the line be drawn between satisfaction of basic needs and having more. The trade off between economic prosperity and environmental education is quite apparent and it is difficult and complicated to strike a balance between the two. The most important issue in the context of both peace education and environmental education is perhaps reducing consumption and practicing restrain. Because researches have revealed that awareness about environmental pollution or the plight of people do not always activate people to behave in pro environmental ways. Stern (2000) had offered a Causal Model of Environment Related Behaviour.

- First, the environment related behaviour lies at the end of the causal chain consisting of personal and contextual factors
- At the intermediate point lies the factor of predisposition towards pro environment behaviour.
- Several interacting factors like environmental concern, attitude, information, beliefs, abilities and external conditions within the chain determine pro environment behaviour.
- All these factors either facilitate or impede environment related behaviour depending on their nature.
- It has also been observed that the weaker the external conditions, the stronger is the attitude-behaviour correspond.

Stern further stated that interdisciplinary research should be undertaken to understand the role of different factors like population growth, migration, economic expansion, culture, individual values, small group norms, political institution and international market on people's environment related behaviour. These issues could be referred as socio-economic determinants of environmental behaviour. Hines et.al (1987) on the other hand stressed more on personal factors like intention to act, locus of control, attitude, knowledge and personal responsibility for initiating environmental behaviour.

Of course the social factors and personal factors should not be considered in isolation as the two are integrated. Nevertheless personal norm and value system are powerful forces behind pro environmental behaviour.

The objectives of sustainable development were highlighted in the UN declaration of the decade of education for sustainable development (2005-2015). These include

- Social progress that recognises the needs of everyone
- Effective protection of environment
- Prudent use of natural resources

- Maintenance of high and stable levels of economic growth and development.

As a matter of fact SD occurs when we acknowledge the relationship between human needs and natural environment. Linking social, economic and environmental concerns are crucial aspects of SD. It depends on fostering creativity and innovation and being sensitive to ethic, value system and the value of cultural identity. (Ospina 2000)

Values for a sustainable earth and culture of peace: Values are abstract ideas about things or objects cherished. They may be good or bad, better or worse, and are considered to be standard of behavior judgment. Values are worth studying as attitudes are formed on the basis of values which again are reflected in behaviour. Thus instilling right values in the minds of children are the objectives of peace education and environmental education as well.

The Earth and Peace Education Association International (2003) mentioned the following values for a sustainable earth and culture of peace. These are:

- Ecological sustainability
- Non violence
- Social justice
- Intergenerational Equity
- Participatory democracy.

It is to be noted that the values of environmental education and peace education are interconnected and always discussed together. These values in positive term denote respect for others regardless of race, gender, age, nationality, class, appearance, political and religious belief, physical or mental ability. It implies commitment to equality and non-violence, appreciation and respect for diversity, empathy and of course concern for environment and understanding of our place in ecological system.

The United Nations (2004) declared the fundamental values which underlie the Millennium Declaration. These are freedom and dignity. By freedom it is meant freedom from hunger, fear and violence.

According to Page (2008) the rationale of peace education and of course environmental education can be located in virtue ethics, consequentialist ethic, conservative policy ethic, aesthetic ethic and ethics of care. Hence for the achievement of objectives of peace education relevant values are to be implicated.

The Role of Educational Institutions in Peace Education and Environmental Education

Education for Sustainable Development has now replaced the term environmental education which was though to be narrow in scope. This is now a key challenge to the system of education.The fundamental purpose of ESD is to integrate all the values of sustainable development in to all aspects of school learning. This should encourage changes in behaviour enabling a more viable and fairer society for everyone. Five kinds of learning may be mentioned here namely learning to know, to do, to be, to live together, to transform oneself and society. To realise these objectives it is imperative that education should be based on two principles namely

- Philosophy
- Skill

The system of education must teach and preach the philosophy of non-violence, love, compassion, reverence for all life. On the other hand both environmental education and peace education should ensure the development of skills like listening, reflecting. problem solving, conflict resolution, cooperation etc. More research works are needed to understand the philosophical basis of peace of education which somewhat lacks philosophical underpinning. (Page 2008). In the Western countries it is mostly based on Kantian philosophy. But in India we have long spiritual tradition which could be suitably integrated in the curricula of different stages of education. There is an urgent need to acquaint our students with our ancient treatises which contain such invaluable messages regarding environment and social justice. The most important virtue and state of mind has been eulogised in the founder of Bah'I faith, Baha'u'llah 's qutation which goes like this—it is not for him to pride himself who loveth his own country, but rather for him who loveth the whole world. Earth is one country and mankind is its citizen.

Education for sustainable development is not so much about becoming aware and knowledgeable about environmental/social issues but primarily a matter of culture, the culture of peace and sustainability. Environment has to be presented as source of value awareness and clarification and where such issues as intra-generational justice are explored. (Gough et.al 2001). This calls for drastic change in school practices. The curriculum transaction has to be supplemented with whole school activities to imbibe social and environmental ethics in the minds of the students. Learning for sustainability has to involve pupils and take learning beyond the classroom to show that they can change things for better.

In the UK, the Department of Education and Science (DfES) in national framework of curriculum envisaged the concept of sustainable school. The basic principles of sustainable school are care for oneself and each other (across culture, distances and time) and environment (both far and near). The whole school approach was suggested on the basis of eight doorways *viz.*

- *Food and drink*—model supplies of healthy locally produced and sustainable food and drinks for the students and staff.
- *Energy and water*—signifies energy management by reducing consumption of electricity and water and reducing green house gas emission. The curriculum has to be tailored for this purpose.
- *Travel and traffic*—schools are to be models of sustainable transport.

- *Purchasing and waste*—it means waste minimisation by recycling and sustainable procurement.
- *Building and ground*—sustainable building design to be adopted with the school ground being the mode of learning about natural world.
- *Inclusion and participation*—The school will enable all students to participate fully in school activities
- *Local well being*—the school gives good corporate citizenship training within their local areas.
- Global dimension of school activities.

Thus sustainable development can be embedded into whole school management and help in providing practical guidance. These types of school practices will help to develop pro social behaviour among the students by social learning theory which are essential for peace education and environmental education (Eisenberg and Mussen 1989). In this way peace education, population education, environmental education, life skill education and education for conflict resolution can all be integrated to improve the quality of human life and natural environment as well.

REFERENCES

1. Annual Review of Environmental Resources 2006, Vol. 31.
2. Baha'u'llah. Gleanings from the Writing of Baha'u'llah. (CXVI, p. 250) Baha'I Publishing Trust 1976.
3. Billimoria.P (1995) Indian Religious Tradition. In Spirit of the Environment. Ed. Palmer, J.A. and Cooper. D.E. London. Routlege.
4. Delors J.(1993) Learning: The Treasure Within. Report to UNESCO of International Conference on Education for 21st Century.
5. Dalai Lama www.http://brainyquote.com
6. Devall. W. Session, G., (1985) Deep Ecology: Living as if Nature Really Mattered, Salt Lake City: Peregrine Smith
7. Earth Charter 2000 http://www.earthcharter.org.
8. Earth and Peace Education Association International 2003. http://www.globalepe.org

9. Earth Summit (1992) United Nations Conference on Environment And Development.Rio De Jeneiro.
10. Eisenberg, N., Mussen. P.H. (1989) Roots of Pro-social Behaviour in Children. Cambridge. Cambridge University Press.
11. Gough, S., Walker, K., and Scott. W., (2001) Life-long Learning: Towards a Theory of Practices for Formal and Non-formal Environmental Education and Training. Canadian Journal of Environmental Education 6, 178-196.
12. Hardin. G. (1968) The Tragedy of Commons. Science 162, 1243-1248.
13. Hines. J.M., Hungerford, H.R. and Tomera, A.N. (1986/1987) Analysis and Synthesis of Research on Responsible Environmental Behaviour: A Meta Analysis. The Journal of Environmental Education 18, 1-8.
14. Hinduism and Ecology at http://holeys7.tripod.com.
http://www.teachersnet.gov.uk/sustainableschools. Retrieved on 1.10.09
15. Lahn. B.T, (2004)www.hhmi.org/news/pdf retrieved on 5.10.09
16. Leopold. A. (1949) A Sand Country Almanac: with Essays on Conservation from Round River. New York OUP.
17. Naess, A. (1988) The Basics of Deep Ecology : Resurgence. 126 4-7
18. Ospina. G.L., (2000) Education for Sustainable Development: A Local and International Challenge. Prospects XXX 31-40.
19. Page. J.S. (2008) Peace Education: Exploring Ethical And Philosophical Foundation. Charlotte. Information Age Publishing, p. 189.
20. Pearce, D., 2007b Sustainable Development. In Clark, D.A. (Ed) The Elgar Companion to Development Studies. Edward Elgar, Cheltenham, UK.
21. Seed., J (2000) www.stumbleupon.co/url/www.../anthropocentrism.html.
22. Stern. P.C. (2000) Psychology and Science of Human—Environment Interaction. American Psychologist 55, 523-530.
23. Spinoza.B. Theological Political Treatise 1670.
24. World Commission on Environment and Development (WCED Brundtland Report) 1987. Our Common Future. OUP. Oxford.
25. UN 2004. Millennium Development Goal Indicators data base *http://millenniumindicators.un.org/unsd* retrieved on 15th October 2009.
26. UNESCO 2005. International Implementation Plan: United Nations Decade of Education for Sustainable Development, 2005-2014, Paris.
27. White., L. Jr. The Historical Roots of our Ecological Crisis. Science 155: 1203-1207.

CHAPTER 18

Environmental Education Curriculum Towards Enriching Peace Education Issues and Policies

*Dr. A.G. Matani

Introduction

Education is a methodical effort towards learning basic facts about humanity. Value education is important to help everyone in improving the value system that he/she holds and put them to use. It's our duty to uphold the various types of values in life such as cultural values, universal values, personal values and social values.

Thus, value education is always essential to shape a student's life and to give him an opportunity of performing himself on the global stage. The need for value education among the parents, children, teachers etc, is constantly increasing due to increasing violent activities, behavioural disorder and lack of unity in society.

The Main Causes of Moral Degeneration

- Abuse of alcohol and drugs.
- Abuse of women and children, and other vulnerable members of society.
- Breakdown of parental control of children in families
- Crime and corruption.
- Lack of respect for other people and property.
- Lack of respect for the sanctity of human life.

* Lecturer in Mechanical Engineering Department in Government College of Engineering Amravati-(MS).

- Lack of respect for authority, seen through the brazen breaking of the law.
- Total disregard for rules and regulations.

To solve all these type problems it is necessary to know the main causes of the above problems. Hence by using science and technology in the proper way it is easier to solve all the problems of the non-moral and value things.

Present Scenario

- Absence of specific secondary school course on environment protection that is capable of capturing the interest of young people and orienting them toward choosing a career in this field.
- Lack of coordination among the diversified activities related to environment education within the education field.
- At the university level, very little information is available concerning prerequisites and the procedures that could lead to a degree or training programme in the environment education area.
- Training needs in the area of environment education are poorly defined.
- Very less information is available concerning needed training programmes to be initiated specific technical as well as practical courses, advanced education, summer schools, etc.
- Poor distribution of research and training centers is another issue.

ENVIRONMENT PROTECTION INITIATIVES THE WORLD SCENARIO

American Association of State Colleges and Universities (AASCU) Encouraging Roles of Institutions

AASCU devoted its July/August 2006 Public Purpose magazine to cover the issues related to sustainability at public higher education institutions. The issue highlighted role of various institutions implementing sustainability policies on its campuses, in its classrooms and bridging them to the business world.

Bedford College in Southern England Providing Training

Bedford College in Southern England is a centre for excellence in green energy, providing training for small businesses in installing and maintaining solar panels, wind turbines and bio-mass technology.

Canadian Industry Programme For Energy Conservation (CIPEC) Developing Comprehensive Projects

The Canadian Industry Programme for Energy Conservation (CIPEC) with representation of 294 companies, and 24 sector task forces is active in developing comprehensive projects to improve conservation in their municipal operations. Non-governmental organisations are implementing community-wide programmes for improving the conservation in existing and new buildings, and at developing integrated, fuel efficient transportation schemes.

Florida Gulf Coast University Reducing Operating Expenses

National Center for Academic Transformation implements effective uses for information technology in order to improve student learning and reduce the cost of higher education. By redesign their coursework schools reduced costs by an average of 37 per cent, saving of $3.1 million in operating expenses each year.

Park Lane College In Leeds Offering Courses On Climate Change

Park Lane College in Leeds offers a *"reduce your carbon footprint"* course managed by a team of conservation and environmental tutors through practical energy saving techniques, and the science behind climate change.

Texas State Energy Conservation Office (SECO) Encouraging Energy-efficiency Projects

Oil Overcharge Funds used for energy efficiency and renewable energy projects are consistent with settlement guidelines and approved by the U.S. Department of Energy (DOE). This energy efficiency retrofit program has saved Texas taxpayers more than $199 million through energy-efficiency projects for state agencies, institutions of higher education, school districts, county hospitals and local governments. Energy education programmes of SECO promote energy conservation and efficiency through education. Over 2,500 teachers have attended these workshops and utilised the materials in their classrooms reaching over 375,000 students.

The Wisconsin Environmental Education Board and the University of Wisconsin-Stevens Point Utilises Community Resources

K–12 Energy Education Programme (KEEP) encourages school-to-career skills and the use of a rich set of community resources including professionals, businesses, environmental organisations, and institutions of higher education. Wisconsin students are now competent enough to cope with difficult decisions about energy and its relationship to environmental, socio-political, and economic issues.

University of Nîmes in Southern France Organising Programmes for Eco-citizens

University of Nîmes in Southern France, in March 2007, organised a programme to promote the behaviour of "eco-citizens". Concentrating on the promotion of waste management and economising on energy use a university wide campaign for providing practical demonstrations of environmental awareness linked to social psychology theory.

York University Encouraging Green Buildings

The Computer Sciences Building of York University is an ideal example of a 'green' building built at no cost premium. Raising the standards for new buildings and major renovations is the most economical means of conserving energy in new buildings and avoids the lost opportunity cost associated with retrofitting improvements after the building is constructed.

Possible Areas of Development

Possible areas and actions for the development of general knowledge programmes should include:

- Organising seminars, workshops or summer schools for decision makers and experts related to environment education and allied fields.
- Reporting on the prospects of renewable energies in scientific and economic journals.
- Organising technical visits to the most outstanding solar energy installations.
- Producing audio-visual materials that illustrate existing solar installations, as well as future prospects for these technologies.
- Publishing information, in the form of study articles and comprehensive, well documented reports, on solar energy and its prospects.
- Distribute such information and/or documentation to consumer associations.
- Produce and broadcast programmes and documentary films for television.
- Encourage teaching of environment education and renewable energy technologies in primary and secondary schools.

Conclusion

A diversified training programme is needed to meet increasing demands for qualified personnel in the developing countries. This training should consider the latest developments in science and technology. It must strengthen competence and technical polyvalence, in such a way as to produce a technical staff of high quality in judgment and decision-making. Both of these qualities are necessary for project planning and management, and for being able to identify the most appropriate application and utilisation for local conditions. For greening of the curriculum and carbon emissions reduction, teachers and researchers require encouragement of climate change research and its impact on the world. Conservation principles need to be embedded in government policy, programmes and regulations. Education not only gives us a platform to succeed, but also the knowledge of social conduct, strength, character and self respect. Value based education is a tool which not only provides us a profession which we can pursue but also a purpose in life. Creating Environmental awareness and knowing about the problems related with Environment, training about the various aspects of environment will bring in some peace not only in our society and nation but throughout the world.

REFERENCES

1. Basak, N.: Environmental Engineering, McGraw-Hill Education (India), New Delhi, 2005 Edition.
2. Dutta Subijoy: Environmental Treatment Technologies for Hazardous and Medical Wastes: Remedial Scope and Efficacy: McGraw Hill Education, New Delhi, 2006 Edition.
3. Dr. S. Amal Raj: Introduction To Environmental Science and Technology: Laxmi Publications, New Delhi, 2006 Edition.
4. Garg K: Solar Energy: Fundamentals And Applications: McGraw Hill Education, New Delhi, 2005 Edition.
5. Jery A Nathanson: Basic Environmental Technology, 4th Edition: Prentice Hall of India Pvt. Ltd. New Delhi, 2004.
6. J A Salvato: Environmental Engineering and Sanitation, 4th Edition, John Wiley and Sons Inc, New York, 1992.
7. Kothari D P: Energy Engineering: Theory and Practice: S Chand and Company Ltd., New Delhi, 2005 Edition.

8. M L Davis, D A Cornwell: Introduction to Environmental Engineering, McGraw Hill Inc., New York, 2nd Edition, 1991.
9. N. DeNevers: Air Pollution Control Engineering, McGraw Hill Inc, New York, 1995.
10. P. Meenakshi: Elements of Environmental Science and Engineering: Prentice Hall of India Pvt. Ltd. New Delhi, 2005 Edition.
11. R K Rajput: Basic Electrical Engineering: Laxmi Publications, New Delhi, 2006 Edition.
12. Thomas R. Koballa Jr.: *Designing A Likert-Type Scale to Assess Attitude Toward Energy Conservation: A Nine Step Process, Journal* of Research In Science Teaching 1963-1995 Vol. 21, Issue 7, pp. 709-723.
13. http://www.oregon.gov/
14. http://www.aascu.org/
15. http://www.uwsp.edu/
16. http://nces.ed.gov
17. http://valueeducation.nic.in
18. http://theviewspaper.net

CHAPTER 19

Establishing Peace on the Pillars of Jain Philosophy

*Aditi Jain

We all are very well aware of the fact that today's era is of science and technology where men have attained a remarkable position in various fields like medical science, space science, electronic gazettes and so on. He is running blindly behind materialism. That materialism, which only offers rest in the grave, to the individual. This materialism is responsible for much of our greed and covetousness and through them for our hateful deeds. In this blind race man has sacrificed his assets of values, morals and even his mental peace. Today people are living together to serve their utility purposes. They have even forgotten the basic ideal of 'Live and Let Live'. Their viewpoint is getting so rigid that they can't see beyond self-glorification and their own benefits. This narrow vision is responsible for the development of negative feelings like hatred, anger, fear ultimately giving rise to the violent attitude in them.

The roots of violence are so deep that to destroy them completely is really a difficult task, if not impossible. Today we are in dire need of mental peace, integrated personality and a co-operative social environment. In order to achieve all the above mentioned components it is necessary to aware the up-coming generation about peace. Thus it may be said that modern man is in the dire need of such philosophy of life that is built upon the foundations of and is conducive to world

* Asst. Professor, College of Professional Education, Meerut (U.P.).

peace. The philosophy which promotes the doctrine of '*Vasudheva Kutumbakam*'.

Indian philosophy with its eternal ideal is therefore the obvious need of the hour, the urgently required panacea to the ills of modern society the key to a balanced and purposeful development. Jainism one of the heterodox systems of Indian philosophy has an important place in Indian Philosophy. Non-Violence in ethics, Non-Absolutism (*Anekanta*) in thought, Qualified assertions (*Syadvada*) in speech and Non-possessiveness (*Aparigraha*) in society are the four pillars on which the whole Jaina philosophy is resting.

These four jewels of Jainism if rightly implemented in all walks of life and Nation can be proved harbingers of Peace-individual as well as social. The present article endeavours to explicate the Jain philosophy and explore their indispensability towards attaining the central ideal of 'World Peace'.

Ahimsa

A look into some of major world events seems pertinent before one can visualise the modern-day threat to peace. Terrorism today is breaking the globe into pieces: Terrorist attack in America, London and several places in India such as Mumbai, Jaipur and Delhi even last year have reiterate that we cannot take peace for granted. The definition of Peace says that it is the complete absence of war, freedom from quarrels, harmonious relations among citizens of the same and different Nations and so on. Thus the first and foremost element required for the establishment of peace is Non-violence (*Ahimsa*).

Ahimsa is the sheet anchor of Jainism. It is the first vow out of the five vows that are to be followed by all the Jains, whether saints or the laymen. It is considered as *Param Dharma* or highest religion by the great Tirthankars. According to Jain philosophy, Ahimsa is a rule of conduct that bars the killing or injuring of living beings. It is closely connected with the notion that all kinds of violence entail negative karmic consequences. In simple words Ahimsa means not hurting, not injuring anyone by words, thought or deed moreover, one must not even entertain the desire to hurt anyone. For the doctrine is equally applicable to all the three stages of evil doing, namely intention, preparation and actual commission of wrong deeds. (*Krita, Karita, Anumodna*). This ahimsa is not limited to humanity on contrary; its application must be extended to all living beings, may it be animal or plants. It can be better understand as if one has no love for the life in the animal, one will not have it for man either. There is no such thing as a sudden rush for affection for one form of life at once.

The true meaning of Ahimsa is generosity, love for all, not incurring pain to others in all the efforts so to emulate the life of Mahavira. It actually allows everyone to enjoy life, unhampered, unmolested by anyone else, for life is dear to all.

Some say, 'War is necessary to end war,' or Himsa is necessary to establish Ahimsa, but if the aim is to bring peace on earth and goodwill amongst mankind, it must always emphasise the ultimate good and declare evil as evil even if it may appear to be unavoidable at a particular time or in a particular set of circumstances. Good cannot come out of evil. The Ahimsite way of life is the sure panacea for all moral, social, economic and political ills of human civilization. In short Jaina philosophy considers all souls to be equal and thus insists one to follow the line of Ahimsa (Universal Love), which is the surest path to human happiness.

It will purify, ennoble and sweeten life in all departments and establish brotherly relations among men and communities and Nations, as surely as it will purge the heart of all evil inclinations and trait for Ahimsa is love and nothing but love.

The seed of all forms of sorrows and violence lies in the partial, adamant, selfish, restricted and misguided thoughts and actions, the understanding of the doctrines of Anekanta and Syadvada can lead the humanity towards the ideal of world peace.

Both of these doctrines develops an understanding of other's view point and holds that no one is perfectly right or wrong. It is due to the limitation of the senses, that men are unable to know anything in its complete form. Thus their claim of perfection is not correct but simultaneously it cannot be said that they are completely wrong as they are supporting one face out of many realities. So we must respect and welcome everyone's view.

Anekanta

Jain metaphysics believes in independent existence of innumerable material atoms and innumerable individual souls. Further, it says that each atom as also each soul has infinite characteristics of its own. Thus according to Jainism reality is complex. It can be looked at and understood from various view-points or angles. Different people think about different aspects of the same reality and therefore their partial findings are contradictory to one another. The term Dravya or substance is used for the things that possess varying characteristics *viz.* attributes and modes. The attributes are the permanent and inseparable qualities of a substance where as the modes are the changing and separable qualities of a substance. Now, in keeping with this doctrine of the *'many ness of reality'* or *Anekanta,* Jain philosophers define reality as unity and difference or difference and unity.

If we look at a substance from the point of view of substance it is factual, enduring and one whereas if we view it from the point of view of modes, it is illusory, impermanent and many. Thus we can know and describe the reality only from a certain angle or viewpoint. Though every angle can claim that it gives a true picture of reality, yet it gives only a partial and relative picture or reality. We must accept that the views of our opponents may also be true from some other angle. The Jain theory of Anekanta emphasises that all the approaches to understand reality gives a partial but true picture of reality, and due to their truth value from a certain angle one should have regard for other's ideologies and faiths.

This can be better understood with the help of an example: There were six blind people, each of them was standing near an elephant they all touched it but from different angles. After this they all describe elephant in their own different ways. Now the Question that arises is this, was anyone out of six, wrong. The answer to this is that no they all were right in one form or the other. This is what the theory of Anekanta says.

It forbids to be dogmatic and one-sided in our approach. It preaches us a broader outlook and greater open-mindedness, which is more essential to solve the conflicts taking place due to the differences in ideologies and faiths. Anekanta brings the spirit of intellectual and social tolerance.

Syadvada

The logical and epistemological side of the Jain concept of reality is *Syadvada* or the doctrine of relativity of knowledge, this doctrine explains that, since reality is infinitely complex and thus indeterminable by ordinary mortal means, human judgments are necessarily relative, conditional as also restricted. Thus word 'syat' denoting the relative ness and doubtlessness must precede all our judgments. The infinitely complex reality is real as also unreal, enduring as also illusory, universal as also particular, one as also many. Syadvada is also known as SaptaBhangi, it explains that there can be seven ways of saying the same thing

1. ***Syad asti*** (A thing is) : A thing exists in the context of its self or from the perception of a preceptor. You saw a tree through your own eyes at a particular place in your backyard and so you know from your experience that the tree of such and such type, shape, colour and size exists at such and such place and time.
2. ***Syad nasti*** (A thing is not) : A thing does not exist in the context of other forms, other substance, another place or another time. The same tree that you saw does not exist as another type, shape, colour and size tree

or at a different place or time. Simply, a thing does not exit other than what it is. (Hope this is not rather too much for you to understand.)

3. ***Syad asti nasti*** (A thing is and is not) : A thing may or may not exist at the same time. It may exist from one point of view and many not exist from another point of view. If you see an object with your eyes it exists, but if you close your eyes and want to perceive it with your hearing, it may not exist. Also if you are preoccupied with some other matter, you may not see it even if it is there. Similarly, if you are familiar with the concept of a tree, you would say the tree that you saw is a tree. But if you are not at all familiar with the concept of a tree, you would perhaps argue that what you saw was something else.

4. ***Syad avyaktaya*** (A thing is simply inexpressible) : A thing is inexpressible when we try to express in term other than what it is. For example I cannot speak about a tree other than what it is or I cannot speak about a tree other than in its own terms.

5. ***Syad asti avyaktaya*** (A thing is simply inexpressible) : A thing exists but I cannot express it. A tree exists but certain aspects of it are indescribable. We know that some of the things that exist in the universe are inexpressible, either because we do not know about them or because we do not have the capacity to express them or because of our own limitations. This is a predicament many of us experience. Sometime we know for sure something exists, but we do not have adequate words to express it or the means to express it. This is especially true about abstract concepts that are difficult to express.

6. ***Syad nasti avyaktaya*** (A thing is not but and inexpressible) : The thing does not exist, and also cannot be expressed. If the tree does not exist from my vantage point, how can I express it? We can speak about things

that exist. But how can we speak about things that do not exist at all? We can speak about existence. But what can we say about non-existence? We can express what is known and perceivable. But how can we speak about what is unknown and what is not? So we cannot express that which does not exist.

7. ***Syad asti nasti avyaktaya*** (A thing Is inexpressible) : A thing is there and also not there at the time and it is inexpressible. The tree exists in the present. It might not have existed in the past. The tree exists when I am standing near it and does not exist when I am far away from it. When the same thing exists and also does not exist, how can it be expressed correctly without losing the truth of its simultaneous existence and non-existence?

Thus, we may say that according to Jainism we can make many statements or draw many conclusions about the same truth. A thing may exist in the context of its own form, substance, place and time. Similarly, a thing may not exist in the context of another form, another substance, another place and another time.

Aparigraha

No doubts that wealth plays an important role in our lives and is considered as one of the four purusarthas *i.e.* the pursuits of life, yet it cannot be maintained as the sole, end of life. Accumulation of wealth and lust for worldly enjoyment are jointly responsible for the emergence of present day materialistic attitude. A tremendous advancement of the means of worldly enjoyment and amenities of life has made us crazy for them.

21st century is witnessing a continuous rise in the level as well as frequency of the crimes such as robbery, murder, kidnapping, physical extortions and so on. One of the main reasons for such acts may be the never ending, never satisfying desires. Even the terrorist attacks that are taking place all over the world are the result of the lust of expanding their empire and of self-glorification. All beings have certain needs in order imply remain, beyond that, we may have the additional needs in order to remain healthy. We probably have still more needs in order to be radiant. Men is not satisfied with what he has, on contrary he is ready to sacrifice his own life as well as his relations to lead a luxurious life. Human desires are endless. The more we possess the more we want. When we think of the word 'possessive', we think of someone grasping desperately, someone short-sighted and who refuses to share what they have. Aparigraha (Non-possessiveness) directs us to avoid this desperate state. *Aparigraha* means non-hoarding, not desiring more than we need to limit possession to what is necessary or important. Thus *Aparigraha* is one of the direct means of establishing peace.

Like Ahimsa, Aparigraha is also one of the five basic vows, which have to be followed by all those who believe in Jainism. The limit to which these vows are to be followed has been defined clearly in the Holy books. The laymen is required to follow these vows in the form of *anuvrat* (*vrat ka ek desh palan*) which encourages one to consider the possessions with attention and awareness, where as the ascetics follow these vows as *Mahavrats*, which means sacrifice to the utmost level. They even give up their clothes in order to follow this vow, as Jain philosophy have firm believe that even a single non-required addition to one's possession is a step ahead towards Hell.

To conclude it may be said that the world is like a joint family in which people with different interests, aptitude, attitude, visions, liking and disliking reside. What we need in order to lead a happy and prosperous life is to develop an understanding for their specific behaviors. To help us understand this we have several doctrines, but the value of such jewels is still to be recognized. Some of these jewels are Ahimsa, Anekanta, Syadvada and Aparigraha. They are the guardians of Peace, prosperity and wisdom. Ahimsa is the highest religion for all, it has to be regarded equally by everyone, as its efficacy is not limited to any particular sect or Dharma it is equally good for every living being as it teaches us, not to hurt anyone intentionally or unintentionally by words, thoughts and deeds. Now a days even the most materialistic and developed country like America is stepping towards Ahimsa for animals and consequently have banned meat-eating, which will surely lead to a healthy, peaceful and prosperous life.

Anekanta and *Syadvada* enables us to understand respect and accommodate others feelings. They teach us to understand the limitations of our thoughts. One's ego, tolerance and violent attitude evaporate when he or she is able to appreciate and understand the differences in our world. The feeling of universal brotherhood is encouraged when we realise that an individual or a community is the result of its own specific environment and, therefore, the differences are natural. It is, in fact unwise to expect similar views and reactions from people under dissimilar conditions. In addition to these doctrines the doctrine of *Aparigraha* which emphasises that one should remain happy in what he has and should limit his desires as there is no end to these desires needs to be followed by all. In short, it can be said that if these doctrines becomes an integral part of human personality the ever growing problem of dissatisfaction, non-understanding and violence can be reduced to minimum. Thus Jain philosophy provides us with such pillars on which the building of most desired peace can be built.

REFERENCES

1. Dr. Singh,Jaya. Towards World Peace on the Wheels of '*Anekantavada* and *Syadvada*'. *Sramana*. Research Journal Vol. LVIII No. II-III Parswanatha Vidyapitha: Varanasi.
2. Jain, Sudeep. 1996. *Prakrit-Vidya*. Shri Kund-Kund Bharti: New Delhi.
3. Dr. Jain, J.P. 1982. Bhagwan Mahavira Life, Times and Teachings. Ratna Printing: Varanasi.

4. Upadhayay, Muni Guptisagar.1999 *Ahimsa Aaina:* Luknow.

5. Upadhayay, Muni Nirnaysagar.2007. *Antaryatra.* Nirgranth Granthmala Samiti: New Delhi.

6. see http://www.worldpeaceforum.ca/.

7. see http://www.jainsamaj.org.

8. seehttp://dictionary.reference.com/browse/peace.

9. Dr. Srivastava. K. 2007. *Jain Darshnik Chintan Ka Aitihasik Vikas-Krama*. Journal *Sramana*. Parswanath Vidyapitha: Varanasi.

CHAPTER 20

Attainment of World Peace through Practice of Buddhism

*Prof. Susanta Kumar Pathy

Introduction

Buddhism teaches that whether we have global peace or global war is up to us at every moment. The situation is not hopeless and out of our hands. If we don't do anything, who will? Peace or war is our decision. The fundamental goal of Buddhism is peace, not only peace in this world but peace in all worlds. The Buddha taught that the first step on the path to peace is understanding the causality of peace. When we understand what causes peace, we know where to direct our efforts. No matter how vigorously we stir a boiling pot of soup on a fire, the soup will not cool. When we remove the pot from the fire, it will cool on its own, and our stirring will hasten the process. Stirring causes the soup to cool, but only if we first remove the soup from the fire. In other words, we can take many actions in our quest for peace that may be helpful. But if we do not first address the fundamental issues, all other actions will come to naught.

The Buddha taught that peaceful minds lead to peaceful speech and peaceful actions. If the minds of living beings are

* Department of Education, Lingaya's University, Faridabad, Haryana.

at peace, the world will be at peace. Who has a mind at peace, you say? The overwhelming majority of us live in the midst of mental maelstroms that subside only for brief and treasured moments. We could probably count on the fingers of both hands the number of those rare, holy persons whose minds are truly, permanently at peace. If we wait for all beings in the world to become sages, what chance is there of a peaceful world for us? Even if our minds are not completely peaceful, is there any possibility of reducing the levels of violence in the world and of successfully abating the winds of war?

To answer these questions, let us look first at the Buddha's vision of the world, including the causality of its operations. Then, in that context, we can trace the causes of war. When the causes are identified, the Buddha's suggestions for dealing with them and eliminating them can be discussed. Finally, having developed a Buddhist theoretical framework for understanding the nature of the problem and its solution, we can try to apply the basic principles in searching for concrete applications that we can actually put into practice in our own daily lives.

Some Aspects of the Buddhist World-view

The Buddha taught that all forms of life partake of the same fundamental spiritual source, which he called the enlightened nature or the Buddha-nature. He did not admit to any essential division in the spiritual condition of human beings and other forms of life. In fact, according to Buddhist teachings, after death a human being is reborn, perhaps again as a human being or possibly in the animal realms or in other realms. Likewise, animals can, in certain circumstances, be reborn as human beings. All sentient beings are seen as passing through the unending cycle of the wheel of rebirth. They are born, they grow old, become sick, and die. They are reborn, grow old, get sick and die, over and over and over again.

What determines how you are reborn is karma. Whether you obtain a human body, whether male or female, or that of an animal or some other life—form is karma. Whether you have a body that is healthy or sickly, whether you are intelligent or stupid, whether your family is rich or poor, whether your parents are compassionate or hard-hearted—all that is karma. Karma is a Sanskrit word that is derived from the semantic root meaning 'to do'. It refers to activity—mental, verbal, and physical—as governed by complex patterns of cause and effect. There are two basic kinds of karma—individual and shared.

Individual karma is not limited to a single lifetime. What you did in your past lives determines your situation in your present life. If you did good deeds in past lives, the result will be an auspicious rebirth. If your actions in past lives were predominantly bad, your situation in the present will be inauspicious. If in this life you act more like an animal than a human being, your next rebirth will be as an animal.

Shared karma refers to our net of inter-relationship with other people, non-human beings, and our environment. A certain category of beings live in a certain location and tend to perceive their environment in much the same way, because that particular shared situation is the fruition of their former actions.

The doctrine of karma is not deterministic. Rather it is a doctrine of radical personal responsibility. Although your present situation in every moment is determined by your past actions, your action in the present moment, in the present circumstances, can be totally unconditioned and, therefore, totally free. It is true that you may mindlessly react according to the strengths of your various habit-patterns, but that need not be the case. The potential for you to act mindfully and freely is always there. It is up to you to realise that you have the choice and to make it. This realisation is the beginning of true spiritual growth.

The Buddha taught that the fundamental cause of all suffering is ignorance. The basic ignorance is our failure to understand that the self, which is at the center of all of our lives, which determines the way in which we see the world, which directs our actions for our own ease and benefit, is an illusion. The illusion of the self is the cause of all our suffering. We want to protect our self from the dangers of the constant flux of life. We want to exempt our self from change, when nothing in the world is exempt from change.

Life centered on self naturally tends toward the selfish. Selfishness poisons us with desire and greed. When they are not fulfilled, we tend to become angry and hateful. These basic emotional conditions cover the luminous depths of our minds and cut us off from our own intuitive wisdom and compassion; our thoughts and actions then emanate from deluded and superficial views.

The Causes of War

The causes of war are too numerous even to list, let alone

discuss intelligently. What we discuss here are what the Buddha considered the most fundamental, the fire under the boiling pot of soup.

War is not something abstract. War is waged between one group of individuals and another. The reasons for war are also not abstract. [We have not yet had a war started and directed according to logical paradigms programmed into a computer.] It is individuals who decide to wage war. Even if the war is global, its beginning can be traced back to the decisions of individuals. And so before we talk about global war, let us first talk about war on the level of the individual.

Wars begin because the people of one country, or at least their rulers, have unfulfilled desires—they are greedy for benefits or wealth (*i.e.*, economic greed) or power, or they are angry or hateful. Either their desires have been thwarted or their pride, their sense of self, has been offended. This can also manifest as racial or national arrogance. They wrongly feel that the answer to problems, which are essentially within their own minds, a matter of attitudes, can be sought externally, through the use of force.

The Story of the Water War

Four years after his [the Buddha's] attainment of enlightenment, a war took place between the city-state of Kapilavastu and that of Kilivastu over the use of water. Being told of this, [the Buddha] Sakyamuni hastened back to Kapilavastu and stood between the two great armies about to start fighting. At the sight of Sakyamuni, there was a great commotion among the warriors, who said, "Now that we see the World-Honoured One, we cannot shoot the arrows at our enemies," and they threw down their weapons. Summoning the chiefs of the two armies, he asked them, "Why are you gathered here like this?" "To fight," was their reply. "For what cause do you fight?" he queried. "To get water for irrigation." Then, asked Sakyamuni again, "How much value do you think water has in comparison with the lives of men?" "The value of water is very slight" was the reply. "Why do you destroy lives which are valuable for valueless water?" he asked. Then, giving some allegories, Sakyamuni taught them as follows: "Since people cause war through misunderstanding, thereby harming and killing each other, they should try to understand each other in the right manner." In other words, misunderstanding will lead all people to a tragic end, and Sakyamuni exhorted them to pay attention to this. Thus the armies of the two city-states were dissuaded from fighting each other.

The doctrine of karma teaches that force and violence, even to the level of killing, never solves anything. Killing generates fear and anger, which generates more killing, more fear, and more anger, in a vicious cycle without end. If you kill your enemy in this life, he is reborn, seeks revenge, and kills you in the next life. When the people of one nation invade and kill or subjugate the people of another nation, sooner or later the opportunity will present itself for the people of the conquered nation to wreak their revenge upon the conquerors. Has there ever been a war that has, in the long run, really resolved any problem in a positive manner? In modern times the so-called 'war to end all wars' has only led to progressively larger and more destructive wars.

The emotions of killing translate into more and more deaths as the weapons of killing become more and more sophisticated. In prehistoric times, a caveman could explode with anger, take up his club, and bludgeon a few people to death. Nowadays, if, for example, the President of the United States loses his temper, who can tell how many will lose their lives as the result of the employment of our modern weaponry. And in the present we are on the brink of a global war that threatens to extinguish permanently all life on the planet. When will that happen? Perhaps when the collective selfishness of individuals to pursue their own desires—greed for sex, wealth and power; the venting of frustrations through anger, hatred and brutal self-assertion—overcomes the collective compassion of individuals for others, overcomes their respect for the lives and aspirations of others. Then the unseen collective pressure of mind on mind will tip the precarious balance, causing the finger, controlled ostensibly by an individual mind, to press the button that will bring about nuclear Armageddon. When the individual minds of all living beings are weighted, if peaceful minds are more predominant, the world will tend to be at peace; if violent minds are more predominant, the world will tend to be at war.

Buddhist Prescriptions

Providing people with physical well-being and wealth does not necessarily lead to peace. Lewis Lapham recently wrote:

Apparently it is not poverty that causes crime, but rather the resentment of poverty. This latter condition is as likely to embitter the 'subjectively deprived' in a rich society as the 'objectively deprived' in a poor society.

Mental attitudes and the actions to which they lead are the key.

Buddhists believe that the minds of all living beings are totally interconnected and interrelated, whether they are consciously aware of it or not. To use a simple analogy for the interconnection, each being has his or her own transmitting and receiving station and is constantly broadcasting to all others his or her state of mind and is constantly receiving broadcasts from all others. Even the most insignificant thoughts in our minds have some effect on all other beings. How much the more so do our strong negative emotions and our acting out of them in direct or indirect forms of physical violence! In other words, each thought in the mind of each and every one of us brings the world either a little closer to the brink of global disaster or helps to move the world a little farther away from the brink. If each time we feel irritated, annoyed, thwarted, outraged, or just plain frustrated, we reflect on the consequences of our thoughts, words and actions, perhaps that reflection in itself will help to lead us to behave in a way that will contribute to global peace. If every time we get angry at our wife or husband, girl friend or boy friend, parents or children, we are aware that we are driving the entire world toward the brink of war, maybe we will think twice and wonder whether our anger is worth the consequences. Even if we feel our cause is just, if we in thought, word, and deed make war against injustice, we are still part of the problem and not contributing to the solution. On the other hand, if we concentrate on putting our own minds at peace, then we can broadcast peace mentally and generate peace through our actions. We should use a peaceful mind to act for peace in the world.

As to the interrelations between the minds of beings, the being we may be about to harm or even kill, from a Buddhist point of view, may well be our own parents, children, wives or husbands, or dearest friends from former lives.

Because Buddhists see the problem of war as a karmic one, the solution is seen as the practicing and teaching of correct ethical behaviour. Good deeds lead to good consequences, bad deeds to bad. If you plant bean seeds, you get beans; if you plant melon seeds, you get melons. If you plant the seeds of war, you get war; if you plant the seeds of peace, you get peace.

The most fundamental moral precept in Buddhist teaching is respect for life and the prohibition against taking life. Generally speaking, all living beings want to live and are afraid of death. The strongest desire is for life, and when that desire is thwarted, the response is unbelievably powerful anger. Unlike almost all other religions, Buddhism teaches that there are no exceptions to this prohibition and no expedient arguments are admitted. The taking of life not only covers human life but all sentient beings. Reducing the karma of killing is equivalent to putting out the fire under the pot of boiling soup. If we end killing, the world will be at peace.

The prohibition against stealing says, more literally, that one must not take what is not given. Stealing, whether it is by individuals, corporations, or nations, occurs because of selfish greed. From the time of the Trojan War, sexual misconduct has also been a cause of war, as has been lying. National leaders whose minds have been clouded by drugs are not rare in history either—their conduct is rarely just and peaceful. The international drug trade in itself has become a major impediment to peace in most parts of the world. The taking of intoxicating substances is also prohibited by fundamental Buddhist teachings.

The Buddhist vision is a world in which all life is sacred, in which selfishness, in the guise of greed, anger and foolishness, does not interfere with the basic interconnectedness of all living beings. That interconnectedness, when freed from the distortion of selfishness, is based upon the potential for enlightenment that every being shares.

Practical Applications

A beautiful vision, some might say. But how can such a peace be realised in a world such as ours? Isn't it mere impractical fantasy? No, it is not. Now the time has come to outline some concrete and practical steps that can be taken towards making it a reality. As a beginning, here are three steps.

Step One

If the karma of killing is the flame beneath the soup pot, by reducing it, we directly affect the boiling turmoil of violence and war. We need to reduce the atmosphere of killing and violence, both in our society and in our own lives. Each one of us can reduce the level of killing in our own lives by the very simple act of becoming vegetarian. An ancient sage once said:

For hundreds of thousands of years
The stew in the pot
Has brewed hatred and resentment
That is difficult to stop.
If you wish to know why there are disasters
Of armies and weapons in the world,
Listen to the piteous cries
From the slaughterhouse at midnight.

In a more contemporary vein George Bernard Shaw wrote a "Song of Peace:"

We are the living graves of murdered beasts,
Slaughtered to satisfy our appetites.
We never pause to wonder at our feasts
If animals, like men, can possibly have rights.
We pray on Sundays that we may have light,
To guide our footsteps on the paths we tread.
We're sick of war, we do not want to fight,
The thought of it now fills our hearts with dread
And yet we gorge ourselves upon the dead.
Like carrion crows, we live and feed on meat,
Regardless of the suffering and pain
We cause by doing so. If thus we treat
Defenceless animals for sport or gain,

How can we hope in this world to attain
The Peace we say we are so anxious for?
We pray for it, o'r hecatombs of slain,
To God, while outraging the moral law,
Thus cruelty begets its offspring—War.

For those who still do not see the logical relationships, I shall try to spell them out more clearly. Non-human life is not qualitatively different than human life, according to Buddhist teachings. Just as when a human is killed, an animal too most often responds to its death with thoughts of resentment, hatred and revenge. While it is dying, these thoughts or emotions poison its flesh. After it is dead, its disembodied consciousness continues to broadcast thoughts of resentment, hatred and revenge to the minds of its killers and those for whom it was killed. Think of the billions of cows, pigs, chickens and sheep that are killed for consumption each year in the United States alone. Those of you who have passed the slaughter yards on the interstate highway near Coalinga, California, have probably noticed not only the stench but also the dark cloud of fear and violence that hangs over the place. The general mental atmosphere of that entire county is thick with thoughts of violence with which such thoughts within our own minds can all too easily resonate.

One of the problems of modern society is that the karma we generate is often indirect and not immediately obvious to us, even though it can be quite powerful. We are no less responsible for the death of the animals when we buy meat wrapped in plastic in the supermarket than if we had killed them ourselves. We are no less responsible for the environmental poisoning of people by chemicals that we pour down our drains or by industries we work for or whose products we buy, than if we had personally added the poison to their food. So too we may not be directly aware of the ways in which we may be providing support for many conflicts and wars around the world. Of course, it is much worse to do something wrong, clearly knowing that it is wrong than to do it in ignorance. Yet ignorance does not absolve us of blame.

Step Two

Since war can come about when the general level of violence in the population reaches the boiling point and can either manifest in civil war or be channeled into foreign wars, anything we can do to reduce the general level of violence in the population will certainly be most helpful. One of the major teachers of violence in our society is television. Turn off your TV—permanently. Michael Nagler has written:

- 96 per cent of American homes have at least one television set. The average home has a set going six hours a day.
- In 'ordinary' viewing, there are 8 violent episodes an hour.
- Between the ages of five and fifteen the average American child has watched the killing of 13,000 people. By age eighteen he or she will have logged more than 15,000 hours of this kind of exposure and taken in more than 20,000 acts of violence... .

- 97 per cent of cartoons intended for children include acts of violence. By the criteria of the Media Action Research Center, an act of aggression occurs every three and a half minutes during children's Saturday morning programmes. Dr. George Gerbner counts one every two minutes by similar criteria.
- In a typical recent year "children . . . witness, on prime time television, 5,000 murders, rapes, beatings and stabbings, 1,300 acts of adultery, and 2,700 sexually aggressive comments," according to a group of concerned mothers.

How can all this be helping the cause of world peace? From an early age our citizens are learning that violence the best solution to their problems, that violence is a socially acceptable and socially approved way of dealing with problems both personal and interpersonal. Turn off the TV!

Step Three

By constantly being mindful of your own thoughts, words and actions and by constantly trying to purify them, we can become part of the force for peace rather than part of the force for war. Teachings about karma indicate to us that no matter how just our cause, no matter how right our ideas, if they are accompanied by anger and hate, they will merely generate more anger and hate. If our minds are inundated with the emotions of war, we aid the cause of war, no matter how noble our cause. Buddhist teachings about karma indicate unequivocally that a fundamentally moral life is a necessary prerequisite for ridding our minds of negative emotions, for transforming them into selfless compassion for all. There are many selfless endeavours that we can take upon ourselves to stir the soup and help cool the pot. But we should remember to be constantly mindful of our own mental attitudes. If we are not, no matter how hard we stir, we may also be unconsciously helping to turn up the flames.

How do we change our own mental attitudes; how do we rid our minds of those strong negative emotions that cause turbidity in our minds? Part of the Bodhisattva Path consists of the practice of giving as an antidote to desire, greed, stinginess, and craving; the practice of patience as an antidote for anger; and the practice of wisdom as an antidote for foolishness.

Step Four

We should work on the systematic extension of compassion towards others. From the level of our own minds, to our speech and then our actions, we can work on generating compassion to those who are closest to us, the members of our own familes, and then progressively extend our compassion to our communities, countries, and the entire world.

Many of you may be disappointed in these suggestions. Perhaps you are looking for something more exciting or stimulating. However, I hope that you will realise that there is some indication that these Buddhist ideas do really work. King Asoka, the Mauryan emperor of India who was coronated in 268 BC, was converted to Buddhism after experiencing personal revulsion in the aftermath of his bloody conquest of Kalinga. Thereafter he prohibited any form of killing and encouraged humane treatment of all peoples and also animals. The Tibetans were bloodthirsty and warlike before conversion to Buddhism. Likewise, their neighbours the Mongols, particularly the armies of Ghengis Khan, terrorised many peoples, from China to the gates of Vienna. It would be hard to find people more fierce and bloodthirsty. Buddhist missionaries subsequently transformed the Mongols into one of the most peaceful peoples of Asia. Buddhists have never advocated war and have never sanctioned the idea of religious war. The ideal of the Bodhisattva (an enlightened being who devotes himself or herself to the enlightenment of all beings) is to voluntarily return, life after life, to our world of suffering to teach the Way to permanent inner peace, which is the only way to true peace in the world. Whether for us or for the great sages of the world, peace can only be brought to the world one thought at a time in the minds of each one of us. Only on that basis, can our actions for peace, also performed one at a time, be truly effective.

Let me quote the words of a great son of India, Shri Jawaharlal Nehru.

> If we follow the principles
>
> enunciated by the Buddha
>
> We will ultimately win
>
> peace and tranquillity for the world

If all of us gathered here today make a determined effort to develop *loving-kindness* and radiate it to the world,

I am sure we can achieve our target to create a world of peace and harmony.

May all living beings be well and happy.

REFERENCES

1. Http://www.dangdang.com/product/7411/7411446.shtml
2. Http://www.ewen.cc/cache/books/view/29/view020010000960329.htm
3. Http://www.fidh.bnznews/HTML/bnznew_2000923083807.html
4. Http://www.sacu.org/religion.html
5. Http://www.sacu.org/religion2.html

CHAPTER

21

Towards the Revival of Value-based Education : Looking for Objective Solutions

*Dr. Meenakshi Singhal

Introduction

It is a well known saying that the progress of human race is the outcome of value-based knowledge or education. Education lays foundation for man's life and it evolves man to attain a physical, mental and spiritual well-being. Education is the fundamental right for every human being. Full-fledged effective education will assist in nation's growth by laying a conceptual base.

While the society is passing through the phase of disintegration. Today human and moral values like faith, believe, peace and courtesy seem to lose their existence. Today an individual finds himself alone in the crowd. Family bonds are becoming weak. Consumerism and materialism have become the biggest values. Now we are living in the Modern, Scientific and Technological world. Science and Technology have brought enormous changes in the society, in the attitudes

* Head, Centre for Communication, University of Petroleum and Energy Studies, Dehradun.

of the people and also the changes in the day-to-day life of human beings.

Modern mass society presents a sharp contrast, as the young grow up. They are faced with confusions, delays and discontinuities. Adolescents in particular are uncertain about themselves. Some are in conflict with themselves, bewildered and insecure. In today's multi-cultural and multi-racial society, with its changing social norms and expectations, it can be difficult for a young person to know what is right. To enable young people to appreciate themselves and others, and to take greater responsibility for their actions and for the world around them it is necessary to give importance to human values in the present era of globalisation.

The process of education is considered so important in our society that no parents, who can afford it, can imagine having their children go uneducated. It has become such an integral part of our lives that for most people, completing the process of education appears to be a matter of habit. Others, who have so far remained outside this process, are now being covered by the literacy programmes of the government and various non-governmental organisations. Extending the privilege to everybody in the country seems to be a top priority for various governments representing political thought of different shades. Those outside the education system see it as a desirable thing and are quite eager to take advantage of the opportunity offered to them. But, why exactly is education so indispensable?

Need for Value-based Education

Values are the guiding principles, decisive in day-to-day behaviours and also in critical life situations. Values are a set of principles or standards of behaviour. Values are regarded desirable, important and held in high esteem by a particular society in which a person lives.

Values are usually influenced by the changing philosophical ideologies, cultural and religious perspectives, social, political and geographical conditions. In modern emerging society, there has been a revolutionary change in the field of values due to many factors in addition to the influence of modern culture, industrialisation, modernisation, urbanisation, globalisation and multinationals.

Value education means inculcating in the children a sense humanism, a deep concern for the well-being of others and the nation. This can be accomplished only when we instill in the children a deep feeling of commitment to values that would build this country and bring back to the people pride in work that brings order, security and assured progress.

Value education refers to a programme of planned educational action aimed at the development of value and character. Every action and thought of ours leaves an impression in our mind. These impressions determine in our behaviour at a given moment and our responses to a given situation. The sum total of all our impressions is what determines our character. The past has determined the present and our present thoughts and actions will shape our future.

This is a key principle, governing personality development. The human values are resolved having lasting impact necessary for bringing about a change in thought and conduct, in the 21st century.

Flawed Education System

The ground reality is that in most of the schools and colleges of India, students, teachers and administrators are indifferent towards the process of education, fraudulent ways are being adopted to complete the process and a large number of educated youth find themselves without jobs. It is quite strange that when the people, government and those involved in implementing it, consider the education to be a desirable thing, they choose to ignore the real state of affairs on ground. Policy makers, politicians, social activists and education experts are seen taking idealist positions when talking about education, most of the time. Education as an activity seems to be going on without any direction.

More precisely, the perceived goal of education to make the individual and the society 'better' in some qualitative sense, seems to be missing in its current form. In our rush to get everybody educated, we are forgetting the values attached with education. Education is perceived to be a desirable thing because education makes people progressive in some sense and is necessary for the advancement of a civilised society, it imparts knowledge and it provides employment opportunities. When parents send their children to school they are essentially seeking a 'secure future' for them, which basically means that their children upon getting educated would become eligible for salaried jobs.

Since the education system is designed to produce merely a 'clerical' class, upon the completion of their education programmes the youth seek fixed salary and low risk secure jobs. The top priority is often government jobs because there is remote possibility of getting thrown out of them, in addition to other financial and material benefits offered by them. However, the number of such salaried jobs is limited.

To present the idea of education in its current form as a desirable thing and involving large masses of people in it through literacy programmes, thereby making them aspirants in a limited (salaried) job market, is an irresponsible behaviour. Even though it could be argued that economic liberalisation programmes are creating more job opportunities, the number of people receiving education and going without a job is growing at a faster rate.

Since what is needed to demonstrate when applying for a job is the certificate and not actual competence, people have devised ways of completing the process of obtaining the certificates without actually putting in the hard work to go through the entire exercise involved in the process of education.

Since examinations can now be passed without a rigorous programme of studies, the entire process of classroom teaching has been short-circuited. The teachers are content drawing their salaries. As the number of people possessing certificates, diplomas and degrees has gone up, so has the competition for jobs and the number of unemployed. Since the education system prepares a job mentality in people, a person is called unemployed if he/she is not in a salaried job.

It is only the dream of getting these small number of high salaried coveted jobs that has sustained the view that education opens up more job opportunities. If we consider the hard reality, education system today makes many more people jobless than it is able to provide jobs to. In fact, the process of education is so lop-sided and strangulating that it saps the person of all his/her imagination and enthusiasm making him/her unfit for any other work. The crippling effect of getting low paid jobs can only lead to frustration among the people who are unfortunate enough not to secure a good salaried job. The government and political parties only make the situation worse by creating an illusion that they can create more jobs. They only fuel the rat race of people going through the education system and then contending for jobs.

Way Forward

If we are to channelise the energy of our youth for constructive activity in society then we work to dispel the notion that education opens up more job opportunities. The sooner we agree to examine the myth that the present education system is a desirable thing, the better it would be for our society. A completely new form of education system with a different purpose altogether, has to be worked out for creating a healthy society. Fortunately we are forced to re-examine our education system because, firstly, it is failing to provide jobs to everybody, and, secondly, to the people it has provided jobs, it is failing to provide satisfaction. In any case, the myth that education opens up more job opportunities needs to be dispensed with.

The government has to take proper steps in order to improve the efficiency of students by making improvement in the quality of education. The student drop-out rate has been high in low-income family. The government must provide continuous support to the poor young people in order to reduce the drop-out rate because of poverty.

The school syllabus has to be reformed in such a way that it will provide practical knowledge to the students and meets the needs of industries. The academic performance of a student can be increased only by an effective teaching. Hence proper training has to be provided to the teachers in order to keep the knowledge uptodate.

The education process cannot be effective if the classes are overcrowded. Only an effective education can reduce poverty and improve the quality of life of Indians.

The government can offer free vocational education for poor student's in order to bring out the productivity of young minds. Communication skills and computer skills training should be offered to them to meet the growing demands of the ever changing world.

Equality has to be promoted at school. The teaching staff must motivate young people to achieve their potential. Quality improvement is necessary in higher education.

Initiatives have to be taken and systematic approach towards improved teaching and learning has to be overlaid. The government must also judge the syllabus pattern of the universities by making an educational committee with experts.

It is necessary to start more number of schools and colleges in the nation to have an impressive growth in education. The government must take steps to reduce the gap between the male and female enrollment rates in higher education. Scholarships must be provided to the meritorious students in all educational levels. It is true that the education can alone create a strong society, better lives for people and even the future economy.

It is necessary to analyse the current education system and plan towards the improvement. School improvement activities have to be carried out. The universities must make plans and efforts towards continuous improvement of quality. The learning pattern can be effective only if they apply what they have learnt in work or life. The student must be taught to learn with certainty and ease. The educational barrier has to be confronted. The working hours of teachers in school and the allocation for the education has to be increased as the present level of investment is not adequate. The education department must estimate the requirement and act accordingly.

Education transfers a student to a great society man in future. The educational system must be changed from theoretical level to more practical and technical level to focus on career prospects.

The student must develop a clear insight or key skills in technology at the primary level. For that Government must reform the educational system to establish meaningful linkages with the business, corporate and service sectors. The ancient technology must be incorporated into modern science to meet the society requirements. An improvement in the technology has to be addressed to the needs of students.

The university education must be in such a way that the graduates can be able to tie-up with international jobs. The educational institutions must impart challenged learning which ensures uniformity to all citizens. Indian government must ban child labour and ensure that every child must get education at least to the secondary level. Profession based vocational training helps students to attain skills to meet the competitive world. The best ways to foster learning has to be identified and then the educational system has to be reformed.

Technical, Research and development activities must be emphasised to enrich the technical knowledge of the learners. There must be a synergy between education and practice for effective transformation of students to corporate leaders. The educational system must be structured and updated on a regular basis to incorporate latest changes of society and technology. Technical projects must be included in school education to address the corporate or society needs.

In addition to professional education, value-based education must be incorporated in the curriculum to nurture the values of students thereby imparting social responsibility.

Successfully reforming education cannot be easily achieved. The flaw in an educational system is to be considered as an economic flaw. Steady and stable steps have to be taken to reform the structure else the quick move will often result in failure. The main idea of reform has to be structured. Then the ideas have to be tested before the implementation step. Technology changes each and everyday. Hence new updates have to be constantly added in the technical sectors. The youth educational system must be employable.

In order to reform education, the views of teachers and students have to be evaluated. There should be a system of sharing ideas and information with the public which will help in better reforming. The government associate has to seek the help of professional universities or colleges to better structure the education. Only the teaching staff can provide deep insight as they have direct contact with students and subject matters to make the reforming process more effective. For a renaissance of Indian education, the industry leaders and educationalists must have a commitment to improve the present system. In a survey, it is known that world's largest population of illiterate citizens exists here in India. The educational ministers must make agenda to improve the quality and quantity of education.

The educational system remains to be privatised on a massive scale. Comprehensive programmes have to be designed by both private sectors and government to change the pattern of education. The educational policy has to be prepared in such a manner that both the low income people and the middle class get benefited. Educational sector should be a non-profitable sector. Teachers development and orientation programmes have to be conducted regularly for teaching staffs to meet the demands of a changed education to make the teaching process effective. The educational system must transform students for an increasingly diverse and technological world. To reduce the number of educated unemployed young people in India a radical reconstruction of the present system is mandatory.

The educational programme has to be meticulously reformed with a planned and progressive syllabus that facilitates holistic development of students to reach a higher level in society. Educational system has to be reformed taking into consideration the student's future and also requirements of the corporate industries.

REFERENCES

1. Value Education, Dr. Venkataiah, Editor, APH Publishing Corporation, 5, Ansari Road, Daryaganj, New Delhi-110 002, First Edition, 1998.
2. Value Education in India, Usha Rai Negi, Editor, Published by Association of Indian Universities, AIU House, 16 Kotla Mark, New Delhi-110 002, 2000.
3. National Institute of Child Health and Human Development. (2000). The National Reading Panel: Reports of the Subgro.

CHAPTER 22

Peace Education through Yoga : Need of the Day

*Ms. Amar Jyoti
**Mr. Hitesh Kumar Sharma

Peace means being one with life itself. Having no fear or bitterness. Peace is more than merely sitting still or in silence. Peace therefore is a state of mind. Tagore rightly said *"Where the mind is without fear and the head is held high, into that kingdom of freedom my father let my country awake"*

Peace is simply having a feeling of security, calm and restfulness. We often tend to think of peace as being an international issue, far from our daily life, but we do not realise that global peace can only be achieved if each country is settled and at peace. The peace and happiness of each country can only be achieved if every citizen is at peace. This follows therefore that a country can be peaceful and progress if her people live in harmony. We all want peace of mind.

Is peace of mind possible at all in our rushed life? It is up to us. We must come to grip with ourselves. Though the world may be full of problems and distress we must see the positive side of it all. We must accept the problem as an opportunity not as a problem. Just as you destroy an enemy and make him your friend you can destroy a problem and turn it into joy. When there is no peace among the persons, then peace in society is threatened. Sometimes this leads to chain of violence. Lack of peace destroys the identity of a country.

* Lecturer, Vivek College of Education in Bijnor (U.P.).

** Lecturer and Admn. Officer in Vivek College of Management and Technology in Bijnor (U.P.).

The mental and creative energies of citizens are diverted from useful activities to destructive one.

The need of the hour is to develop the young generation with peace consciousness. Irreparable damage has been done to the present generation by our system of government the political system and the religious leaders who exploit emotions for their immediate gains. It may not be possible to change the attitude of the present generation but it is possible to mould the future generation for the good of the nation and for mankind. We all talk about the fissiparous tendencies that come up in our country in the name of religion, place and community, which in fact are man made barriers used in the name of God. We the educationist should think ways and means to inculcate the spirit of unity and integrity.

Neither our society nor our educational system has any scope for highlighting the importance of peace. In every walk of life our attention is focussed on violence, confrontation, competition, self interest and the greed to win. The history of wars is not longer than peace. It looks the impact of two world wars and the Hiroshima bomb disaster for human kind to begin to perceive the concept of peace as the primary goal.

Peace has become an important area of concern in the present day world. Peace is a state of harmony, the absence of hostility and it is generally agreed that a culture of peace is an essential precondition for the development of human beings both as individuals and as a collectivity so the inculcation of the value of peace in the minds of growing generation assumes great significance. For this, peace must become an integral part of education that is why peace education is given an important place in today's educational programme. It may be said that peace education is a system of education directed towards the generation of peace.

What we need today is education that is capable of saving mankind from the present predicament of violence and disorders prevailing in the society. But unfortunately the education system in India does not give adequate importance to the component of peace in its curriculum in modern times. Many eminent educationists have pointed out the serious drawback in the system. Hence it is highly desirable that peace component is included in the process of education to build a world of peace and harmony. Peace education is more effective and meaningful when is adopted according to the social and cultural context and the needs of a country. It should be enriched by its cultural and spiritual values together with the universal human values. The importance of yoga is to be stressed here as it is regarded highly contributive to the eternal calm and happiness. Yoga is a way of life, an art of righteous living or an integrated system for the benefit of the body, mind and inner spirit.

Yoga—A Historical Vision

The history of yoga spans from four to 8000 years ago to the current age. It is an integral subjective science. It is spiritual, mental and physical import that can not be separated from each other according to Panini, the grammarian, the word Yoga is derived from two roots, viz, *Vizur* and *Vuja* one referring to yoking (*Vuujir* yoga) and the other referring to mental concentration (*Yuj Samadhan*) and to sense control (*Viz Samjamane*). Yoga standing for mental consideration, is the theme of entire Indian system dealing with yogas. It also implies the control of senses. Thus, the second derivation of the word yoga consist in *'citta vrittivirodhah'* i.e. the silencing of (all) activities in the minds substance. According to Vedanta, yoga means supreme realisation. Yoga is the reunion of the living self with the supreme self. According to Puranas, that particular inclination of the mind, which is accompanied by an active desire to know the self and which needs to unite with the principle is called yoga.

In ancient time, Yoga techniques were kept secret and were never written down or exposed to public view. They were passed on from teacher or Guru to disciple by word of mouth. In this way, there was a clean understanding of their meaning and aim. Through personal experiences, yogis and sages were able to guide sincere aspirants along the correct path, removing any confusion, misunderstanding and excessive intellectual contemplation.

Yoga does not believe in temporary cure of the patient because "the old troubles often reappear in different forms". It, therefore, the scribes total eradication of mental conflicts, unpleasant urges and tendencies through yogic methods. It claims complete cure of neurotics and psychotics by yogic exercise. Sage Patanjali's yoga consist of eight steps:

1. *Yama:* refers to abstention from violence, falsehood, dishonesty and acquisitive tendencies.
2. *Nyrama:* refers to observance of purity, contentment austerity, self study and resignation.
3. *Asana* or Physical Posture: conies.
4. *Pranayam:* refers to control of inspiration and expression.
5. *Pratyahara :* withdrawal of the mind(senses) from objects.
6. *Dharna :* refers to concentration.
7. *Dhyana :* uninterrupted focus of the mind on one point.
8. *Samadhi :* deep meditation is the final stage.

These eight steps are to be followed in order. Unless one follows and practice all of them together in an integrated manner, one will not be able to derive full benefit from yoga. The first two are related to social and personal behaviour. The third and fourth are the yogic exercise. The last four are the stages of the meditation (Udupa, 1985).

The yogic exercise are both preventive and curative in their nature these include the benefits as follows:

- Harmonious development of all muscles.
- The tripod of life, i.e. heart, lung and brain are kept in healthy condition.
- Improved blood circulation

- Flexibility in whole body
- Strengthens spine
- Cleans throat, lungs
- Improves digestion
- Proper functioning of different glands, i.e. thyroids, pituitary, pineal etc.
- Improves memory and concentration.
- Provides mental stability and emotional maturity
- Reduces stress and anxiety
- Enhances motor reflexes and sharpen perception

Yoga—A Best Way for Exploring Peace

Peace is not sold in the market. Peace is personal as well as universal. Today society is awaking to the reality of lending a hand this is a good sign of a hope. All of us have to put over shoulders to the wheel if we want a better tomorrow.

Yoga for Peace

Mind itself is the cause of diseases. Yoga is no more and no less than a better way of living. Yoga balances the state of mind generating the right kind of attitude. Yoga contribute significantly many have come out of depression and negative attitude.

Yoga is bunch of physical exercise called Asanas. These help to calm the nerves which in turn gives us peace. It help us to control our temper and anger. Yoga uses the techniques of relaxation of the body and mind. It is a technique of awareness which makes an objective evaluation of life's problems. Yoga help in giving direction to human activities that lead to the joy of fulfillment.

The first attempt in Yoga is to calm oneself so that one sees thing clearly. Calmness creates enough clarity to throw up essential queries.

ASANAS

(1) Sukhasana

Sit cross-legged on the mat. Put the palms on the knees in the relaxed way. Maintain the spine, the neck and the head erect. Draw the abdomen in. close the eyes watch your normal inhaling and exhaling. Sit still. Let no thoughts come to your mind.

Benefits : Spreads a feeling of general quietude. With peace and calm comes clarity and understanding which helps in better coordination of the days' work

(2) Nishpandabhava

Sit relaxed and in a comfortable position. Have soft slow music played. Remain passive and get completely absorbed in the sound.

Benefits : Trains the mind. Releases tension, physical and mental relaxation and quietude. There are certain activities that go well at certain hours of the day. The early hours at dawn are good for quiet thinking and contemplation. This is an asset for those who live in cities. They will be better off with reflection and recollection.

(3) Vajrasana

Sit kneeling. Slip toes to join at the back heels apart. Place buttocks in the cavity formed keeping thighs together. Place hands on thighs. Keep spine erect, head and neck straight. Reflect on the previous days events in sequence and with detachment trying to learn form the events and reactions.

This reflection gives a fresh perspective, which is helpful for future behaviour. The important point here is that one learns to create a distance between oneself and the events. Ordinarily one gets emotionally involved. Thus one falls a prey for fears.

Benefits : Feeling of quietude and turning the mind inwards acts as preparation for meditation and concentration. The fear for fear is our only real enemy.

(4) Sithaprarthana

Stand, join feet together, close eyes, join hands silently, pray or create good thoughts. Remain in this position for 5 to 7 minutes.

Benefits : Adds to steadiness and on pointedness.

(5) Bhadarsana

This is a good Asana. It is very good meditative posture. It is said that the mind in this Asana transforms physical energy into subtle psychic energy. Sit on the floor with the legs nearer to the body while still keeping the legs in contact with the floor with knees bent outwards and the soles of the feet together with the abdomen controlled and inhale for 3 seconds. Bring the feet with the toes pointing outwards close to the body. Place the hands on the knees pressing them down. Exhale for 3 seconds. Keep the body erect.

Benefits : Will very important when a person wants to change. A very strong urge is required.

Need of Yoga for Adolescents

"Yoga is methodical effort to attain perfection, through to the control of different elements of human nature, physical and psychical".

—*Patanjali*

Today we are living in the age of explosims and paradox. We have conquered the enquired the unconquerable and achieved things beyond the wildest dream of ancestors. Due to ever increasing ambitions, desires and competitions, restiveness and maddening tension have also increased by leaps and bounds. Ever increasing diseases of insomnia, mental deformity, impulse, opposing ethical values and destructive instincts are some of the common physiological and psychological problems faced by man of today the modern world, which is said to be world of achievements, is also a world of stress (Kaul, 1989).

It is well said that if we want to have real peace in this world we shall have to begin with the children. Main victim of today's stress is our adolescent. Adolescent itself is a stage of 3s *stress, storm* and *strife*. The person encounters change at the physical, mental, psychological and social level, which is bit natural. But our education system of other pressures such as vast syllabus and curriculum, examination fear, neck to neck competition etc. peer pressure and prenatal pressure and tons of their problems. Their self worth gets wrapped around their academic performance.

Adolescents are particularly vulnerable to suicide on account of emotional immaturity and temperamental instability. Parental expectations are largely incongruent with their children's ability which leads to frustration and depressions. Students attempt to commit suicide due to feeling of worthlessness and to escape social disapproval. The causality graph of adolescents peaks sharply during examination days and the time when result is declared. Academic stress and examination anxiety are cited as causal factors. Parents and teachers perpetuate the feelings of shame by scolding and beating but worse methods like withdrawal precipitates and worsens the situation. When there is no one to share the pain and anxiety, stress gets out the bounds (Garewal, 2003). In India several studies focussed on the problem of mental health among children suffer from problems. These studies further revealed that 15-19 years of age group is most vulnerable stage for developing mental disorder. It begin an age of storms is likely to shatter the homeostasis of a growing individual (Basu-1962; Chacko 1969, Surya 1964, Dube -1970, Srinivasamurthy-1974, Rao-1978, John -1980, Jiloha and Srinivasamurthy-1981, Shariff-1982 and ICMR-1984).

Review of Literature

Research studies revealed that yoga practical led to reduction in anxiety, neuroticism and hostility (Vinod-1984) and improvement in attitude, self-esteem and self confidence (Joshi-1984). Yoga decreased emotional disturbance spells (Dhoundeal, 1984) and helped in some psychological parameters (Singh and Madhav, 1987). Asanas were effective in curbing anxiety (Vicente-1987) Yoga helped through is more effective in comparison to drug therapy in combating anxiety and neuroticism (Shashi Mohan and Kanchan-1989) Yoga group was more effective when compared with chemotherapy group in reducing anxiety, neuroticism and depression (Grover it at, 1989) Yoga helped to create harmony between inner and outer world of the individual which is an important and neglected aspect of education (Flak-1990) Systolic blood pressure also decreased during treatment phases (Latha and Kaliappan-1991)

Yogic practices helped to deal with delinquency and criminal behaviour and improved academic performance (Samprasad, 1991) Yoga was helpful to deal with headache, meditation intake and symptoms of stress perception) Latha and Kaliappa-1992). Yoga help to solved the confusion between self deal disparity and ideal self (Rani and Ras-1992). Yoga helped to decreased anxiety levelling the gymnastic group (Annakali -1993). It helped to improve the mental health and emotional maturity of adolescent girls (Sharma-1994). *Hatha* yoga improved and fastened a psycho-physical balance (Yadav, 1998). Yoga and meditation enhance self esteem, self disclosure, improve emotional intelligence and enhance social adjustment of jail inmates (Sharma, 2004) and helped to decrease depression (Rani and Rao, 2005) So yogic practices help to improve physical health, reduce anxiety, depression and stress and improve mental health, self concept and emotional maturity of individuals.

Epilogue

Peace and stress-free life for today's students appears to be a mirage. He is caught in a dynamic technological whirlpool and seems to be precariously poised on the brink of disaster. In a school situation there is lot of academic pressure. At adolescent stage, students worry about their future, what course they will get admission and so on. Will they be able to have a secure job? Because, today even if one gets high distinction marks, there is no guarantee that he/she will get admission in the course/institution of their choice. In order to lead a happy and prosperous life with almost harmony in the society, Yoga can play an important role in helping adolescent to combat stress and pressure from parents, peers and society. Yoga can help individuals to adapt themselves to the changing world and thus lessen some social stress. Yogic practices help to academic anxiety, as has been shown in the present study. Yogic exercises help to release shown muscle tension (Grossman, 1967).

The science of yoga applies to all aspects of life. The basic yogic practices including *asanas* (postures), *pranayamas* (breathing techniques), *mudras* (positions or gestures) which represent the psyche; *bandas* (locks for channeling energy) and *satkarmas* (cleaning practices)—purity the body, mind and energy system to prepare the ground for higher practices of meditation and for the ultimate experience of cosmic consciousness. Scientists and doctors not only in India but also around the world are currently researching the effects of yogic practices during and after performance. Their results show that *asanas, pranayamas, mudras* and *bandas* are a potent means to restore and maintain physical and mental health. In the near future we hope to see an increasing application of yoga in all walks of life.

Yoga is the science of right living and, as such is intended to be incorporated in daily life. When practiced faithfully, under the guidance of a competent teacher, this technique will expand the individual's consciousness. It works on all aspects of the person: the physical, mental, emotional, physic and spiritual. So yoga helps in all round development of an individual, which is the main aim of education.

Everybody's life is full of ups and down and we cannot get rid of stressful situation. But we can make ourselves strong enough to face the stressful life situation with the help of yoga. Yoga deals with the practical aspects of our life and makes us aware and experience the higher 'dimensions of our nature or self. This leads to the unity of higher self. Swami Shivananda said "An ounce of practices more precious than tons of theory". Yoga kills our negative thoughts and fills optimisms and enthusiasm within. The body and mind are energised by freshness and become ready to take initiatives to accept the challenges. The outlook towards life and world becomes positive and progressive. Yoga makes the men self disciplined. A combination of *Asans, Pranayam, Pratyahara, Mudra, Bandha, Mantra, Kriyas, Yog Nidra, Meditation Trataka* etc. developed the ability to remain active and alert at physical as well as mental level. The person achieve the strength to experience his own in a power in the most demanding situations the life and world can throw on him.

At a time when the world seems to be at a loss, rejecting past values without being able to establish new ones, yoga provides a means for people especially the adolescents to find their own way of connecting with their true selves. Yoga is helpful for all, especially adolescents. Yoga helps to discipline the mind for an integrated and harmonious development of an individual. Yoga provides internal peace, happiness, develops positive thinking, self-confidence, positive approach to life, state of mind emotional stability and strong will power. Jayasree, P.G. and Suramya Mathai (2009) Conducted a study to find out "Effectiveness of Yoga as an educational strategy for practicing peace education among student teachers". It revealed that yoga is highly effective in internalising peace behaviour.

To sum up, we can say that yoga is a way for the harmonious development of human being (Body, Mind and

Spirit) the ultimate aim of education and which would help in leading a peaceful leaving.

REFERENCES

1. Annakili, C.M. (1993) A Comparative Study of Yoga Asanas and Gymnastic in Selected Physical Physiology and Physiological Variables, Unpublished M. Phil Thesis, Alagappa University.
2. Barnes, B.L. and Nagarkar, S. (1989) Yoga Education and Scholastic Achievement. Indian Journal of Clinical Psychology, Vol. 16(2), 96-98.
3. Basu, D.M.(1962) "Analysis of Care Attending Child Psychotherapy centre, Indian Journal of Psychiatry Vol. No. 4, p. 139
4. Chacko, R (1969) Psychiatric Problems in Children. Indian Journal of Psychiatry, Vol. 3, p. 147.
5. Dhar, H.L. (1977) Health and Aging. India Journal of Medical Sciences, Vol. 51(10), pp. 373-377.
6. Dubey, K.C., (1970) "Study of Prevalence and Bio-sociable Variable in Mental Illness in a Rural and Urban Community in UP, India. Acta Psychiatrica Scandinavia, Vol. 6, p. 327.
7. Dhoundial, V. (1984) Home Environment and Emotional Disturbance Among Adolescents. Indian Journal of Psychology, Vol. 59 (1&2), 19-22.
8. Flak M. (1990) Yogabhakti Exploring Ways to Introduce RYE Techniques into U.K. Schools. Paper presented in seminar at London, October. In Bihar school of yoga.com.
9. Grossman, B.P. (1967) Textbook of Physiological Psychology. London: John Willey and Sons. Inc.
10. Garewal, Geetinder (2003) Self Worth not Buy Academic Performance alone. The Tribune April 8, p. 13.
11. Dr. Nayyar, Gopinath "Peace Education and Conflict Resolution in School" Health Administrator Vol: XVII, No. 1, pp. 38-42.
12. Grover. V.P. and Verma, S.K. (1989) Factors Influencing Treatment Acceptance in Neurotic Patients Referring for Yoga Therapy—An Exploratory Study. Indian Journal of Psychometric, Vol. 31(3), 250-257.
13. ICMR (1984)Project Report by the Task Force on Multi Centre of Patterns of Child and Adolescent Psychiatric Disorder (1981-1983) Micro Graphed ICMR New Delhi.

14. Jiloha, R.C. and Srenivasamurthy, R(1983) " Socially Disadvantaged Children is Their Mental Health at Risk?" In Dubey, S and Suchdev, P.S.(eds.) Mental Health Problem of the Society, Disadvantaged. New Delhi, Tata Mc Graw Hill.

15. Joahi, K.S. (1984) Yogic Pranayama Breathing for Long Life and Good Health. Delhi : Udayana Publications.

16. John, P (1980) Psychiatric Morbidity in Children Epidemiological study. M.D. Thesis Submitted to Banglore University, Banglore.

17. Kaul, H.K. (1989) Yoga in Hindu Scriptures. Surjeet Publications, New Delhi.

18. Latha and Kaliappan, K.V. (1992) Efficacy of Yoga Therapy in the Management of Headaches. Journal of Indian Psychology, Vol. 10(2), 41-47.

19. NCERT (2000) NCF for School Education, New Delhi NCERT.

20. Rao, P.N. (1978) Psychiatric Morbidity in Adolescence M.D. Thesis Submitted to Banglore Univresity Banglore.

21. Rani, J.N and Rao, K.V.P. (1992) Effect of Yogic Practices on Self-ideal Disparity (SID) Journal of Indian Psychology, Vol. 10, (I&2), 35-41.

22. Rani, J.N and Rao, K.V.P. (2005) Impact of Yoga Training on Body Image and Depression. Andhra University, Vishkhapatnam, Psychological Studies, Vol. 50(1), 98-100.

23. Sharma, C. (1994) Effect of Selected Yogic Practices on Mental Health. Unpublished Doctoral Thesis, Physical Education, Panjab University, Chandigarh.

24. Sharma, S. (2004) Effect of Yoga and Meditation Practices on Self-esteem, Self-disclosure, Emotional Intelligence and Social Adjustment of Criminals at Model Jail. Unpublished Doctoral Thesis (Education) Panjab University, Chandigarh.

25. Shashi, G.D., Mohan and Kochar, C.(1989) Effectiveness of Yogic Techniques in the Management of Anxiety, Journal of Personality and Clinical Studies,Vol. 5(1), 51-55.

26. Singh, A. and Madhu, (1987) A Study of the Effect of Yogic Practices on Certain Psychological Parameters. Indian Journal of Clinical Psychology, Vol. 14, 82-83.

27. Sunita (2002) Effect of Yoga Experience on Self-concept and Mental Health of Secondary School Students. Unpublished M.Ed. Dissertation, Panjab University, Chandigarh.

28. Shariff, I.A.(1992) A Study of Psychological Problems of Young Learner Ph.D. Thesis, Karnataka University Dharmand.

29. Shrinivasmurthy, R. (1974) Behaviour Disorder of Childhood and Adolescents. Indian Journal of Psychiatry Vol. 16, p. 229.
30. Surya N.C. (1964) 300 Families, A Psychiatric Survey. Journal of Psychiatric Vol. 09, p. 280.
31. Vicente, P.D. (1987) Role of Yoga Therapy in Anxiety Neurosis and Depression. Yoga Mimansa, Vol. 20(3-4).
32. Vinod (1984) Effect of Yogic Practices Performed on Adolescent Anxiety and Certain Personality Traits. Yoga and Research International Conference Abstracts, Yoga Mimansa, Vol. 28(29), 33-34.
33. Yadav, H. (1994) A Study of Hathayoga Practices in Treatment of Anxiety and Pain in Cancer Patients, Chd. PGIMER. Unpublished Doctor Thesis, 616-914.
34. Jayasree, P.G. & Suramya Mathai(2009) Conducted a Study to Find Out " Effectiveness of Yoga as an Educational Strategy for Practicing Peace Education Among Student Teachers". Edutracks, June 2009 Vol. 08, No. 10, pp. 40-41.
35. Kauts, Amit and Sharma Neelam (2008) Yoga and Student Performance" University News Vol. 46, No. 07, pp. 5-11.
36. Dr Mehra, Vandana & Dr. Sharma Anjali (2009)" Effect of Yogic Practice on Social Stress and Academic Stress of Female Adolescents" Edutracks Vol. 7, No. 7, pp. 32-39.
37. Jayasree, P.G. and Suramya Mathai(2009) " Effectiveness of Yoga as an Educational Strategy for Practicing Peace Education Among Student Teachers" Edutracks, Vol. 8, No. 10, pp. 40-41.
38. Prasad, S.N. (1998) " Development of Peace Education in India Since Independence. Reports-research Sweden Lund University.
39. www.indianyoga.org
40. www.peaceworkmagzine.org
41. www.haguepeace.org
42. www.ncte.india.org

CHAPTER 23

Relevance of Higher Education for Peace

*Dr. Sanjay Marotra Dalvi

The Indian education scene has been witness to many changes. During the course of its growth, the number of universities has reached to more than 254 universities and 11,000 colleges. Even though, Indian Higher education is second biggest in the world after USA, yet to say that our education system has been dynamic and fully responsive to the dictates of changing times or to the genuine aspirations of the people, would be an overstatement.

Challenges of Higher Education

Education should impart values to the youth that makes them sensitive to fellow human beings and the environs around them. As Nobel Laureate Gurudev Rabindranath Tagore said, *"the highest education is that which does not merely give us information, but makes our life in harmony with all existence."*

For education to be useful it needs to be comprehensive. There are questions on which sometimes less emphasis is placed in our educational system, but they are of enormous importance. This is building the character of the youth. What values should be inculcated in them? How to make them individuals who understand the virtues of hardwork, discipline and dedication? How to help them understand the importance of the common thread of humanity that binds us all together? This common thread is the universal desire for

* Asst. Professor, Department of Botany, Shri Guru Buddhiswami Mahavidyalaya, Purna, Distt. Parbhani, Maharastra.

peace and harmony—it is like the thread that holds together a beautiful garland of flowers of many colours, fragrance and variety. Different faiths, languages, ethnicities, races that exist in the world should come together as a garland of peace. This requires that we must have respect and tolerance for each other's views and backgrounds. These attitudes are important and higher education should promote such commonalities and strengths.

The goals and objectives of academic institutions while Pandit Nehru way back in 1947, mentioned in his address to the graduates of the Allahabad University as:

> *"A university stands for humanism, for tolerance, for reason, for the adventure of ideas and for the search for truth. It stands for the onward march of the human race towards higher objectives. Universities are place for ideals and idealism. If the universities discharge their duties adequately, then, it is well with the nation and the people.*

Goals of Higher Education for the Society

Peaceful and prosperous nations are predicated on an educated, well-informed and well-meaning population. All countries should set up progressive and well-regulated education systems that impart quality education, while meeting the aspirations of all segments of society. This challenge translates itself to the target of providing increased opportunities of higher education in a wide range of subjects. Universities and institutes among others, of technology, science, engineering, medicine, law, management and vocational training have a critical role in meeting the requirements of a country for trained professionals with a sound knowledge of their respective disciplines and of a skilled human resource base. According to Her Excellency the President of India, Shrimati Pratibha Devisingh Patil, at the inauguration of the international conference on the theme "facing global and local challenges: the new dynamics of higher education" *(New Delhi, 25th February, 2009),*

'Education should empower the people of a country to meet the challenges of a knowledge based society of the 21st century. It should prepare them to contribute constructively—as enlightened citizens not only to nation building but also to the world',

Socrates believes that goodness and truth, positive essences and pure ethical and moral instincts are placed there divinely in the soul. However, they are not brought to consciousness unless they are awakened or learned. Therefore, consensus on the important things in life is just below the surface waiting to be acknowledged. It is the destiny of mankind to seek out virtue such as courage and self-control, or propriety over the desires of ambitions or emotions that cloud the quest for truth. Formal education is necessary for the acquisition of authentic and useful knowledge. It can, then, be said that education has a foremost role in shaping civilised and peaceful societies. Higher education, besides providing solid platform for professional life, helps build positive mindset, brings in rationality and balanced thought, breeds reason and logic instead of asserting one's point of view, enables one to appreciate and observe moral and cultural values, and on top of it all lets sanity prevail in all spheres of decision-making. India is a case in point, where even after sixty years of independence, the basic rights violations, ethnic violence, religious intolerance, corruption, crime, and the latest being terrorism are some serious problems. India is facing problems on both the fronts, external and internal.

Education brings in sanity, wisdom and reason which form basis of any civilised and peaceful society. Over the years India has improved its educational infrastructure; higher education has improved, contributing to industrial progress; so one can see better management at national level, however, peace building and reconciliatory processes have not matured in India as yet. In contrast, South Korea, Malaysia and Singapore have emerged as 'tiger economies' in the region. Much of the progress is attributed to education. As a result crime, anarchy, intolerance, ethnicity is very low in these countries. People are aware of their rights and are law-abiding citizens. Higher education has contributed a lot in shaping these societies. Undue exploitation by the Governments and by the public is minimal. Violence is negligible. Europe and USA are much better off so far as general law and order, crime rate, corruption, ethnicity and terrorism are concerned. Prime reason is education; access to basic and higher education is much easier and cheaper in these developed nations; as a result general public is saner, wiser and reasonable in their actions and attitudes. Public cannot be fooled or hoodwinked by the Governments. Public protests are peaceful and effective. An ordinary voter in USA or Europe is much more educated, aware and mature as compared to a voter in India who could be a selling commodity. In India ignorant and uneducated are still the real voters as they are larger in number and their loyalties could be bent anyway, compared to educated voters who are fewer in number and would like to see and discuss objectives of political parties.

The Role of Education in Peace building

Today world is encountering threat to human security despite having made technological advancement, and that this can be dealt with peace-building through education. Of course it is a time-taking process but probably a sound way of cultivating 'Wisdom' and harvesting 'Peace'. It is also pertinent to mention that education is only one input to peace-building processes; others may be political, social, economic, cultural and/or psychological. However, education is certainly at the center point. It has far reaching impact on every aspect of human life. Minds have to be transformed, ideologies need to be clarified and peace has to be inculcated.

Globalisation and Economic warfare owe, largely, to the technological advancement. The socio-political dynamics of modern world are controlled by technological imperatives. The development, sustenance, implementation and continual improvement in technology rely heavily on higher education. However, higher education in isolation from industry may not bring about desired results, especially in technological progress. USA and Western European countries have not only successfully experimented this but also showed positive results. This linkage between industry and academia is also imperative for socio-economic development. Post World War-II era has witnessed sharp rise in higher education, especially in USA and Europe. Asia and Pacific region though has followed the suit but it is yet to bloom. These countries are pursuing to build knowledge-based economies by expanding their higher education. Issues like knowledge production, research policy and research management have come to the lime light. Internationalisation and integration of higher education has been a parallel development during the later half of the twentieth century. It can be said that phenomenon of globalisation has also engulfed the higher education. International accreditations, linkages between universities, split degree programmes and collaborations broken through the geographical frontiers. The impact has also been felt in developing countries. Need for the development of knowledge-based economies has gained significant importance in today's world. Socio-political development is finding its roots in knowledge-based economies. Although societies are adapting fast to the technological developments, yet the issues like security and safety of human life and property have cropped up in the last seven years or so. The post 9/11 era has been more volatile compared to the periods of World Wars in very specific ways.

Education may be the starting point in bringing about much elusive peace, but one has to remember that it is a time-taking process. Significance of higher education: 'Socrates believes that goodness and truth, positive essences and pure ethical and moral instincts are placed there divinely in the soul. However, they are not brought to consciousness unless they are awakened or learned. Therefore, consensus on the important things in life is just below the surface waiting to be acknowledged. It is the destiny of mankind to seek out virtue such as courage and self-control, or propriety over the desires of ambitions or emotions that cloud the quest for truth. The concept of ignorance is what stands in the way of consensus, and that once one realises that he does not know, a change in any disagreement can occur.' [www.san.beck.org]

Significance of Higher Education

Significance of higher education is further highlighted in one of the UNESCO's resolutions which states: 'In our complex and rapidly changing global society, higher education must contribute to the building of peace founded on a process of development and predicated on equity, justice, solidarity and liberty. To attain this objective, access on the basis of merit, the renovation of systems and institutions, and service to society, including closer links to the world of work, must be the basis of renewal and renovation in this level of education. This requires that higher education enjoy autonomy and freedom exercised with responsibility.' [UNESCO (1998) "World Conference on Higher Education"] Although lack of education is not the only contributing factor to this volatile situation yet its importance cannot be denied. Areas which are termed as hub of 'terrorist' activity have least literacy rate and women are almost illiterate. 'Education is a significant social investment in preventing a recurrence of conflict. Over the past forty years around half of all civil wars have resulted from post-conflict relapses, 40 per cent of them within the first decade. Investing in education in post-conflict situations pays high dividends, as it gives people confidence in peace by signalling that that the benefits are going to be long-term and widespread.

It is generally observed that countries having low levels of education development face more conflict situations compared to those with high level of education. Education inculcates wisdom, sanity, rationality, patience, discipline, integrity, harmony and reconciliation within individuals, families, communities, societies and the world. Education has paid high dividends in western countries and USA. The technological advancement and high economic growth and comparatively better peace situation can be attributed to education. Academia has strong links with industry. Research and Development in American universities is driven by the industry and industry also reaps the fruits of university research. Democracy has also flourished in these societies and general public feels empowered. Where education brings wisdom and sanity, it also paves way for decent living; an illiterate person can easily be attracted to crime just for earning livelihood. As mentioned earlier education is one of the tools to bring in peace and harmony in society. It also helps establish democracy which actually empowers people. *'The true development of human beings involves much more than mere economic growth. At its heart there must be a sense of empowerment and inner fulfillment. This alone will ensure that human and cultural values remain paramount in a world where political leadership is often synonymous with tyranny and the rule of narrow elite. People's participation in social transformation is the central issue of our time. This can only be achieved through the establishment of societies, which place human worth above power, and liberation above control. In this paradigm development requires democracy, the genuine empowerment of the people.'* [AUNG, San Suu Kyi, (1994), November]

Higher Education and Peace-building: Way Forward

'Since wars begin in the minds of men, it is in the minds of men that the defenses of peace must be constructed.' [UNESCO CONSTITUTION] It is imperative to provide physical security besides good governance and socioeconomic foundations for long-term peace. Basically human being, regardless of religion or set of beliefs, is peace-loving. Peace is, however, disturbed due to conflicts arising out of differences between individuals, families, societies and countries. A sound strategy should be in place to ascertain the nature of conflict, its causes, how it could be managed and resolved and how it could be averted in future. Such a strategy could be formulated with the help of intellectuals in academia, governance, practitioners and contemporary opinion leaders. Universities could provide the platform where issues could be debated upon, causes of conflicts could be analysed and strategies could be formulated

to resolve or manage the conflicts. It, however, requires an atmosphere which is conducive enough to reap positive results; otherwise such exercises could only be theoretical and probably fruitless. This is one way where universities can play their role but if this is done voluntarily, and it may prove to be beneficial in post-conflict scenario or in emergency situation. Instead of having a reactive approach, pro-active measures should be taken *i.e.* prevention prior to the outbreak of conflict or violence. Conflict could be dealt with in three stages: Prevention prior to conflict or violence Managing conflict during conflict; and Post-conflict peace-building process. In order to formulate sound strategies to ensure all of the above measures, there is a need to have peace education or education for peace built in the curriculum of formal studies at higher education level or even at lower levels of education. But then there is also a need of teachers who are trained enough to impart such education. 'It is important in post-conflict contexts to pay special attention to the curriculum and, in particular, to prioritise peace education programmes so that distrust and hatred between groups is overcome and citizens are equipped with the tools for peaceful conflict resolution.

Furthermore, higher education institutions need to assess their relationship with wider society and the world, so that they could promote rights of poor and marginalised sectors in the context of justice, intercultural respect, sustainable development, human security and global solidarity. The recommendations include training of educators/teachers whereby they could be able to impart peace education and on top of it act as role models to impress upon effectively what they are advocating. [Symposium Recommendations (2005) "International Symposium" Griffith University, Australia, August.] It has also been discussed internationally that so far curriculum has been functional which helps get jobs and good earnings, rather than developing ethical character and nurturing seeds of peace and compassion within all human beings. Educational programmes should actively help develop values and promote ethical formation among learners that reject corruption and the abuse of power that aggravates the inequitable distribution of basic needs and resources among all members of societies and the world.

Conclusion

After having established that higher education can be the best tool to control, manage and resolve conflicts; how could it be done effectively and efficiently comes next. As mentioned earlier curriculum needs to be blended with ethical values based on culture of peace and harmony. Teachers need to be trained to impart such education. Universities need to reach out societies surrounding them to get the real picture of state of human beings, especially the poor and marginalised. The way this 'war on terror' is being fought, possibility of peace and reconciliation seems remote. Where it is the responsibility of Governments to initiate dialogue amongst warring factions, higher education institutions can play a pivotal role. Peace education or education for peace should be made part of the formal education.

As said earlier, this could be done in a disciplined manner through educational institutions. Such education would not only promote peace and reconciliation but would also strengthen national institutions. Technical and vocational education and training, especially for those who are from remote areas would pave way for decent jobs and inclination to crime, if any, could be averted. This would not only bring prosperity amongst these deprived classes but would have positive impact on national economy. Sense of deprivation and being left out in the cold are some factors which nourish and breed resentment and sometimes hatred. 'Have-nots' of society see no point in living a miserable life; it is then that they become vulnerable to brain-washing and eventually are persuaded to take arms. Education in the right perspective and provision of jobs can work wonders. Idea is to empower people to build institutions and thus strengthen the nation. Lessons of humanity and morality should be learnt by all.

Wisdom and sanity through education should not be used to condemn and criticise only rather find solutions to problems.

REFERENCES

- AUNG, San Suu Kyi, (1994), November.
- CHAUVET and COLLIER (2007).
- CHOMSKY, Noam (2003) "Wars of Terror" *New Political Science*, March.
- MINOW (2002).
- Symposium Recommendations (2005) "International Symposium" Griffith University, Australia, August.
- UNESCO (1998) "World Conference on Higher Education".
- UNESCO (2008) "Global Monitoring Report".
- UNESCO Constitution.
- www.san.beck.org.

CHAPTER 24

Teacher Preparation for Peace Education

*Dr. Lokanath Mishra

Introduction

Peace is possible for life at all stages and it is up to man to choose his destiny or to suffer from the horrors of war. 'Today mankind is at the cross road were he has to choose with courage, determination and imagination—(*Federico major*). The 21st country is characterised by events of most unprecedented nature and emergency of information era which has brought humankind into the age of universal communication by abolishing distance, with easy access to most sophisticated information technology today the most accurate up to date information can be made available to any one anywhere in the world within a mouse click. The case with which money and information can now cross frontiers has facilitated illegal trade of drugs, arms, nuclear armaments and even human beings as well as encouraging a criminal network.

Violence is emerging in an unprecedented manner in human society. Lookers at the world today any sensible person facts disheartened and even horrified to see the kind of violent acts being committed by man against man and nature. It is sad to realise that we live in the era of unprecedented violence in the forms of terrorism, war, crimes, injustice and apprehension and exploitation amidst a seemingly outward development enjoyed by a fact. The majority of mankind lives in stark poverty struggling for bare survival. The saddest

* Principal, Vivek Colleve, Bijnor (U.P.)

part of the research is that this state of disorder and confusion in the society is affecting the children's innocent minds, children naturally absorb the sprit of violence in the atmosphere and will soon grow to be the next generation of perpetual of violence. Therefore the need to nurture peace in the hearts of children has arisen as urgent issues.

Now-a-days subjected centered and examination-oriented learning at school, the purpose and the beauty of the whole education seems to have lost. The joy of learning is taken away from children. They are trained to cape with rate of the society.

Today school, college and university is no more a place of leisure or of peace. Today teachers of various institute complain about increasing disciplinary problems in the institutions. The public criticises the youth whom we produce at schools as insensitive to the problems of society, selfish, narrow-minded, lacking in intellectual depth and susceptible to the violent and corrupt. Social pressures – R.D Laing (1978) puts it this way:

> *"A child born today in the U.K stands a ten times greater chance of being admitted to a mental hospital than a university. We are driving mad our children more effectively than we are genuinely educating them".*

Under the present predicament there is a growing realisation in the world of education today that children should be educated in the art of peaceful living. As a result, more and more peace concepts, attitudes, values and behavioural skills are being integrated into school curricula in many countries. There is also renewed interest to develop peace-related disciplines such as value education, moral education, global education., etc. In the past we seemed to have assumed that the more knowledge people have the better they are. Accordingly we stressed cognitive learning in schools at the cost of developing children's emotional, social, moral and humanistic aspects. The consequence of such imbalance learning is evident today in the forms of youth unrest with their anti-social attitudes and behavioural problems.

This teacher's guide introduces an educational approach, by the name of Peace. Education which can undo certain basic negative effects discussed above. It attempts to do so by way of bringing in core human values essential for peaceful and health living. It provides a wide range of interesting active methods of teaching and learning to deliver the curriculum effectively alongside with a focus on core human values. This approach has been tried out by educationists and teachers in different countries and found effective. For instance, a student in such a school in Sri Lanka, writes; 'This programme strongly influenced my mind· I was enlightened on how to lead a contented life, to live a conflict-free life in school, to build up mutual co-operation and make our future happy and successful and most of all, to live as a peaceful citizen' (National Institute of Education (2000) Bulletin on Education for Conflict Resolution Programme).

A teacher who had received a short course training on peace education said a the end 'I have never received such a wonderful experience and knowledge in my teaching career I have become a changed person with good attitudes. This is indeed a useful programme which could bring about peace and harmony to our country' (Ibid).

Robin Montz, another teacher, who tried out such an approach in America writes : 'School started, and I began to weave into our curriculum some of the effective exercises I had experienced or read about. And I saw some "miraculous" things begin to take place. I saw students form meaningful relationships in the classroom. I saw students who had been bored and in trouble much of the time begin to learn. I saw myself and my own role as teacher begin to change and to take on new meanings. And I saw genuine relationships begin to develop between myself and my students, not so much as teacher and pupil but as people human beings meeting each other and learning from each other.

The Real Meaning of Peace

There once was a king who offered a prize to the artist who would paint the best picture of peace. Many artists tried. The king looked at all the pictures. But there were only two he really liked, and he had to choose between them.

One picture was of a calm lake. The lake was a perfect mirror for peaceful towering mountains all around it. Overhead was a blue sky with fluffy white clouds. All who saw this picture thought that it was a perfect picture of peace.

The other picture had mountains, too. But these were rugged and bare. Above was an angry sky, from which rain fell and in which lightning played. Down the side of the mountain tumbled a foaming waterfall. This did not look peaceful at all.

But when the king looked closely, he saw behind the waterfall a tiny bush growing in a crack in the rock. In the bush a mother bird had built her nest. There, in the midst of the rush of angry water, sat the mother bird on her nest—in perfect peace.

Which picture do you think won the prize? The king chose the second picture. Do you know why?

"Because," explained the king, "peace does not mean to be in a place where there is no noise, trouble, or hard work. Peace means to be in the midst of all *those things and still be calm in your heart. That is the real meaning of peace."* 'Peace' is a word that is uttered almost as frequently as 'truth,' 'beauty,' and 'love.' It may be just as elusive to define as these other virtues. Common synonyms for 'peace' include 'amity,' 'friendship,' 'harmony,' 'concord,' 'tranquility,' 'repose,' 'quiescence,' 'truce,' 'pacification,' and 'neutrality.' Likewise, the peacemaker is the pacifier, mediator, intermediary, and intercessor. While some of these descriptions are appropriate, they are still quite limited in describing both the nature of peace and the role of the peacemaker. Any attempt to articulate the nature of peace and peacemaking, therefore, must address those conditions which are favorable to their emergence. Freedom, human rights, and justice are among such prerequisites. Also included are proactive strategies such as conflict resolution, non-violent action, community building, and democratisation of authority.

Peace education involves the use of teaching tools designed to bring about a more peaceful society. Topics addressed may include philosophical and practical issues such as *human rights,* conflict management, international relations, *development,* and the *environment.* Peace education has also been used in order to facilitate gender equality. These programmes focus on income, health, and *power disparities* between men and women as well as examining the traditions and structures that have led to the disadvantaged position of women. At its core, peace education emphasises *empowerment* and *non-violence* and involves building a *democratic* community, teaching cooperation, developing moral sensitivity, promoting self-esteem, and stimulating critical thinking.

A number of key components of an effective peace education programme have been identified—

- *First,* programmes should be compulsory and integrated to facilitate interaction with those from other groups in order to build positive relationships.
- *Second,* there needs to be a recognition that opponents will come to the programme with incompatible agendas and perceptions, but this may be turned into an opportunity.
- *Third* emphasis is on fostering *civic values.* It appears that generating scenarios in which different groups come into contact in a *safe setting* can be beneficial in developing more cooperative relations. Following Allport's contact hypothesis, if conditions are optimal, namely *working collaboratively* to achieve common goals, intergroup contact may promote altered intergroup attitudes. *Trust* and cooperative relations may be built amongst opponents through such things a *dialogue,*

sharing personal experiences, and collaborating on projects for mutual benefit Competitive situations should be avoided and interaction needs to go beyond superficial exchanges.

- *Fourth,* a sense of shared goals and common fate needs to be established as well as an acceptance that the fruits will be justly distributed in order to ultimately build a common *identity*. Developing strong and empathic interpersonal *relationships* appears to be important in appreciating the viewpoint of the other.
- *Fifth,* many advocate the constructive controversy procedure, which helps develop skills to make difficult decisions and to engage in political discourse. However, forcing programme participants to adopt their opponent's viewpoint, particularly while the conflict is ongoing, will likely be viewed as threatening. Drawing lessons from other conflicts, however, appears to be more effective.
- A *sixth* key component is teaching *integrative negotiation* and peer *mediation* as a means of constructively resolving conflicts.
- *Seventh,* peace education requires continued reinforcement to withstand the forces of division and time. This supports research that suggests while workshops are effective in changing hearts and minds, they typically provide meager support for changing behaviour particularly once one is back in one's own group.
- Peace education is relevant for a range of *conflict stages* from *latent hostility* to the height of violent conflict to *peace building* efforts. For those in danger of falling into conflict, *dialogue* may generate inter group understanding in order to *hinder conflict escalation*. It may also help expose the use of education, particularly of history, in fomenting instability and *distrust*. For those in the midst of conflict, peace education may sow

> the seeds of understanding and provide nonviolent tools where violence is the accepted norm. For those who are emerging from conflict, peace education presents an opportunity to confront the historical myths that often contribute to conflict. Transitional periods often also present opportunities to reform education.

The international role in peace education is also expanding. There is a recognition that education has been used politically and, unless challenged, the persistence of divergent views of history can be a source of latent conflict. Aid agencies are interested in providing peace education to school-aged *refugees* who may be displaced by conflict or natural disaster which may itself sow the seeds of conflict. Much attention has also focussed on *civic education* on the assumption that buying into democratic values will reduce destructive conflict.

Components of Peaceful Society

Literature on non-violence has a suggested that the concept of non-violence has at least eight components—Peace, Equality, Fearlessness, Humility, Love, Self control, Truth and Tolerance. Off course these components are not exclusive of each other and peace appears to be the salient attribute of non-violence. However peace cannot be achieved if oppression and exploitation of man by man continues. Through a healthy and learning environment in schools that encourages tolerance, gender equity, cooperative group work, broadening of social imagination and skills of reserving conflicts, a culture of peace may be developed among children. The role of schools, therefore needs to be redefined from institutions involve in social reproduction, replication, to potential sites for negotiating cultures of peace and harmony. Schools in the recent passed have ceased to inculcate long-term goals of human values and moral principles in the quest for producing more and more literature man power who can be employed as skilled or semi-skilled work force in various walks of life. Mahatma Gandhi had once said "whatever education we give to children it should be constructive and creative ... the ancient aphorism education is that which liberates is as a true today as it was before". Education has been considered as an indispensable asset in the attempt to attain the ideas of peace, freedom and social justice.

Definition of Peace Education

Peace education is more effective and meaningful when it is adopted according to the social and cultural context and the needs of a country. It should be enriched by its cultural and spiritual values together with the universal human values. It should also be globally relevant. Peace education could defined in many ways. There is no universally accepted definition as such. Here are some good definitions from peace literature.

"A Peace education is an attempt to respond to problems of conflict and violence on scales ranging from the global and national to the local and personal. It is about exploring ways of creating more just and sustainable futures."

—R.D Laing (1978)

In the words of *Fran Schmidt and Alice Friedman (1988) :* "Peace education is holistic. It embraces the physical, emotional, intellectual and social growth of children within a framework deeply rooted in traditional human values. It is based on philosophy that teaches love, compassion, trust, fairness, co-operation and reverence for the human family and all life on our beautiful planet.

Peace education is skill building. It empowers children to join creative and non-destructive ways to settle conflict and to live in harmony with themselves, others and their world ... Peace building is the task of every human being and the challenge of the human family."

—Fran Schmidt and Alice Friedman (1988)

The basic concepts embedded in the above definitions are that peace education is a remedial measure to protect children from falling into the ways of violence in society. It aims at the total development of the child. It tries to inculcate higher human and social values in the mind of the child. In essence it attempts to develop a set of behavioural skills necessary for peaceful living and peace building from which the whole of humanity will benefit.

In fact two out of the four pillars of education suggested by the *Dolor Report* namely learning to live together and learning to be are related to peaceful living. Namely such efforts as peace education is not always necessary. What matters is integrating peaceful attitudes, values and skills into the teaching and learning process in school and makes it a part of the total curriculum. Certain countries and institutes have it in the form of subjects such as Values Education, (Malaysia and Philippines), Citizenship Education (U.S.A). Education for Mutual Understanding (Ireland) and Developmental Education (UNICEF). Apart from such subject names it can be integrated into the formal curriculum and co-curriculum of schools. Through applying peace education and creating a peace culture, it has been observed that schools can have the following benefits (as reported by teachers and principals who have used the peace approach in their schools in Sri Lanka. Source Education for Conflict Resolution Project. National Institute of Education. Sri Lanka).

Models of Peace Education

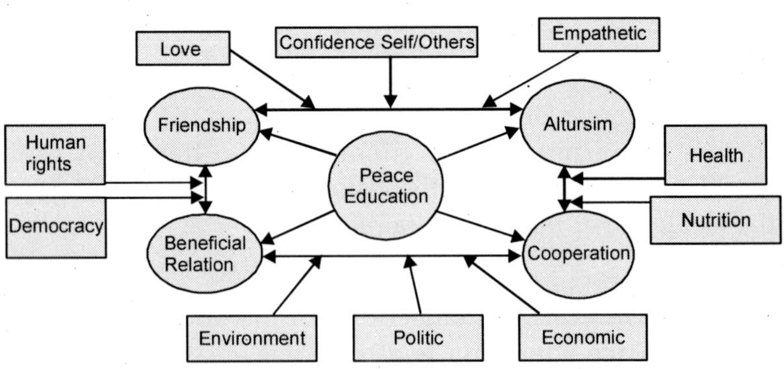

Branches of Peace Education

Peace Education is a broader discipline, Disarmament Education, Human Right Education, Environmental Education, Education for non-violence, Education for international understanding and Global Education are the branches of peace education.

Development of Peace Education

There are several universities in Europe and America, and also in some parts of Asia, where separate peace research institute and centers have been established. However peace education has a long history. IN 1919, the peace association of Swedish school was founded. Several teachers many of them women were engaged in peace movement. Propagating for the inclusion of elements of peace ideas in school education. In 1920s and 1930s the men concerned of the teachers involved was to support the league of national and to counteract tendencies of fascism and nazism by intensified instruction in democracy. In Australia, the international peoples college at Helsingor was founded in 1921 by Peter Manniche as an experiment in peace education "A miniature league of Nation". In India peace studies having introduced in the discipline of Gandhian studies. Besides this, Gujurat Vidyapitha and Vishwa Bharati University also provided M.A. and Ph.D. level course and studies in peace and non-violence. J.N.U., New-Delhi had created Rajiv Gandhi Chair for studies in Peace. The National council of education Research and Training (NCERT) and University Grants Commission (UGC) are working for the inclusion of human rights education at the school and higher level respectively.

In tracing the recent development of peace education, we begin to see that in the past it had been an integral part of education at all times and in all cultures. Every culture regards peace as a noble ideal to attain. However with the advent of Western secularism at the beginning of the 20th century through the guise of a positive, its scientific outlook to education, moral and human values including peace were slowly discouraged away from school curricula. Under the ideal of value free positivist and reduction knowledge, the whole education was viewed narrowly as teaching facts of various subjects.

However in spite of such materialistic views, the thinking of such humanists like Rousseau, Henry Thoreau, Tolstoy and Maria Montessori kept the sense of education alive. With the witness of the horrors of the First and Second World Wars there was–a reawakening to the need of developing the humanistic side of education at least among a few educationists. In this context Maria Montessori's loud and tireless reiteration on the need for educating for peace should be mentioned here with respect and appreciation. At the beginning of the 21st century today we are only rediscovering her vision of peace education which she tried to tell the world in the 1930s. For instance she said in one of her public talks :

Those who want war prepare young people for war; but those, who want peace have neglected young children and adolescents so that they are unable to organise them for peace.

Her vision of education provides a meaningful sound basis for peace education. She looked at education as a tool of rebuilding World Peace. To her peace is the guiding pencil of man and nature. Any attempt to deviate from the principle will only bring about destruction. However it has never been investigated seriously so far. Peace should be studied as a science identifying its direct and indirect complex factors. She also observed that man had neglected to realise his inner sources of energies. Mastery over the external world alone is inadequate in bringing about a peaceful world. Peace is not only cessation of war. There are many positive qualities in peace. She said that violence destroys the moral perception inherited in man. She described her time as an era of insidious madness, which demanded man to return to reason immediately. Like Rousseau. She believed that man is intrinsically pure by nature. The child's natural innocence has to be preserved from being sidetracked or spoilt by society. To her the child is the promise of mankind. The child 's has real vision a bright little flame of enlightenment that brings us a gift. Constructive education for peace must aim to reform humanity so as to permit the inner development of human personality and develop a more conscious vision of the mission of mankind and the present conditions of social life. What we need today is an education that is capable of saving mankind from the present predicament. Such an education involves the spiritual development of man and the enhancement of his value as an individual and prepares the young people to understand the time in which they live. At school we must construct an environment in which children can be actively engaged in learning.

Curricular Issues in Peace Education

All education programmes at developing children through the provision and facilitation of certain learning experiences. Tanner and Tanner 1975 define curriculum as the planned and guided learning experiences and intended learning out comes, formulated through the systematic reconstruction of knowledge and experiences under the auspices of the schools for the learners continuous and willful growth in personal and social competency.

In this manner the teacher educator of peace education have to develop clear vision for an effective programme. This model consist of 10 basic themes which can accommodate many peace values and concept most meaningful in the present global context. Here we discussed Mishra's Thematic Model of peace education.

To begin with *Think Positive,* the theme aims at developing a positive mindset in children. Positive thinking is the first characteristic of a peaceful person. It involves building a positive self-concept in oneself. Having a positive outlook helps the child to not only value himself but also to value life in all forms. It also build attitudes towards accepting others with respect. And appreciating them honestly. This is a self-empowering concept that helps children to develop positive attitude towards themselves as individuals and their country and humanity.

Be Compassionate and Do No Harm tries to inculcate empathetic qualities such as, kindness, friendliness and so on. These qualities are primarily important to respond to the violence in society.

Discover Inner Peace as a theme is concerned with resolution of one's own psychological conflicts and problems and discovering the peace of mind. Under this theme ways of understanding self and the process of thought, controlling emotions such as anger, art of soothing the mind could be discussed. It also addresses children's spiritual needs and provides experiences of inner peace. Learning to Live Together is so important today in a world where there is so much polarization of human beings on the increase. Children need to learn to work harmoniously in groups with others. The theme can accommodate such subtopics as sharing, mutual help, trust building, taking group responsibility, leading and following. Learning co-operation reduces egoistic competitive tendencies in children.

The next theme *Respect Human Dignity* is based on the concepts of Human Rights, Duties and Justice, It attempts to develop a consciousness that recognises, respects one's own and others rights.

The concept in the theme *Be Your True Self,* means the strength of the character to be honest and direct in expressing one's needs, feelings and thoughts without letting others down. The skills in such behaviour are necessary for resolving conflicts and effective social interaction.

Developing Critical Thinking is an essential intellectual skill helpful to problem solving. It also includes decision-making skills. Critical thinking on the part of the citizens is a necessary feature of a democratic society. It involves analysis, syntheses, looking at the other sides of an issue, searching for alternatives and logical thinking. Resolve Conflict Non-violently encompasses such skills necessary for conflict resolution as conflict analyses, negotiation, active listening, mediation, creative problem–solving and alternative solution seeking. It is a basic component of peace education.

Build Peace in Community as a theme provides an opportunity for children to be exposed to social realities and understand peoples problems and work with them. School can organise various peace-building projects in the community. Attitudes towards the Swing for the Planet is a global educational need not only for children but for the masses as well. The health of the planet has direct and immediate influence on the destiny of mankind. Under this theme several interesting activities, projects and assignments could be organised in school. The above thematic framework provides a comprehensive content area for peace education. The themes could be developed from grade to grade in depth and width spirally. For instance the first theme, *i.e.* positive thinking could be developed in the following manner:

Understanding myself
Self – esteem and ways of developing it
Meaning of positive thinking
Effect of negative thoughts
Philosophy and psychology of positive thinking
Positive thinking in our culture and religion.

The above model is simple and easy for curriculum developers to use as a guide to select peace concepts. Having such a model helps teachers to identify peace concepts in the curriculum. Through in-service training teachers can be equipped evidence to show that it improves to quality of teaching and learning, discipline and helps emotional development in children.

Framework for Peace Education

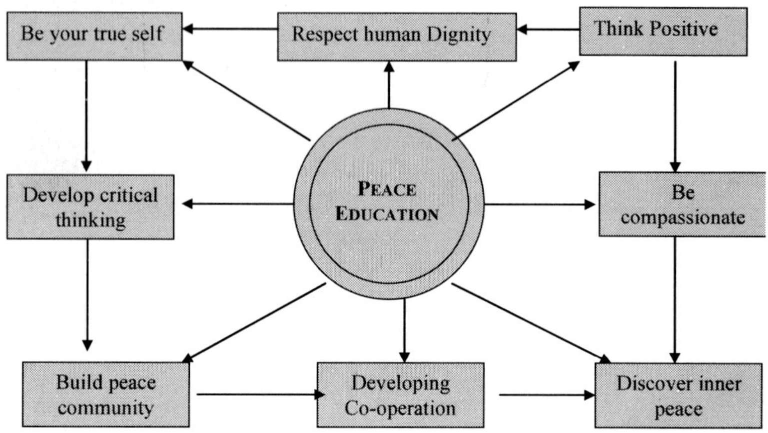

Mishra's Thematic Framework of Peace Education)

Teacher Education For Promoting Peace Education

Teacher Education plays a vital role in sensitising teaches about peace education programme, It also aims at enabling teachers to initiate Peace Education Programme with commitment to guide the direction of student inquiry to promote learns participation in exploring peace to prefer peace in solving complex problems to imbibe and reflect Peace in day-to-day life. The teachers involvement in designing constructivist learning environment is encouraged with a view to helping learners in independent thinking, reflection of ideas and crucial issues, exploring peace, collaboration efforts in solving problems and interpretation of experiences which may contribute to development of peace.

The teacher education for peace project which is of several years durations is being implemented in the Asia-Pacific region by the Institute of Internal Education, the Flinders University, Alelaide in close collaboration with UNESCO's Asia-Pacific Center of Education. Innovation for Development (ACEID) Bangkok and National Institute of Education Research (NIER) of Japan. The teacher education for peace is based on eight assumptions :

1. Development of cross cultural understanding and tolerance is an essential component of peace building process.
2. School is a logical starting place for this kind of peace building.
3. Teachers can play a constructive role in this process only if they themselves are free from racial intolerance and prejudice.
4. Cross-cultural understanding develops only when individuals have a firm sense of their own cultural identity.
5. Pre-service and in-service education of teachers are the most effective ways of developing and enhancing cultural identity, tolerance and cross cultural understanding.
6. Local processes of knowledge analysis and acquisition offer opportunities to develop more holistic, inter-dependent and harmonious approaches to teaching and learning.
7. The project therefore should focus on teacher education institutions targeting both teacher educator and the programme they offer, and
8. The project should address the process of teaching and learning as much as the content to maximise its impact. It should therefore target the entire teacher education curriculum not just particular courses or units.

Developed on these eight assumptions the 'Teacher Education for Peace Project' aims at to promote teaching of peace, tolerance and international understanding through.

- Strengthening the cultural identity of teacher educators and teacher trainees
- Enhancing the cultural identity of teacher educators and teacher trainees.

- Enabling teacher trainees on completion of their studies to facilitate the development of cultural identity and develop such understanding and tolerance among the students they teach.

Proposed Course Content of Teacher Education for Peace Education

Unit –1 Meaning, Nature and Definition of Peace, Types of Peace, Relationship between Non-violence and Peace and Peace education.

Unit –2 Concept of Peace Education, Need and Significance of Peace Education at School stage with special emphasis on Non-violence sociological Religions and Philosophical dimension of peace education.

Unit –3 Branches of peace education, Aims of peace Education, Gandian thoughts on Non-violence Moral Development, R.J. Having hurts their character development, Human Rights and responsibilities, tolerance, International co-operation, sustainable development, Human dignity, El. Zahar model for peace education, Educational thoughts of Rosseu, Henry Thoreaue, Tolstoy and Meria Montessori.

Unit-4 Peace Education Curriculum. Peace Development as a component of hidden curriculum, Development of peace associated with subject curriculum. Objectives and organisation of curriculum for peace education and International understanding.

Unit –5 Peace education strategic, *via-a–vis* construction, Different methods and approved of peace education Development, self study, Yoga and Meditation peace analysis model, community participation Role play, simulation and Gaming, visit to Peace Education Institutes.

Unit-6 Assessment and Evaluation of peace Development of learners. Continuous and comprehensive evaluator of peace education in the context of total curriculum, Monitoring of peace education activities Internal Evaluation of Projects, group activities community Intervention Services, Evaluation of connective components. Rating and gradation of peace Development.

Learning Resources for Peace Education of Teachers

Different kinds of learning resources can be made available which accommodate contextual factors. Some of them read as biographic, scriptures, proverbs, hymns, thoughts of great personalities on socio-political system, stories moral dilemmas, institution of experiences on implementation of peace education programmes, project reports on peace education submitted by school/ college students teachers and teacher trainees, recorded personal experience group experiences in dealing with contextual problems intervention strategies on conducting social service environmental education, protection of human rights etc. Such resources need to be explored by trainees through self-initiations at local level institutional level as well as at a wider level. The role of ICT is significant in this context.

Learning Activities

Various kinds of learning activities can be explored and organised in promotion of peace with emphasis on cognitive affective and action dimensions. Some of such activities, which may be organised with involvement of trainees.

- Develop a more humanistic management approach Yoga, Meditation, Prayer, Self study, and Scriptures classical stories.
- Problem solving exercises.
- Peace Discussion/Classification of conflict.
- Improve human relation between, teach-student, teacher–teacher, student–student etc.

- Improve students discipline and moral behaviour.
- Developing creativity both students and teachers.
- Role play, Drama, Poetic recitals dealing with peace conflicts in virtual environment.
- Visit to missionary organisation. Peace Education Institutions and interaction with eminent personality.
- Group project, group discussion, workshops, community service, hospital service, sramadan, blood donation, serving needy literacy activities, cleaning the campus, visit to place of worship of different faith, tolerance, sacrifice etc.

Framework of Evaluation

Self assessment exercises, Peer Evaluation Sessions, Continuous monitoring of learning as well as daily activities, feedback mechanism. Peer/teacher evaluation and internal evaluation of peace education. Practical/Projects needs to be given 60 per cent credit weightage while the remaining 40 per cent weightage may be given to the components of curriculum.

Conclusion

It is the high time to strengthen Peace Education Component in teacher education which can serve two purpose. *First* is to orient teachers on Peace Education *second* is to empower them for development and implementation of Peace Education curriculum at school level. Emphasis on participating and experimental learning can serve the purpose of Peace Education. Which aims at protecting children's minds from being imbued by violence in the society. Peace Education prepares the teachers, as well as students for building a peaceful world by empowering them while necessary knowledge attitudes and skills. It humanises the teachers, teaching and learning and schools. Teacher trying institutions can directly benefit by adopting Peace Education. There is ample evidence to show that it improves the quality of teaching and learning, discipline and helps emotional development of teacher educations as well as students.

REFERENCES

1. *Gaining, J (1996).* Some Basic Assumption of Peace Thinking, Mimco International Peace Research.
2. *Mayer. F (1995).* Peace Education an Innovative Proposal Annual Meeting Research Association San Francisco, CA, 18-23 April.
3. *Montz, R (1998).* Affective Learning Techniques, American Psychological Association, p. 168.
4. *Pandey. S (2000).* Teacher Education for Peace, University News Vol. 38, No. 21, May 22, 2000.
5. *Qamar, Jahan (2002).* Relevance of Educational Ideas of Mahatma Gandhi in 21st Century, Global Peace, Vol. 2, No. 2.
6. *Sahoo P.K. (2005).* Teacher Preparation for Value Education Anweshika NCTE Vol. 2, No. 2.
7. *Yerankar. S.K. (2003).* Peace Education Yojana Vol. 47, No. 9 Sept.
8. *Zahhan. N (1996).* Peace and Peace Education. Paper. presented at International Seminar of Peace Education, Arab Region of the WOSM Cairo—3-9 April, 1996. Egypt.

CHAPTER 25

Human Rights Education for Approaching Peace in Society

*Jitandera Kumar Singh
**Jyoti Singh
***Vishal Agarwal

Peace education is a buzz-word today and number of approaches to 'peace education' has been put forth by leading experts in this field. The approaches are distinguished by their assumptions that peace education is primarily either (*a*) knowledge-based subject that can be directly taught in the school curriculum; (*b*) a set of skills and attitudes that can be explicitly taught or more subtly infused in a variety of educational contexts; or (*c*) some combination of the two.

A. The Knowledge–base Subject Approach

The U.S.-based Consortium on Peace Research, Education and Development emphasises the knowledge component of peace education, defining peace as a "multi-disciplinary academic and moral quest for solutions to the problems of war and injustice with the consequential development of institutions and movements that will contribute to a peace that is based on justice and reconciliation". (1986, COPRED).

B. The Skills and Attitudes Approach

Cremin (1993) places a greater emphasis on skills and attitudes, defining peace education as "a global term applying to all education endeavours and activities which take as their focus

* Research Scholar, Department of Education, Gokul Das Hindu Girls College, Moradabad.
** Research Scholar, Department of Education in S.S.P.G. College, Shajahpur.
*** Research Scholar, Department of Education, C.S.J.M.University, Kanpur

the promotion of a knowledge of peace and of peace-building and which promote, in the learner, attitudes of tolerance and emathy as well as skills in cooperation, conflict avoidance and conflict resolution so that the learners will have the capacity and motivation, individually and collectively, to live in peace with others."

C. Combining Knowledge, Skills and Attitudes

The assumption that peace education must combine knowledge, skills and attitudes is perhaps the dominant one in the field at this time. Reardon (1988) sees peace education as a process that prepares young people for global responsibility; enables them to understand the nature and implications of global interdependence; and helps them to accept responsibility to work for a just, peaceful and viable global community. Central themes for Reardon are stewardship, citizenship and inter-group relationships, with the ultimate aim of addressing both overt and structural violence in society. Classroom practice and the instructional process are also essential for Reardon, who sees cooperative learning as fundamental to peace education (1993).

Hicks (1985) defines peace education as activities that develop the knowledge, skills and attitudes needed to explore concepts of peace, enquire into the obstacles to peace (both in individuals and societies), to resolve conflicts in a just and non-violent way, and to study ways of constructing just and sustainable alternative futures.

But the definition given by UNICEF is very comprehensive, noteworthy and reflective of a number of theorists in this field and of much peace education work that has been carried out in industrialised countries. In UNICEF, peace education refers to the process of promoting the knowledge, skills, attitudes and values needed to bring about behaviour changes that will enable children, youth and adults to prevent conflict and violence, both overt and structural; to resolve conflict peacefully; and to create the conditions conducive to peace, whether at an intrapersonal, interpersonal, intergroup, national or international level.

Peace education has a place in all societies not only in countries undergoing armed conflict or emergencies. Because lasting behaviour change in children and adults only occurs over time, effective peace education is necessarily a long-term process, not a short-term intervention. While often based in schools and other learning environments, peace education should ideally involve the entire community.

Peace education is an integral part of the quality basis education. The 1990 World Declaration on Education for All clearly states that basic learning needs compromise not only essential tools such as literacy and numeracy, but also the knowledge, skills, attitudes and values required to live and work in dignity and to participate in development. It further states that the satisfaction of those needs implies a responsibility to promote social justice, acceptance of differences, and peace. Since 1990, a number of documents related to the field have confirmed this vision of basic education as a process that encompasses the knowledge, skills, attitudes and values needed to live peacefully in an interdependent world. Peace education, then, is best thought of not as a distinct 'subject' in the curriculum, nor as an initiative separate from basic education, but as process to be mainstreamed into all quality educational experiences.

The term 'education' in this context refers to any process—whether in schools, or in informal or non-formal educational contexts—that develops in children or adults the knowledge, skills, attitudes and values leading to behaviour charge.

'Structural violence' is a term that is used to refer to injustices such as poverty, discrimination and unequal access to opportunities, which are at the root of much conflict. The following diagram helps visualise the core relationship between violence and peace:

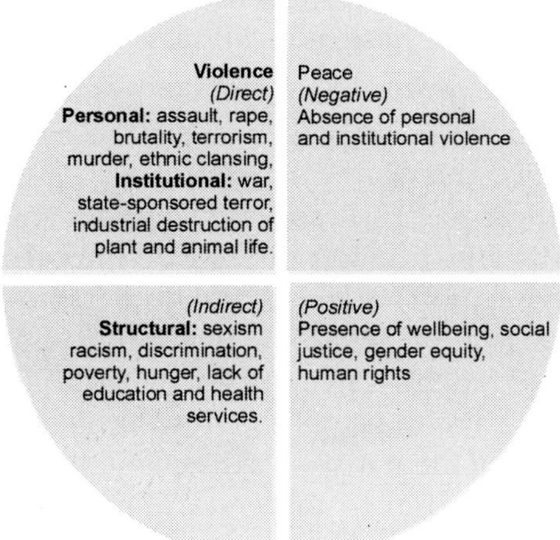

Structural violence is perhaps the most basic obstacle to peace, which by definition can't exist in a society in which fundamental human rights are violated. The Convention on the Rights of the Child, like other major human rights treaties, calls for the elimination of all forms of both overt and structural violence, and the creation of a society based on the principles of justice and peace.

Peace education must address the prevention and resolution of all forms of conflict and violence, whether overt or structural, from the interpersonal level to the societal and global level. It is significant that the framers of the CRC viewed the promotion of understanding, peace and tolerance through education as a fundamental right of all children, not an optional extra-curricular activity.

It is important to note here that a number of educational initiatives have areas of overlap with peace education, and with each other. These include children's rights/human rights education, conflict resolution, multicultural education, world order studies, education for development, gender training, global education, life skills education, landmine awareness, psycho-social rehabilitation, and more recently, environmental education. Each can be thought of as providing another lens or perspective through which to examine how peace can be 'mainstreamed' in the basic education.

Each of these approaches responds to a particular set of problems that have been perceived as the causes of social injustice, conflict and war. Each could also be classified as preventive education "as it seeks to prevent the occurrence of the problems which inspire it." More importantly each is conceived as education for peace, and thus acknowledges that it is intended to be a means to the realisation of a set of social values. Although each relates to peace in the sense of social cohesion and the avoidance of the form of violence to which it responds, none of them displays the elements of prescription and holism so essential to understanding the increasingly conflictual interdependent, planetary social system from which peace is to be wrought from. Each is primarily responsive, particularistic and problem focussed.

Even that strand of peace education that sees itself devoted specifically to learning about 'peace making' has been primarily problem centered, focussing on 'negative peace', the reduction, avoidance and elimination of warfare. As such it has been devoted more to a study directed toward eliminating the causes of war than to creating the conditions of peace, more to negative circumstances of what should not be than to the positive possibilities of what could be. So it is that peace education and peace studies (as the field is known in universities) has been a bit of a 'downer' for all but those students who are either 'positive thinkers' by nature, drawn to social action fields, or simply curious about the study of the 'impossible'.

Human rights education is not only a corrective complement to education for peace but that it is essential to the development of peace making capacities and should be integrated into all forms of peace education. It is through human rights education that learners are provided with the knowledge and opportunities for specific corrective action that can fulfill the prescriptive requirements of education for peace.

Human rights education, fast becoming another global educational phenomenon, appears to be developing along equally varied, but more substantively focused and prescriptive lines. It comprehends some of the same normative goals espoused by peace education, provides a dimension of concrete possibilities for alternatives to current world conditions, and offers a constructive action dimension to complement and apply to all the diverse forms of peace education. Many recent world developments similar to those that have produced the existing approaches to peace education have been articulated as human rights issues and problems, so that some peace educators are adding human rights to the list of approaches. While the addition is certainly necessary, it is far from sufficient and fails to exploit the essential contribution that human rights can make to peace education, namely providing the basis for a prescriptive, holistic yet particularised approach that would make peace education not only more comprehensive, but also far more comprehensible. The actual human experiences that comprise much of human rights education are more readily understood than the theoretical and analytical content of peace education.

The conceptual core of peace education is violence, its control, reduction, and elimination. The conceptual core of human rights education is human dignity, its recognition, fulfillment, and universalisation. Human rights are most readily adaptable to the study of positive peace, the social, political and economic conditions most likely to provide the environment and process for social cohesion and non-violent conflict resolution. Education for peace should be primarily prescriptive, and human rights offers the most appropriate route through which to move from problem to prescription in all the various approaches to peace education. Positive peace, conceptualised by the peace research community to extend the definition of peace beyond the limitation avoidance or absence of war to include issues of justice, poverty, and freedom, is the concept of peace that is the foundational principle of the Universal Declaration of Human Rights. The inextricable relationship between human rights and peace is articulated in the very first sentence of the Preamble to the Declaration, "...... recognition of the inherent dignity and of the equal and inalienable rights of all members of the human family is the foundation of freedom, justice, and peace in the world." Since the core and seminal document for all current standards of human rights, to which all members of the United Nations are assumed to assent, acknowledges this principle, surely education for peace should also do so. Certainly, both peace researchers and activists and human rights scholars and advocates can agree that violence in all its forms is terms an assault on human dignity.

Peace research now recognises several particular forms of violence as the conceptual rubrics under which data are gathered and knowledge derived: physical or behavioural violence including war, and other uses of direct force to destroy or weaken or otherwise harm another nation, group or individual; structural violence that refers to the poverty and deprivation that results from unjust and inequitable social and economic structures. The political violence of oppressive systems that enslave, intimidate, and abuse dissenters as well as the poor, powerless and marginalised; and cultural violence, the devaluing and destruction of particular human identities and ways of life, the violence of racism, sexism, ethnocentrism, colonial ideology, and other forms of moral exclusion that rationalise, aggression, domination, inequity, and oppression. All of these forms of violence can be made most apparent and comprehensible within a human rights framework. Analysing these forms of violence as violations of particular human rights standards provides a constructive alternative to presenting them as abstract concepts as is often the case in peace education. It is for just such reasons that some educators teaching in the fields of conflict resolution, multiculturalism, development education, and world order studies and a limited number of environmental educators are now integrating human rights issues and standards into their curricula as subject matter content, as perspectives for the development of critical capacities, and as areas for experiential learning. To each of these forms of peace education, human rights bring not only the element of concrete experience and observable social conditions but also a much needed normative and prescriptive dimension. We can say that the ensuring of basic right is essential to bringing about peace and without the help of human rights education worthwhile peace education cannot be provided as in fact human rights education and peace education are closely linked activities that complement and support each other.

REFERENCES

1. Andrepoulos, G. J. and Claude, R. P. (1997). "Human Rights Education for the Twenty First Century", University of Pennsylvania Presss: Philadelphia.
2. Consortium on Peace Research, Education and Development (1986). "Report on the Juniata Process", COPERD Peace Chronicle.
3. Cremin, P. (1993). "Promoting Education for Peace", in Cremin, P. (ed.1993), Education for Peace, Educational Studies Association of Ireland and the Irish Peace Institute.
4. Galtung, J. and Ikeda, D. (1995). "Choose Peace", Pluto Press: London.
5. Hicks, D. (1985). "Education for Peace: Issues, Dilemmas and Alternatives", St. Martin's College:Lancaster.
6. Janke, R. and Palmer, K. R. (2005). "Effecting Practices for Infusing Human Rights and Peace Education at the Elementary Level", www.humanrightsandpeacestore.org.
7. Reardon, B. (1993). "Pedagogy as Purpose: Peace Education in the Context of Violence", in Cremin, P. (ed.1993), Education for Peace, Educational Studies Association of Ireland and the Irish Peace Institute.
8. UNICEF (1994). "I Dream of Peace", Harper-Collins: New York.
9. United Nations General Assembly (1989). The Convention on the Right of the Child.

CHAPTER 26

Lets Know Peace Education

*Dinanath Thakur

Peace is generally understood as absence of conflicts and violence in society. Conflicts are pervasive in the society and are held in place due to uneven distribution of socio-economic political power, resources, religious and regional differences. Though conflicts among culturally or politically diverse groups cannot be wished away but management and effective resolution of conflicts lies at the bottom of peace. So that the relationships across these diverse groups may not be broken. Peace education is about empowerment of self so that individuals are equipped with knowledge, competencies and skills of conflicts resolution, such individuals will have self-awareness, values of tolerance and compassion. In order to develop these attitudes, skills and competencies among pupils.

The institutions of family and school have to be oriented to make conscious efforts to promote peace related skills. Development of peace-skills and attitudes would entail inspiring the entire atmosphere of school, personnel and staff to nurture attitudes and competencies for peace. Teachers being central to the entire gamut of all relationships at school, their orientation are most crucial. This programmes was proposed to train teachers to develop their knowledge, attitudes and values relevant for peace .Peace was

Defined as upholding non-violence, human dignity, respect for all, equality, justice prevailing within and-across

* Lecturer, P D M College of Education, Bahadurgadh, Haryana.

societies, and cultures, and nations. etc. Peaces presuppose harmony at all levels within individuals, their families and inter relationships, working environments as well. Peace is a dynamic concept because it is related to human beings who have recurrent needs, which are contextual, full of variety and urgency. Democracy, freedom and equality for all is not enough; social justice and inequalities have to be understood and attend to. Human rights and responsibilities need to be respected. Inner peace or intrapersonal peace is reflected in the behaviour *viz.* physical, social-emotional, health, productivity, and relationships. The outside changes, however, begin from individual, who are pro-peace. What are the characteristics of individuals who could work for upholding peace in the society at different levels? Such questions were posed to the participants. They were encouraged to share their views; many expressed doubts about what can one do in the face of frequent instances of injustice and suffering which are beyond one's control and cause inner disturbances.

Peace means being one with life itself. Having no fear or bitterness. Peace is more than merely sitting still or in silence. Peace therefore, is a state of mind. Tagore rightly said "Where the mind is without fear and the head is held high, into that kingdom of freedom my father Let my country awake"

Peace education may be defined as the process of acquiring the values, the knowledge and developing the attitudes, skills, and behaviours to live in harmony with oneself, with others, and with the natural environment.Peace education is based on a philosophy that teaches non-violence, love, compassion, trust, fairness, cooperation and reverence for the human family and all life on our planet

The concept of peace that is so central to each of the various versions of peace education needs to be analysed diachronically and synchronically, within pre-modern, modern and post-modern arenas. Its philosophical, cultural and political functions may fruitfully be distinctively elaborated in light of (1) a culture that is occupied with the presence of

God; (2) in an arena occupied with the awareness of the bursting of the alternative to this rich presence; (3) in arenas that are free of both God and the killing of God. Gnosis and post-modernism manifest this trend in distinct ways.

Modern peace education and its concept of peace are settled on the act or on the process of the killing of God. Modern philosophies have secularised theology and have much in common with the pre-modern concept of God as it is revealed in central concepts such as 'progress' and 'peace'.

James Page suggests peace education be thought of as "encouraging a commitment to peace as a settled disposition and enhancing the confidence of the individual as an individual agent of peace; as informing the student on the consequences of war and social injustice; as informing the student on the value of peaceful and just social structures and working to uphold or develop such social structures; as encouraging the student to leave the world and to imagine a peaceful future; and as caring for the student and encouraging the student to care for others":

- To show people that violence and war are learned and not an intrinsic part of human nature and that it is possible to resolve conflict peacefully.
- To create a more peaceful world where all of us may become agents for change. Education for Peace gives us the skills that will assist in achieving peaceful societies.
- To correct the limited understanding of peace held by many people that it is the absence, however contrived, of direct violence, of wounding and killing.
- To create a better learning environment where conflict and relationships may be explored.

To build, maintain, and restore relationships at all levels of human interaction.

To develop positive approaches towards dealing with conflicts-from the personal to the international.

To create safe environments, both physically and emotionally, that nurtures each individual.

To create a safe world based on justice and human rights.

To build a sustainable environment and protect it from exploitation and war.

Methods For Imparting Peace Education In Schools

The transaction of the various curricular themes had been planned through the experiential expositions, discussions, demonstrations supported by audio-video inputs, study materials, and handouts for inducing reflection among participants. The participants were actively involved in the process of learning so as to practice peace related attitudes, values and behaviour and also promote the same at the school level. The faculty drawn from within NCERT as well as experts and practitioners led the expositions. Each session was of about one and a half hour to two hours and sometimes even three to four hours also, covering both theoretical expositions and practical activities. Towards the close of each day, time was devoted for consolidation, feedback, self-check and making entries in the reflective journal. Open–sessions and visit to institutions and schools were integral part of the course. Planning future Action Plans and evaluation checklist by the participants also formed part of the concluding session.

REFERENCES

1. Ben-Porath, S. (2003). War and Peace Education. *Journal of Philosophy of Education*. 37 (3), 525-533.
2. Ben-Porath, S. (2006). Citizenship Under Fire – Democratic Education in Times of Conflict. Princeton: Princeton University Press, 57-75.
3. Braidotti, R. (2006). Transpositions – On Nomadic Ethics. Cambridge: Polity Press.
4. Brock-Utre, B. (1983). Educating for Peace: A Feminist Perspective. New York: Pergamon Press.
5. Chetkow-Yanoov, B. (1996). Conflict-resolution Skills can be Thought. *Peabody Journal of Education*, 71, 12-28.
6. Condorcet, A. N. de (1955). *Sketch for a Historical Picture of the Progress of the Human Mind*. Translated by J. Barraclough. London: Weidenfeld and Nicolson.

7. Cooper, M. (2005). Cultivating Wisdom, Harvesting Peace. International Symposium on Peace Education. Griffith University. http://www.griffith.edu.au/centre/mfc/pdf/symposium2005/maxine%20cooper.pdf
8. Ettinger, LB. Coppiesis, Ephemera 5 (X) 2005, pp. 703-713.
9. Ettinger, B. (2008). Compassion and Compassion. http://underfire.eyebeam.org/?q=node/512
10. Freire, P. (1972). *Pedagogy of the Oppressed*. Translated by Ramos-Bergman, M., Augustine, St. (1957). *The City of God Against the Pagans*. London and Cambridge: W. Heinemann.
11. Aduan, S. and Bar-On, D. (Eds.) (2004). Peace Building Under Fire. Beit Jala: Peace Research Institute in the ME.
12. Bar-Tal, D. (2005). Stereotypes and Prejudice in Conflict—Representations of the Arabs in Israeli Jewish Society. Cambridge: Cambridge University Press.
13. Ben-Porath, S. (2003). War and Peace Education. *Journal of Philosophy of Education*. 37 (3), 525-533.
14. Ben-Porath, S. (2006). Citizenship Under Fire – Democratic Education in Times of Conflict. Princeton: Princeton University Press, 57-75.
15. Braidotti, R. (2006). Transpositions – On Nomadic Ethics. Cambridge: Polity Press.
16. Brock-Utre, B. (1983). Educating for Peace: A Feminist Perspective. New York: Pergamon Press.
17. Chetkow-Yanoov, B. (1996). Conflict-resolution Skills can be Thought. *Peabody Journal of Education*, 71, 12-28.
18. Condorcet, A. N. de (1955). *Sketch for a Historical Picture of the Progress of the Human Mind*. Translated by J. Barraclough. London: Weidenfeld and Nicolson.

CHAPTER

27

Education for Attainment of World Peace

*Dr. Manish Chauhan

Worldly life of each of us is unique in thousands of ways yet we all share the common experience of birth and death. It is helpful to realise that though we are exposed to dissimilar aspects of life such as opportunities, challenges and setbacks, however, when it comes to dealing with them we do not find ourselves alone. It is also helpful to understand that we all have varied needs that motivate us to act upon, and over our lifetimes our needs change and so our motivations. What is important here to appreciate is that we, under the effect of ignorance, develop inter conflicting motivations that eventually cause disharmony among us. More awesome is the fact that where on the one hand, people of all nations proclaim not only their readiness but their longing for harmony in the world, simultaneously, on the other hand, uncritical assent is given to the proposition that human beings are incorrigibly selfish and aggressive and thus incapable of erecting a social system that is progressive yet peaceful, dynamic yet harmonious, a system that is giving free space to individual's creativity and initiative and is based on co-operation and reciprocity. It's however inspiring to know that whole human population around the world rely on peace for the survival of humanity. We, as the educators, correctly believe that the peace process must start immediately and from grassroots level itself so that effect of teachings could bring the spontaneous and instant change in the human society.

* Lecturer in Education, SNG PG College, Unnao, U.P.

There are many ways to promote peace in the world but perhaps the first step towards it is the understanding of peace. If the minds of living beings are at peace, the world will be at peace. A change in perception leads to a change in attitude, which leads to a change in behaviour, which further leads to a change in mass behaviour and eventually to the world peace. Process of World Peace necessarily involves phenomenon of internal peace and external peace of a human being, that is, peace within self and peace among human beings.

Internal Peace

Internal peace or peace of mind refers to a state of being mentally and spiritually at peace, with enough knowledge and understanding to keep oneself strong in the face of discord or stress. Peace of mind is generally associated with bliss and happiness. Peace of mind, serenity, and calmness are descriptions of a disposition free from the effects of stress. In some cultures, inner peace is considered a state of consciousness or enlightenment that may be cultivated by various forms of training, such as prayer, and meditation. Many spiritual practices refer to this peace as an experience of knowing oneself. Finding inner peace has often been associated with almost every religion such as Hinduism, Christianity and Buddhism.

Peace and Happiness

"I have come to realise that people are about as happy as they make up their minds to be" —*Abraham Lincoln*

"Happiness is when what you think, what you say, and what you do are in harmony" —*Mahatma Gandhi*

Somehow or other, it seems to make sense that World Peace is inter-related to World Happiness, similar to how inner peace is related to inner happiness. If happiness is truly related to peace then we should be able to turn this new found knowledge into power; the power to make peace a reality in both our lives and the lives of others. Happy people tend to have empathy for those less fortunate than themselves and they tend to volunteer to help others when they can.

Peace and Love

"Love is not primarily a relationship to a specific person; it is an attitude, an orientation of character which determines the relatedness of a person to the world as a whole, not toward one object of love.... If I truly love one person I love all persons, I love the world, I love life. If I can say to somebody else 'I love you,' I must be able to say, 'I love in you everybody, I love through you the world, I love in you also myself."

—*Erich Fromm*

The love that wells within the self, screaming for release, can drive thoughts and actions, and help bring world peace. Affectionate people tend to love life. They tend to love their families. They tend to love their neighbours. They tend to love the world as much they tend to love themselves.

Peace and Enlightenment

It would be inspiring to believe that most people want to be good, honest and helpful. What they just need is the proper love and guidance in order to get back to the side of merit. People need to be reminded that there are much greater rewards for the good than for the evil. They should be taught to realise intuition correctly and to let their conscience be their guide. Having an open mind is also helpful, for the truth can survive only in an open mind; it helps people adjudging good or bad in an absolute manner.

Peace, Mental and Emotional Intelligence

Knowledge comes from learning. Wisdom comes from meditating on knowledge. Real success comes from applying wisdom in our day to day lives. Mental intelligence may have a higher correlation to academic and financial successes but emotional intelligence is more important when seeking the ultimate prizes in life such as happiness, peace, love and joy.

One has to realise that wisdom without compassion is like a body without a soul and therefore he needs both mental and emotional intelligence in order to succeed in life. Recent researches suggest that a balance in mental and emotional intelligence can be achieved through meditation and other stress-reducing techniques. People who learn to handle stress tend to live longer, happier, and healthier lives. With a good degree of preciseness we can state that the mind is capable of healing the body. This is why some people demonstrate pleasant dispositions and others, under the same circumstances, demonstrate negative dispositions.

Peace and Healthy Body

It is worthwhile to know that body is capable of healing the mind. Good health is perquisite for the peace of mind. Recent reports suggest that exercise is as effective at fighting depression as drugs. The balance between work and play has profound effects on one's life. It is yet another good reason to include exercise as part of our daily routine.

External Peace

The fundamental cause of disharmony among people in the world is individual's excessive dissatisfaction and causes of conflicts among civilisations are mainly Poverty, Religion, Race, and Environment. The basic ignorance in this regard is our failure to understand that the life centered on self naturally tends toward the selfishness that eventually poisons us with desire and greed. When they are not fulfilled, we tend to become enraged and hateful. These basic emotional conditions cover the luminous depths of our minds and cut us off from our own intuitive wisdom and compassion; our thoughts and actions then emanate from deluded and superficial views.

Peace and Environmental Misbalances

A variety of environmental problems now affect our entire world. Some of the biggest problems now affecting the world are Acid Rain, Air Pollution, Global Warming, Hazardous

Waste, Ozone Depletion, Smog, Water Pollution, Overpopulation, and Rain Forest Destruction. Human developmental instinct needs to be examined and guided. The specter of outrageous transgression emerges in human beings in the form of greed towards the wealth. The craving to fulfill ourselves with materialistic wealth confront with the law of nature. Materialistic development eventually devours everything that nature gives us to live on without mistreatment. As globalisation continues and the earth's natural processes transform local problems into international issues, the solution necessarily involves proper understanding of people at the every level of socio-economy. A popular whim, that wealthy people are happier, shatters when it's discovered that the level of discontentment is rather higher in those who chase for illusionary materialistic pleasure. An eternal chase of materialistic pleasure is left incontrovertibly unconcluded. At this end we are left with the only choice of handling the issue of pleasure through holistic teachings, we can make ourselves understand the impact of ignorance on our lives.

"When a person labours not for a livelihood but for wealth, that person is a slave. He does not possess wealth; it possesses him". —*Benjamin Franklin.*

Peace and Socio-economic Chasm

Growing socio-economic rift is another great cause of discord among, as well as within, various civilisations. Almost every social evil has its genesis in socio-economic disparities. Widespread poverty, illiteracy and ill-health are some of the reflections of such disparity in our society. If you can find hundreds of million people scarcely earning few rupees in a day so can you find few people earning hundreds of million in a day. Such a society cannot remain stable and happy. Theft, burglary, enmity, murder, kidnapping, drug addiction, prostitution, flesh trading, organ trading are some outcomes we stare at in the retrospect. As we know a balanced society only promises peaceful living we perplexedly wander groping for a peaceful life. Holistic education promises us so much so that we can wake to consciousness and start seeing the world around us with preferred sensitivity. We cannot anymore overlook the issue of growing economic disparity if we sincerely want peace to exist in this world.

Peace and Religious Chasm

It is true that in the auspices of religious teachings every erstwhile human society was tremendously benefited. Most religions teach us that there will be a day of justice and peace in the world, which means, it is achievable. Religion is the organisation of life around the depth dimensions of experience—varied in form, completeness, and clarity in accordance with the environing culture. It is only cultural differences that make it difficult for nations to understand each other.

The problem today we face commonly emerges when the definitions of culture and religion come out of fanatic imaginations, speculations and superstitions. This is the situation when the self has not exposed to ultimate wisdom, has not completely liberated from selfhood and has not attained clear vision still it assumes it has; or an incomplete mind when claims to have ability to describe completeness. It is perhaps the lack of proper understanding about own religion that a section of certain society starts disparaging other's religion. Religious phenomena and religious behaviours can better be defined by avoiding vague intuitive elements or unobservable subjective elements such as vague meanings. We can study and converse together, learn to be fair to the texts, correct longstanding errors, delete the dogmatism that comes from ignorance and fear and endorse that *the ignorant person cannot be pious*. Ignorance of man happens to be greatest enemy of him. A thorough knowledgeable man can fairly deal with the teachings he accomplish from his religion. It is not of even slightest difficulty to realize that religions and cultures have remained a way of peaceful social life. 'My culture and religion offers more peace than yours does' would never create discord and leading to discord would always mean 'I scarcely follow my culture and religion'.

Peace Movement

A peace movement is a social movement that seeks to achieve ideals such as the ending of a particular war (or all wars), minimise inter-human violence in a particular place or type of situation, often linked to the goal of achieving world peace. Means to achieve these ends usually include advocacy of pacifism, non-violent resistance, diplomacy, boycotts, moral purchasing, supporting anti-war political candidates, demonstrations, and National political lobbying groups to create legislation. The political cooperative is an example of an organisation that seeks to merge all peace movement organizations and green organisations which may have some diverse goals, but all of whom have the common goal of peace and humane sustainability.

World Peace Council

The World Peace Council was formed in 1949, replacing the permanent committee of the World Peace Congress, in order to promote peaceful coexistence and nuclear disarmament. It is an anti-imperialist, democratic, independent and non-aligned international movement of mass action. It is an integral part of the world peace movement and acts in cooperation with other international and national movements. As an non-governmental organisation member of the United Nations, the WPC cooperates with United Nations Educational, Scientific and Cultural Organisation (UNESCO), United Nations Conference on Trade and Development (UNCTAD), United Nations Industrial Development Organisation (UNIDO), International Labour Organization (ILO) and other UN specialized agencies, special committees and departments. It also cooperates with the Non-Aligned Movement, the African Union, the League of Arab States and other inter-governmental bodies.

Peace Education

Historically, in various parts of the world, peace education has been referred to as Education for Conflict Resolution, International Understanding, and Human Rights; Global Education; Critical Pedagogy; Education for Liberation and Empowerment; Social Justice Education; Environmental Education; Life Skills Education; Disarmament and Development Education; and more. These various labels illuminate the depth and diversity of the field. Using the term *peace education* helps co-ordinate such global initiatives and unite educators in the common practice of educating for a culture of peace. Through a humanising process of teaching and learning, peace educators facilitate human development. They strive to counteract the dehumanisation of poverty, prejudice, discrimination, rape, violence, and war. Underlying all of this work in the field of peace education are the efforts of committed educators, researchers, activists, and members of global civil society.

Efforts of UN for Peace Education

Peace education by the United Nations has been developed as a means to achieve world peace. It promotes understanding, tolerance and friendship among all nations, racial or religious groups and furthers the activities for the maintenance of peace—*(Article 26, Universal Declaration of Human Rights)*

The Hague Agenda for Peace and Justice for the 21st Century is a significant example of such work. Its appeal is described as "A culture of peace will be achieved when citizens of the world understand global problems, have the skills to resolve conflicts and struggle for justice non-violently, live by international standards of human rights and equity, appreciate cultural diversity, and respect the Earth and each other. Such learning can only be achieved with systematic education for peace." According to the Agenda, their Global Campaign aims to support the United Nations Decade for a

Culture of Peace and Non-violence for the Children of the World and to introduce peace and human rights education into all educational institutions, including medical and law schools. Much of the work of UNESCO is also centered on the promotion of education for peace, human rights, and democracy. The notion of a 'culture of peace' was first elaborated for UNESCO at the International Congress on Peace in the Minds of Men, held at Yamoussoukro, Cote d'Ivoire, in 1989. The Yamoussoukro Declaration called on UNESCO to 'construct a new vision of peace by developing a peace culture based on the universal values of respect for life, liberty, justice, solidarity, tolerance, human rights and equality between women and men' and to promote education and research for a this vision.

Indian Role for Peace Education

From the time immemorial India has been considered across the world the epitome of religious teachings. We uphold Religion as another name for superior conduct and approve the same as the outcome of authentically relevant teachings. Those, who consider universal and scientific values, ideals and traditions to be their religion, who might or might not be religious but are never fanatic, who see God in all humanity and every other living being including plants, and who dedicate their entire life to the service of all creatures and the world and diminishes the sorrow of the world, are considered to be educated in real meaning. Those, who are exposed completely to such education, rise above narrow thinking and love mankind and look upon the whole world as their family and they always keep the feeling of '*Vasudheva Kutumbakam*' in their heart.

From erstwhile Vedas, Buddhism, Jainism, to today's Gandhi, Vivekananda, Tagore, Aurobindo's philosophy almost every one of them elucidated that the fundamental cause of all suffering is the ignorance. The Vedas, the treasure of knowledge and wisdom in the form of *Rigveda, Samveda, Yajurveda,* and *Atharveda,* lay down the importance of transfer of contemporary accumulated human knowledge to next generations to keep them away from much likely ignorance, incontrovertibly proved to be milestone in evolution of human civilisation in present form. Buddha's *Ashtangika Marg* (eight-fold path) containing the principles of Right View, Right Thinking, Right Speech, Right Action, Right Meditation, Right Living, Right Effort, and Right Recollection or Mahavira's *Panchmahavrata* describing *Satya* (truthfulness), *Ahimsa* (non-injury), *Asteya* (non-stealing), *Aparigriha* (non-attachment), and *Brahmcharya* (abstention from materialistic pleasure) all encompass the comprehensive teachings to keep oneself away from worldly sufferings. Whether it was societal reformative teachings through Vedas or individual's enlightenment through Buddhism and Jainism, those teachings ultimately contributed greatly towards erstwhile India's well-being. These teachings and ways to liberate ourselves from sufferings are further described in visionary thoughts of great men in nineteenth and twentieth century. Be it *Viswa Bodh* by Ravindranath Tagore, *Sarvang Yog* Darshan by Aurobindo Gosh, *Adwaita Darshan* by Swami Vivekanand or *Sarvodaya Darshan* by Gandhiji, the attainment of ultimate pleasure through elimination of ignorance happens to be the core substance of guidelines put forth by these visionaries.

Outlook

"Universal brotherhood can be achieved only when there is an equality of opportunity—of opportunity in the social, political and individual life."—*from Bhagat Singh's prison diary*, p. 124

"Without an integrated understanding of life, our individual and collective problems will only deepen and extend. The purpose of education is not to produce mere scholars, technicians and job hunters, but integrated men and women who are free of fear; for only between such human beings can there be enduring peace." —*J. Krishnamurti*

"Modern education is competitive, nationalistic and separative. It has trained the child to regard material values as of major importance, to believe that his nation is also of major importance and superior to other nations and peoples. The general level of world information is high but usually biased, influenced by national prejudices, serving to make us citizens of our nation but not of the world."—*Albert Einstein*

Unprecedented global unification of human knowledge, integration of various socio-economies, and exhaustive exploitation of scientific developments has altogether posed a challenge of regulating the growth of human being in accordance with the sustainability and peace. Collective outcome is downbeat with the environmental threats, unyielding xenophobia, and socio-economical complications. In my opinion a proper solution to all problems pertaining to humanity across the nations in the world generally emanates from the Education. Peace needs to be taught in our schools and in our homes. A new model of holistic education should be adopted. For this a comprehensive compilation of facts leading to discord and suffering should be done. We would be required to design our national policies so as to incorporate the solutions to them. When a line of action is ready we would be needed to define our education policies aiming to respond to national as well as global issues.

Facts About Peace

- Peace is not merely the absence of war and hatred but also the presence of cooperation, compassion and worldwide justice.
- War is a state of hostility between nations or between social, religious and cultural groups within nations characterised by fighting and bloodshed. Wars are often caused by real or perceived injustice, hatred, poverty, and the desire for power. The lack of answerable political institution through which to channel grievances can aggravate the risk of violent

outbursts. Until they become fully consolidated democracies transitional states are at higher risk of violent change.

- Denial of civil and political liberties, the poor level of democracy, and restriction on civil and political rights lead to violent outburst. All of those will eventually lead to disharmony if there are no peaceful alternatives for resolving disputes.
- The distribution of resources along ethnic or identity lines, demographic stresses, and so on, are often precursors of violence.
- Other indicators include economic decline, numerous unemployed young men with no opportunities for the future, high debt burdens, low involvement in international trade. All these factors are associated with a higher risk of state failure.
- It's hard to build democracy on an empty stomach. The countries falling in the bottom half of the Human Development Index are much more likely to experience violent conflict.
- The degradation and depletion of resources can generate tensions in communities. Unequal right on or distribution of natural resources, which is the basic flaw of modern theory of economics, causes all kinds of socio-economic rifts.
- Perhaps the best way to prevent war is Conflict Identification and Prevention; it requires that we eliminate the nature of the hostilities and attempt to create harmony and equality between the various parties. Perceived injustices must be resolved through either negotiation or international laws.

Suggestions for Peace

- We can envision a yearly class on War and Peace which focuses on previous and current conflicts and the reasons for them. If we learn from our mistakes then we can focus on world wide peace efforts which will diminish the need for war. Youth development strategies can help stop our future adults from repeating the mistakes that have led us to war. Our children are the future, teach them right and the future will be all right.

- We must first find Peace within ourselves. By sharing our inner peace with others, peace will spread. By raising our children properly and teaching them to respect and love their neighbours they will learn the joy of peace. The peace process should be a predominantly preventative measure. Peace should likely start as a grassroots movement, thereby creating a "trickle-up" process. Not only can we teach others about peace but also we can compel governments and political leaders to stop advocating war as the main solution to civil and international conflict.
- One nation's problems are problems for all of us. We must learn to see ourselves as one small planet and not be so concerned with our nationality, race or religion. When it comes right down to it we are all human. Think what we could accomplish if we all worked together to create a true world economy. We could end starvation, reduce poverty, create jobs and work towards common goals such as worldwide justice, peace education, and pollution-control.
- Values are important because without positive moral values, others may resent your actions and may not radiate positive energy in your direction. Remember, we all need a minimum level of material possessions but without the wealth of values that come from within, external wealth is nearly meaningless.
- We need to rate others not by the amount of material possessions they have but by the amount of happiness they possess.
- We need to create songs about World Peace. Listening to music can also improve our lives.

- We need films about World Peace. For our visual senses, we need to see less violence and more themes that promote heroes who overcome injustice and mediocrity. We need films that reward strong moral values and have messages that show us ways of achieving peace and success in life.
- Corporations must join the effort and create work environments that address today's changing workforce. With the advent of the Internet and home computers, some jobs could be performed at home allowing for flexible work hours, reduced traffic, improved working conditions and improved productivity. Companies, with employee volunteers, can also start their own non-profit peace organisations that focus on issues in their communities and staff the organisation.
- Philosophy suggests that nations that have found peace should help less peaceful nations by sharing knowledge, food and other resources. Our conscience teaches us that we should treat others the way we want to be treated, with dignity and respect.
- We need a World Flag that we can proudly wave; this will signify that we are growing up as a united world of peace-loving souls. This flag ought to be designed by the children of the world since they are the ones that will benefit most from peace move. We have the futuristic vision of one race (human), on one planet (earth), with two main purposes: Peace and Enlightenment.
- We must learn to accept the fact that others will not always respond to our needs and wants in the way we want them to. Instead of getting upset with them we need to learn to bless them and wish them well, which is exactly what we hope for ourselves.
- We need to learn from our mistakes. Instead of degrading ourselves we must realise that failure and

success go hand in hand. Failure is necessary because it provides obvious lessons to learn from. Analysis of these lessons should improve the chances for future prosperity.

Conclusion

The spiritually ignorant people cannot do justice to any such policy as beneficial to humanity and in this regard it is important here to acknowledge that the *education cannot impart any value until the recipient is awakened.* India should lead the world in the aspect of spiritual stimulation, for this alone can promise the desired outcome. Purity and purpose of Education then will not be ignored at any level. Accountability of educators will automatically take shape according to the various factors, such as economy, climate, religion etc, of the society. However, varying in modes and means the purity and purpose of the education would eventually lead the current world to a peaceful world.

REFERENCES

1. Gandhi, M. K. (1927), *The Story of My Experiments With Truth* (Translated From the Gujarati by Mahadev Desai), Navjivan Publishing House Ahmedabad (Reprinted 1996).
2. Mahathera Narada (1994), *The Buddha and His Teachings, Dharma and Ysushita Sennanayake,* Colombo (Sri Lanka).
3. Radhakrishnan S. (1966), *Indian Philosophy,* London, George Allen & Unwin/
4. Sharma, R.S. (1983), *Material Culture and Social Formation in Ancient India,* New Delhi, Mac Millan India Ltd.
5. *UNESCO and a Culture of Peace,* UNESCO Publishing, 1995.
6. University News, Vol. 45 No. 44, October 29 – November 04, 2007.
7. University News, Vol. 44 No. 12, March 20 – 26, 2006.
8. Vivekanand, S. (1964), *Shiksha Prasanga, Udbodhan Karjalaya.*
9. World Peace News Letter—www.worldpeacenewsletter.com and other World Peace Websites.

CHAPTER

28

Protection of Child Rights in Schools— A Way to Develop Peace Environment

*Dr. Neraja Dhankar

Being human, parents and especially teachers, the topic, area and field of Child Rights is not new for us. Whether we have been taught about child rights or not, we have been safe-guarding them and perhaps sometimes violating them too.

Common examples of violation of child's right to life with dignity, right to health and development are; physical and mental assaults by teachers *i.e.* scolding badly, severely punishing, insulting, naked parading, striping and beating. Of these only a few come into reporting/limelight through the media like newspapers and various T.V. channels, as these are always ready to seek such sensational news. There are news of teachers slapping students so hard that their ear drums are damaged, a teacher threw wooden duster towards a student, breaking his glasses and permanently damaging his eyesight. It is a matter of utter shame but there are incidents of sexual assault of both sexes' students by teachers.

There was reported incident of an eight-year-old student, who committed suicide as he did not want to go to his boarding school because he was afraid of warden/teachers. They were not warm and loving like parents, the child missed his home and family so much that he took this extreme step. Those who are managing residential schools must first of all have love for children so that they can provide warm and loving environment like home to the children.

* Assosiate Professor and Head Department of Education, Sri Guru Ram Rai P.G. College, Dehradun.

Today the drop-out rate from schools is very high, which is a big problem in the way of universalisation of elementary education and one of the biggest reasons that students do not want to attend schools is that they are afraid of their teachers. If the children are afraid of their day time parents, then how they will feel safe, secure and develop, which is so important in these crucial years of physical, intellectual, emotional and social development. Can teachers say that we shall be able to develop love in them if we show violence against them? Here comes the need for peace-education for teachers. Apart from apathetic attitude and behaviour of teachers this is direct violation of the Child's right to education which indirectly effects the overall development of a nation because these children are the future nation builders. Mahatma Gandhi said that fear is the root cause of all other evils. These school drop outs are most likely to develop into anti-social elements for lack of education and employment when they grow up.

The ultimate aim of education is the all round development of child, body; mind and spirit. But this is possible only in a cordial atmosphere, creating which, is the responsibility of the teachers and the management of an educational institution. Teachers need to be non-violent in their thought, behaviour and actions. They need to be at peace within themselves first, then they will be sensitive towards children. They are not supposed to violate child rights. So peace-education for teachers in pre-service and in-service teacher-education is very essential. They are not only to be taught theory of peace and its importance but also to be taught the practice of it through yoga, meditation, breathing exercises, moral education etc.

Every teacher needs to be made sympathetic, sensitive and empathic towards children's needs of love and care. Teachers should be provided with the knowledge of child-rights in theory as well as practice. They need to be sensitised on this crucial issue. They should also be given knowledge of children's needs at all stages of development. Safety education, disaster-management and emergency handling, health and hygiene education, first-aid education for the teachers is must for protection of child rights. Children have special needs, if these are not fulfilled; they feel irritated, unwanted and neglected. By this way leading to depression, which further affects their normal development, sometimes leading to serious personality disorders and even suicidal tendencies.

If possible it would be appreciated if there is aptitude test followed by interviews by specialists such as child-psychologists for all those would be teachers to test whether they deserve to be teachers or not. It may be difficult but not impossible if they are put into real situational tests with children to observe their behaviour with children while managing the class and teaching, while in the playground or any other educational activity with children.

Education is such an important process in the life of a child that it should not be left in the hands of those who are likely to spoil it So there should be careful selection of teachers. And in-service education to sensitise teachers on child rights is an absolute must to revive the good old days of 'Gurukula' system in which teachers were more caring and loving than parents and brought up children as their own for such a long period. Role of teacher is not less important today. Teaching is still considered as a noblest profession. Teachers must keep it such.

Nowadays, there is problem of total lack of individual attention by teachers to their students in the school. Every child has unique personality and individual needs. He or she is not just a role number. Teachers often complain that s/he has to look after sixty to eighty children alone everyday. How can she pay attention individually to each child? Every job has its limitations. Where there is will there is a way. Pre-Primary and Primary teachers are at advantage, as a single teacher remains with the children at least for the whole session and sometimes for two to three sessions altogether. There is enough time to observe, listen to and understand every child and accordingly develop his/her capabilities, potential, and also provide remedial measures to overcome weaknesses of any type academic, emotional or health related in cooperation with parents. For full development of all types children have right to be loved, cared for, listened to, understood, play, recreation, rest and nutritious and balanced diet.

Not a single week goes without news of children falling ill due to consumption of poor quality or carelessly cooked mid-day meals. On January 23, 2009, a dead rat was found in a container of dal which was part of the mid-day meal of a MCD school in New Delhi, 120 kids fell ill after school meal on 26 Nov. 2009 in Delhi. News of this kind have become common. Mid-day meal programme was started with the noble objective of providing healthy meal to school children at least once during day and also to attract poor children to school so that they do not indulge into child-labour at the cost of their study time. But the corruption at various levels and sheer negligence of those in whose hands these job was given is apparent to all. This is gross violence of child right to health and education. The culprit should be identified and severely punished.

A child develops fully if the natural environment is provided to it in the form of open space with trees, plants, flowers, grass, birds, butterflies etc. which the child observes and in the process learns from nature. On one side there are private centrally air-conditioned schools for kids of elite families which provide them with personal computers and an artificial atmosphere which is away from reality and on the other hand for crores of children there are government run schools with no roofs and walls. If these walls and roofs are there—there is risk of their falling any time injuring children. There are no clean and enough toilets. There is no scope for physical activities for children's games and sports especially in the two-room commercial shops of education. In the government funded schools, open spaces are not maintained to be used as playgrounds, there is paucity of teachers, absenteeism among teachers, and lack of basic educational material. Can we say that there is concern about children's right to equality where two parallel systems run, private vis-à-vis government; bringing equality through education? No, here right to equality is being violated through education itself whereas education is considered an egalitarian force.

Yashpal Committee Report 'Learning Without Burden' emphasised on reducing physical and mental burden on the children. But the views remained on the papers. It is a common scene to tiny tots bent double from their backs with the burden of school bags, this daily routine for years sometimes permanently damages their soft body frames and leading to stunt growth. The question is why this much heavy bag has to be carries to and from the school everyday? Why can't it be kept at the school or home and only few needed books and notebooks to be carried everyday? Is it not possible that time table be made such that all this stuff is not to be carried together each day? If the teachers and management of the school is kind and empathetic towards children, it can be done easily. Mental torture of the little kids starts quite at a tender age of three years and sometimes at two plus in the name of play schools and pre-primary education which prepares these kids for the high profile schools. In the difficult interviews which are held for admission into these schools, tiny tots are expected to behave royal and scholarly (as if everything learnt in previous births), the parents are expected to have computers, cars, air-conditions and provide all knowledge and etiquettes at home, as if these children are prepared for royal marriage and not education. Many children are denied admissions and labeled as dulls and duffers by the non-sensitive interviewing authorities who are nothing but shop-owners with a sole motive to make profits by selling such education which is widening gaps between the rich and poor in the society and the irony is that the highly educated parents are becoming the scapegoats of these shopkeepers. Even these educated parents label their children as dull if they fail to respond to the cruel interviewers' questions, affecting children's self concept and personality negatively.

Now, why do the children have to carry water bottles to the schools, which add another one to two kilograms to the weight already being carried to schools? Most of the water bottles are made of plastic which is not considered good for health. Secondly it is not easy to clean these bottles from inside due to their narrow necks. Waters is a basic human necessity. Government provides enough funds to the schools, can't the school authorities provide safe drinking water to their students. Private schools charge hefty amounts from the students in the name of this and that fund, even then the parents do not have faith that their children get safe drinking water in the school so they insist their wards to carry own water-bottle to be on the safe-side as falling ill cannot be afforded in terms of time due to heavy study load. If only the school authotities guarantee safe drinking water to their students, they can be saved from carrying extra weight of carrying water-bottle to school.

Ties are symbols of colonial legacy. Why do we have to strangle our children in the name of smartness ignoring their comfort and ease. Aim of education is helping attain maximum all round development, of which first is physical development which is the basis on which all other types of development depends. It is an unhealthy scene to see lean and anaemic children with ill-maintained tie in their necks which only serves the purpose of pulling and being pulled by each other in quarrels which these frustrated children indulge into. They are overburdened physically and mentally uncomfortable in their school uniforms so they get irritated soon.

Another troubling burden is waist-belt, which hangs uselessly on the non-existing waists of these schools kids, not serving the purpose for which it is meant. Either these belts are so tight that they injure the soft bellies of children by continuously pricking on them, or these are so loose that it has no hold on the clothe it is meant for. It is the duty of the teachers and the school authorities to free these children of these mental and physical burdens so that they are saved from the unnecessary torture. With a little bit of empathy and sympathy for these gifts of God it is possible.

Concept of Common school and neighborhood school given by Kothari Commission as early as in 1963 is necessary to be implemented if these children are to be safeguarded from the dangers of killer buses on the road. Everyday there are incidents of school children being run over by a vehicle while crossing the road or by the sheer negligence of the own school bus driver. Moreover, children are forced to inhale pollution on the roads, suffer traffic jams, tiredness due to long bus journey which has all sorts of ill effects on their health. Common ailments from which children suffer due to everyday travelling are breathing and respiratory problems, eye-infections, back-pains and acute-tiredness. Health of future citizens is being seriously neglected in the name of quality education being provided in few distantly located good schools. Why every school is not considered a good school and why every teacher not a good teacher? There needs to be a standard maintenance in the field of education in every institution of education to protect children's right to life, good health, quality education which provides not only for literacy but also desirable values, recreation, leisure time, fun-time, playtime safety and security to which every child has right. Here I recall a story; there was a saint. Whatever he said turned out to be true. There was a bad man who wanted to downsize the saint. He caught a butterfly and took it to saint, thinking that if the saint would say that the butterfly would die, he will free it and if the saint would say it would live, he will kill it, thus proving him wrong. When he took the butterfly to the saint and asked him if it would die or fly, the saint peacefully replied, it is in your hands. So the moral of the story is that the children's lives are in teachers' hands, they are the saviours of their rights to life and development. Children are like sweet flowers, help them to blossom full and fill this earth with their sweet fragrance of laughter, health and happiness so that this universe becomes a worth place to live in.

REFERENCES

1. National Council of Educational Research and Training. Education for Peace. New Delhi: National Council of Educational Research and Training, 2002.
2. Prasad. D.(1984). Peace Education or Education for Peace. New Delhi: Gandhi Peace Foundation.
3. Pasad, S.N. (1972). Education: Mental Health and World Peace. Varanasi (India): Author.
4. Balvinder Kaur; Peace Education, Deep and Deep Publication. New Delhi 2006 (Chapter 10, Peace Education in India), pp. 232-233.

CHAPTER 29

Culture of Peace—A Need of Present Era

*Dr. Akanksha Singh

Once upon a time an ancient Indian King was obsessed with the desire to find the meaning of peace. What is peace and how can we get it and when we find it what should we do with it were some of the issues that bothered him. Intellectuals in his kingdom were invited to answer the King's questions for a handsome reward. Many tried but none could explain how to find peace and what to do with it. At last someone said the King ought to consult the sage who lived just outside the borders of his Kingdom:

> "He is an old man and very wise," the King was told. "If anyone can answer your questions he can."
>
> The King went to the sage and posed the eternal question. Without a word the sage went into the kitchen and brought a grain of wheat to the King.
>
> "In this you will find the answer to your question," the Sage said as he placed the grain of wheat in the King's outstretched palm.

Puzzled but unwilling to admit his ignorance the King clutched the grain of wheat and returned to his palace. He locked the precious grain in a tiny gold box and placed the box in his safe. Each morning, upon waking, the King would open the box and look at the grain to seek an answer but could find nothing.

* Lecturer, Heera Lal Yadav Balika Degree College, Lucknow.

Weeks later another sage, passing through, stopped to meet the King who eagerly invited him to resolve his dilemma. The King explained how he had asked the eternal question and this sage gave him a grain of wheat instead. "I have been looking for an answer every morning but I find nothing."

The Sage said: "It is quite simple, your honour. Just as this grain represents nourishment for the body, peace represents nourishment for the soul. Now, if you keep this grain locked up in a gold box it will eventually perish without providing nourishment or multiplying. However, if it is allowed to interact with the elements—light, water, air, and soil—it will flourish, multiply and soon you would have a whole field of wheat which will nourish not only you but so many others. This is the meaning of peace.

This story depicts Ancient Indian view on peace and it is always true but if one has to define the word peace it will go like this—

Peace—Peace is commonly understood as the absence of hostility or safety in matters of social or economic welfare. It is the acknowledgment of equality and fairness in social and political relationships.

According to Hague Appeal for Peace *"A culture of peace will be achieved when citizens of the world understand global problems, have the skills to resolve conflicts and struggle for justice non-violently, live by international standards of human rights and equity, appreciate cultural diversity, and respect the Earth and each other. Such learning can only be achieved with systematic education for peace."*

This appeal emphasises the necessity of peace education for our children as they later become the global citizen and only by that peace can be disseminated. According to Article 26, Universal Declaration of Human Rights—*Peace education has developed as a means to achieve these goals. It is education that is "directed to the full development of the human personality and to the strengthening of respect for human rights and fundamental freedoms". It promotes "understanding, tolerance and friendship among all nations, racial or religious groups" and furthers "the activities of the United Nations for the maintenance of peace."*

In other words, peace education is an integral part of the work of the United Nations. Through a humanizing process of teaching and learning, peace educators facilitate human development. Peace education currently addresses the broader objective of building a culture of peace.

UNICEF describes peace education as schooling and other educational initiatives that:

- Function as 'zones of peace', where children are safe from violent conflict.
- Uphold children's basic rights as outlined in the CRC(convention on the rights of the child).
- Develop a climate that models peaceful and respectful behaviour among all members of the learning community.
- Demonstrate the principles of equality and non-discrimination in administrative policies and practices.
- Draw on the knowledge of peace-building that exists in the community, including means of dealing with conflict that are effective, non-violent, and rooted in the local culture.
- Handle conflicts in ways that respect the rights and dignity of all involved.
- Integrate an understanding of peace, human rights, social justice and global issues throughout the curriculum whenever possible.
- Provide a forum for the explicit discussion of values of peace and social justice.
- Use teaching and learning methods that stress participation, cooperation, problem-solving and respect for differences.
- Enable children to put peace-making into practice in the educational setting as well as in the wider community.

- Generate opportunities for continuous reflection and professional development of all educators in relation to issues of peace, justice and rights. (*Peace Education in UNICEF,* Working Paper Series, July 1999)

The action for nurturing and peace building must be located in the educational system. The National Curriculum Framework (NCF), 2005 by NCERT asserts that education must be able to promote values that foster peace, humanness and tolerance in a multicultural society. The aims of education enunciated in the NCF 2005 include developing commitment to democracy and the constitutional values of equality, justice, freedom, secularism, and concern for well-being of others. The practice of education in schools needs review

- to remove systemic violence by way of overloaded curricula.
- Inflexible routines and expectations incongruent with the ability patterns of students.
- The modelling of violent behaviour in and out of the classroom needs to be checked.
- Education for peace aims at proactively nurturing such attitudes values and attributes, which would enable students to avoid violence in their lives.
- NCF(national curriculum framework) says the approach to education for peace at school level should be integrative rather than as additive which means values is integrated into the curricular content and processes of education.

Peace Education in Schools

In the schools aim of peace education is to develop skills, attitudes, and knowledge with co-operative and participatory learning methods. Teachers are already practicing peace education without calling it by name. Historically, in various parts of the world, peace education has been referred to as Education for Conflict Resolution, International Understanding, and Human Rights; Global Education; Critical Pedagogy; Education for Liberation and Empowerment; Social Justice Education; Environmental Education; Life Skills Education; Disarmament and Development Education, and more.

Term peace education helps to coordinate these efforts and unite educators in the common practice of educating for a culture of peace.

Awareness of values and attitudes underpin peace education and need to be addressed through the curriculum and the whole school. There are many ways to promote peace in the world but perhaps the best way is to promote it within ourselves. Peace is a gradual and wonderful event that occurs because compassionate people are inspired to help others discover the joy of peace! Peace, like reading, writing, mathematics, drawing, emotional intelligence and enlightenment ("understanding/comprehension/compassion/meditation/intuition"), are learned skills that improve our knowledge, maturity, health, happiness and longevity. Peace is probably the most important lesson we should learn during our lives and the sooner the better.

Education for Peace should be founded on the following values and attitudes:

- Respect for others regardless of race, gender, age, nationality, class, sexuality, appearance, political or religious belief, physical or mental ability.
- Empathy—a willingness to understand the views of others from their standpoint.
- A belief in positive change by individuals and groups of people.
- Appreciation of and respect for diversity.
- Self esteem-accepting the intrinsic value of oneself.
- Commitment to non-violence, equity and social justice.
- Concern for the environment and understanding of our place in the eco-system.
- Commitment to equality.

Teachers have this responsibility to inculcate these values in child that will automatically inculcate the atmosphere of peace in school and later in society.

REFERENCES

1. www.ncte-india.org
2. www.unicef.org
3. www.ncert.nic.in

CHAPTER

30

Role of Teacher Education for Promoting Culture of Peace

*Dr. Vasudha Vinod Deo

The concept of Peace Education and Teacher Education are specifically mentioned in the National Curriculum Framework 2005 (NCP) document. Today the issue of education for peace is being discussed globally. Betty Reardon has stated that Peace Education could provide knowledge applicable to the problem of reforming and reconstruction of the present conflicting and violent human society to make peaceful infield and violence force. Thus education has to decide upon its goals. Education should be a media through which to create integrated and spiritual human being because children today are the citizens of tomorrow. According to Indian view, contribution the development of peace culture and its contribution in world culture is vitally important. Thus spiritual education and coexistence should be given an important place in education. Unless a human being experiences peace of inner mind it can not be reflected in his conduct. Education for Peace emphasises the mind and intellect to shape inner personality. Education should lead to establishment of eternal peace. Education for Peace is a branch of knowledge through which development of peace culture should be the only goal. Indian philosophy, literature of the Saints and thoughts of the philosophers can contribute largely in this respect. Love at the level of Mind, Knowledge at the level of Intellect and Empowerment at the level of Spirit make the human personality a balanced one which in turn established peace in the society. Teacher

* Government College of Education, Akola, Maharashtra.

Education is also very important as he is the backbone of the education system. He is Philosopher, Guide and Facilitator. A teacher is not a knowledge giving machine or recorder. Swami Chinmayanand says, 'only a teacher can supply a clear vision.' The value of 'working as a team, serving as a preacher and nourishing the culture' has to be imbibed through teacher education. A teacher should be an ideal example of 'pure living'. Thus we have to bring about some changes in Teacher Education. The quality of any education system cannot higher than the quality of the teachers in the system.

The existing education system has led to human development but it has failed to bring about development of humanity. The education has certainly fulfilling the present necessities but what about the eternal needs? How can they be fulfilled? Who is responsible for all these things? Individual? society? Government or education? politics or socialism? All these are debatable subjects.

The Indian culture is ancient while the Indian spiritualism is eternal. If a peaceful human being is to be created through education, we have to create a medium of peaceful culture. Hence we need to inculcate spiritual values. Today we find inculcation of material prosperity but spiritual values are not noticed. Have we lost the ancient goals, values, culture and spiritualism in the quest of modernism?

A teacher has a vital place in education system. He is backbone of the educational system. His role is of integrated human builder. Through training it is emphasised that Knowledge, Skill and Attitude are imbibed in the teacher. The more the foundation strong, the more is the strength of the system. If the teachers have to play the role of human builder, they should command respect from the students. A teacher is not a knowledge giving machine or recorder. Swami Chinmayanand says, 'only a teacher can supply a clear vision.' We have to impart training which in turn will enable the teacher to imbibe peace. Hence some contexts are to be considered which can prove pilot in designing teacher education programmes.

1. The global context of teacher education : *'Satyam, Shivam, Sundaram' i.e.* Truth, Purity and Beauty are the basic values of life. Belief in God is the knowledge of Truth. Science has made our life beautiful but we have to behave scientifically according to our religion. We have to follow religion with faith in God. This faith in God provides knowledge to human race. These help us to maintain the balance of the world. It is through this medium that we can inculcate values in human mind. Education is the powerful medium to bring these to us. Hence these have to included in the realm of teacher education.

2. The national context of teacher education and globalisation : The function of education is to inculcate values in human mind. Education is the powerful medium to make human beings strong. We have to mould a generation through education which will believe in Indian way of life. Hence first of all we have to produce teachers who are inspired by the spirit of nationalism. A nation is not just a geographical region, but a group of people who have it is common traditions, values, standardised ways, and spiritualism and unitedly believe in progress. The philosophy of the nation is the spirit of the nation. The nations self realisation, its spirit and its spiritualism is the self-realisation of India. If we want to see the internal aspects of India we have to revive the Indian spiritualism. Swami Vivekanand has said this. Hence we have to believe in spiritualism as the basis of education. The objective of teacher education should be to determine the proper direction of education system. This national viewpoint can only create globalisation.

3. Social context : We need education which will ignite the inner energy. Every national society has within its a developmental inner energy which has to be given proper direction and ignition. This is in fact the objective of education. Maximum good of maximum people is the basis of education.

Like a person every society has its own personality which is reflected in the national goals.

4. The individual context of teacher education : According to a definition of education, the all round development of a personality is education. A person's personality is multifaceted . The following diagram explains this:

soule

Intellect

Mind

Body

Multi-faceted personality of human being

The realisation of the inner spirit leads to its extension and expansion. It is the effort of human being to achieve the completeness and to become complete. This journey begins from self and ends with the achievement of global personality. Hence we require education to shape the individual personality leading to a global one This is the goal of education in its true sense.

5. The quality context : The source of education has to reach every person. For this we need quality education because basically everyone expects to get qualitative education. All the elements included in teacher education have the context of quality. Through the medium of teacher education we should produce teachers who are completely filled with the feeling of extreme peace. Hence it should be an endeavour of the teachers to participate in the process so as to acquire this peace of mind. In realisation of the source of inner peace, its knowledge and creation of new generation with the help of this knowledge and capacities, lies the test of quality. Only material resources and result cannot be its test but the knowledge and skills to be imparted to teachers in teacher training programmes. It lies similarly in the choice of subjects and activities decided upon to create the required capabilities. The indicators of choosing a subject area will be the national, social and spiritual context of the subject. The application of the course book, syllabus, curriculum and co-curricular activities will be based on these indicators. The quality of teacher education is related with the quality of all the other aspects of life. Again the context of quality is not confined only to the education system but it also touches the principles of human mind and intellect.

These contexts are important at the foundation level of education system. Considering all these aspects we come to the conclusion to find out the exact goals and aims of teacher education. Many questions like which subjects should be included in teacher education, what should be the duration of teacher education programme arise in our mind.

Goals of Teacher Education

Swami Chinmayanand has stated the following qualities to be developed among teachers through the teacher training programme:

1. The practice of what is right and proper as indicated in the scriptures.
2. Living the ideals that have been intellectually comprehended during the status.
3. A spirit of self sacrifice.
4. Control of Sense.
5. Tranquility of mind.
6. Practice of concentration.
7. Doing one's duty towards the humanity.

The development of the above mentioned qualities in teachers is tour primary concern in teacher education. The role of the teacher is also important in this process, hence the teachers should also possess some qualities like:

1. Working as a team;
2. Serving as a preacher; and
3. Nourishing the culture.

It is also needed to develop the following viewpoints in the teachers during training programmes:

1. The teachers' role should be: To give, To sure and To share knowledge;
2. Real education means transformation of knowledge into wisdom;
3. There should be coordination between our knowledge and actions;
4. It is not enough to give factual knowledge or wondrous theory to the young generation, it is our commitment to make them familiar with the ideals of human life;
5. Education means enrichment of character;
6. A good teacher will not be just an instructor, he will be a philosopher guide;
7. It is necessary that the teacher education programme would have the ability to understand Indian culture, values and philosophy;
8. It is necessary to develop the values of global thinking through teacher education;
9. Teacher education should lead to total knowledge of personality development;
10. The spirit of the teacher education should be to make aware of national, cultural, religious, global viewpoints;
11. There should be a feeling of devotion to the profession;
12. A teacher should become creative and innovative through education;
13. The should be coordinative look out towards religion and science;
14. There should be development regarding the study of religion and spiritualism in the learner teacher;
15. Taking into consideration that the present era is one of science and technology, we have to produce Knowledge Master and Wisdom Master;
16. A teaching personality should emerge from the teacher training.

Development of teaching personality should be the goal of teacher education. Following are some of the elements that should find place in the teacher development.

1. Formation of beliefs : Teacher education should produce committed teachers. Following are the factors that indicate this commitment :

(*i*) commitment to Knowledge
(*ii*) commitment to Religion
(*iii*) commitment to Spiritualism
(*iv*) commitment to Nations
(*v*) commitment to Society
(*vi*) commitment to Students
(*vii*) commitment to Nature
(*viii*) commitment to Character
(*ix*) commitment to Values
(*x*) commitment to Peace

2. Development of Perceptions

(*i*) Multifaceted character of a person
(*ii*) Relation between Man and World
(*iii*) Co-relation between Man and the Society
(*iv*) Balance in Physical, Spiritual and Social life
(*v*) National character
(*vi*) National devotion
(*vii*) National integration
(*viii*) Decision-making
(*ix*) Character
(*x*) Global perception

Viewpoints: Teacher education should bring about the following viewpoints in the teacher:

1. Loyalty to Nation and National Integration : A nation is not just living together of human community in a specific geographical region. Common goals, higher education and sharing a common will to progress which lives on a common region are a nation. This is the core of value education. Loyalty towards goal is an inspiration to work. Commitment is a power which creates inspiring environment. Human intellect is usually honest to these feelings hence it is our primary concern that a teacher should be devoted to his nation.

2. Love of discipline : A teacher should love discipline. He should be complete in Self discipline. The outward discipline should turn into inner discipline. Self discipline is nothing but the devotion to one's aims, dedication, social service, purity of heart, development of culture, self-education etc. This self discipline gives an organised personality to the teacher. Self discipline should be on physical, intellectual and emotional level.

3. Character : To put it simply character is organisation of good habits. Good habits depend on the frequency of good behaviour. Good habits also depend on positive thinking. A teacher can organise good thoughts through education.

4. Leadership quality : A teacher leads a society. It will not be wrong to say that an identity of any nation is through a teacher. The society follows only a teacher. Similarly students also draw heavily on their teachers. A teacher needs to have vision. In order to revive the society the teacher needs to have divine qualities within him. He also needs a balanced outlook.

5. Acceptance of novel ideas : Education makes the teacher knowledge master as well as wisdom master. He should develop the spirit of acceptance of advanced science and technology. Our country is father of advanced technological knowledge. To accept these things and to be able to learn and apply them in life, the teacher needs to be positive in his attitude.

3. Developing skills : *1. Teaching skill :* We have to keep balance between the old and new methods of teaching. The teachers have to develop mastery over all the methods. Hence we use various activities during teacher training.

2. *Self-Mastery* : It is necessary for the teachers to develop mastery over self. We find competition in every walk of life today. The prime thought is how one establishes his mastery over others in any field. But how can one establishes his supremacy over the world unless he achieves mastery over his self? For mastery over the self we have to depend on knowledge and high values of life. Unless a teacher has these values in him, he can not transfer them to the next generation.

3. *Creativity* : Creativity has to be developed during teacher training. Today creativity is being discussed globally. The concept of creativity has been widely acknowledged by all. If a teacher can master the factors needed for creativity—intellect, knowledge, personality and environment – he will be enable to impart these into his students. Hence the teachers should be made aware of specific theories of teaching. These include the problem oriented, case studies, simulation, role play, action research, etc. A teacher can achieve the above mentioned goals but for that we have to restructure some of the subjects. The decision to include the subjects must follow careful discussion on their need and importance.

Teacher Education and Curriculum Indicator

The curriculum of teacher education should be theoretical as well as practical. The draft is precisely given below:

1. Draft list of subject's areas with reference to development

- Theoretical foundation of human personality
- Education of Peace
- Mind Management
- Education for eternal development
- Indian Psychology
- Science of Meditation
- Education of self-control

- Arts and handicrafts
- Child Psychology: Principles and Practice

2. Draft of co-related areas : We can enlist some subjects with reference to co-related areas:

- The spiritual foundation of man
- The spiritual foundation of society
- Environment education
- Spiritual foundation of nature
- Education of co-existence
- Education of the rules of existence
- Culture and education

3. Draft of national education : We can suggest some areas for development of nationalism:

- Education for accountability
- Education for citizenship
- History of Education
- Literature of the Saints and Education
- Great educationists
- Universal Philosophy and Education

4. Draft of Religious Education : We can include the following areas under this:

- Education of Co-existence,
- Education of different religions,
- Spiritual Education and Practice,
- Meditation, Yoga, Japyoga.
- Education of Law of Being

5. In order to relate to the new era of scientific advancement we can include these subjects in the syllabus. History of Educational Management and New Trends in Education can be added.

Teaching Methods : Today under this we teach different methods of teaching, models of teaching, content-cum methodology, etc. These can be retained. In addition to these we can have the following areas:

1. Anti-lust method
2. Self-observation Method
3. Thinking Method
4. Cause-effect Method

The above mentioned methods have been recommended in Upanishads. A teaches has to be skilled to learn these subjects. Only these lead to developing ability to create the knowledge.

Evaluation scheme : following aspects should have place in the evaluation in teacher education:

1. Original thinking; and
2. Independent judgment

Different tools of evaluation have to be developed. Instead of emphasis on examination, focus should be on free expression of thoughts and ideas. The evaluation should be three tire :

1. Evaluation by the teachers;
2. Evaluation by the self in the presence of experts; and
3. Evaluation by co-learners.

Evaluation has to be qualitative as well as quantitative. These have to be prepared.

The draft of syllabus of teacher education is suggested here. Based on these lines a thorough syllabus can be designed. This is demand of the times.

REFERENCES

1. Editor (2001). *Sparks From the Fire.* Mumbai : Central Chinmaya Mission Trust.

2. *Ibid.*, (2006).
3. *The Essential Teacher.* Mumbai : Central Chinmaya Mission Trust *Ibid.*, (2006). *The Source of Inspiration.* Mumbai : Central Chinmaya Mission Trust :
    1. Swami Chinmayanand (2005). *Think Again.* Mumbai : C.C.M.T.
    2. Swami Chinmayanand (2002). *As I Think.* Mumbai : C.C.M.T.
    3. *Ibid.*, (2007). *Gitas Words of Guidance.* Mumbai : C.C.M.T.
    4. *Ibid.*, (2006). *Know What You Have.* Mumbai : C.C.M.T.
    5. *Ibid.*, (2006). *The Art of Living.* Mumbai : C.C.M.T.
    6. *Ibid.*, (1995). *Source of Joy.* Mumbai : C.C.M.T.
    7. *Ibid.*, (2004). *Art of Man Making.* Mumbai : C.C.M.T.
    9. *Ibid.*, (1997). *Planet in Crisis Actress to United Nations.* Mumbai : C.C.M.T.
    10. *Ibid.*, (2001). *Future of Country.* Mumbai : C.C.M.T.
    11. Swami (2004). *Right Thinking.* Mumbai : C.C.M.T. Tejomayananda.

Marathi Books

1. Deo Vasudha (2006) Shaikshanik Chintan-Nagpur, Visa Books.
2. Deo Vasudha (2009)—Chinmaya Shikshanopnishad-Nagpur, Mangesh Prakashan.
3. Wanjari Shashi Deo Vasudha (2007)—Udayonmukh Bhartiya Samajatil Shikshan—Nagpur, Visa Books.

Index

F

G

H

L

M

N

S

V

W

Y

Z